Great Digital Media with Windows® XP

Great Digital Media with Windows® XP

Paul Thurrott

Hungry Minds™

Best-Selling Books • Digital Downloads • e-Books • Answer Networks • e-Newsletters • Branded Web Sites • e-Learning

New York, NY ✦ Cleveland, OH ✦ Indianapolis, IN

Great Digital Media with Windows® XP

Published by
Hungry Minds, Inc.
909 Third Avenue
New York, NY 10022
www.hungryminds.com

Library of Congress Control Number: 2001092882

ISBN: 0-7645-3620-6

Printed in the United States of America

10 9 8 7 6 5 4 3 2

1B/RR/QZ/QR/IN

Distributed in the United States by Hungry Minds, Inc.

Distributed by CDG Books Canada Inc. for Canada; by Transworld Publishers Limited in the United Kingdom; by IDG Norge Books for Norway; by IDG Sweden Books for Sweden; by IDG Books Australia Publishing Corporation Pty. Ltd. for Australia and New Zealand; by TransQuest Publishers Pte Ltd. for Singapore, Malaysia, Thailand, Indonesia, and Hong Kong; by Gotop Information Inc. for Taiwan; by ICG Muse, Inc. for Japan; by Intersoft for South Africa; by Eyrolles for France; by International Thomson Publishing for Germany, Austria, and Switzerland; by Distribuidora Cuspide for Argentina; by LR International for Brazil; by Galileo Libros for Chile; by Ediciones ZETA S.C.R. Ltda. for Peru; by WS Computer Publishing Corporation, Inc., for the Philippines; by Contemporanea de Ediciones for Venezuela; by Express Computer Distributors for the Caribbean and West Indies; by Micronesia Media Distributor, Inc. for Micronesia; by Chips Computadoras S.A. de C.V. for Mexico; by Editorial Norma de Panama S.A. for Panama; by American Bookshops for Finland.

For general information on Hungry Minds' products and services please contact our Customer Care department within the U.S. at 800-762-2974, outside the U.S. at 317-572-3993 or fax 317-572-4002.

For sales inquiries and reseller information, including discounts, premium and bulk quantity sales, and foreign-language translations, please contact our Customer Care department at 800-434-3422, fax 317-572-4002 or write to Hungry Minds, Inc., Attn: Customer Care Department, 10475 Crosspoint Boulevard, Indianapolis, IN 46256.

For information on licensing foreign or domestic rights, please contact our Sub-Rights Customer Care department at 212-884-5000.

For information on using Hungry Minds' products and services in the classroom or for ordering examination copies, please contact our Educational Sales department at 800-434-2086 or fax 317-572-4005.

For press review copies, author interviews, or other publicity information, please contact our Public Relations department at 317-572-3168 or fax 317-572-4168.

For authorization to photocopy items for corporate, personal, or educational use, please contact Copyright Clearance Center, 222 Rosewood Drive, Danvers, MA 01923, or fax 978-750-4470.

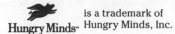

About the Author

Widely acknowledged for his contributions to the Windows community, **Paul Thurrott** is the News Editor for *Windows 2000 Magazine* and *Connected Home Magazine*. Through his work with these magazines and various online publications, Paul reaches over one million readers every month. He is also the author of over a dozen books about Windows and related technologies, including such titles as *Visual InterDev 6 Unleashed* and *VBScript for the World Wide Web*. As the person who first broke the news of Windows XP's existence to the world, Paul has been covering this product since late 1999 (when it was still known as "Neptune") through his daily news stories in WinInfo (www.wininformant.com) and more in-depth coverage at the SuperSite for Windows (www.winsupersite.com). Paul recently returned to his hometown of Dedham, Massachusetts, along with his wife Stephanie and son Mark. You can reach Paul at paul@thurrott.com or thurrott@win2000mag.com.

Credits

Acquisitions Editors
Debra Williams Cauley
Greg Croy

Project Editor
Amanda Munz Peterson

Technical Editors
Sean Alexander
Lee Musick

Copy Editor
Barry Childs-Helton

Editorial Manager
Ami Frank Sullivan

**Senior Vice President,
Technical Publishing**
Richard Swadley

Vice President and Publisher
Mary Bednarek

Project Coordinator
Nancee Reeves

Graphics and Production Specialists
Jill Piscatelli
Kendra Span
Laurie Stevens
Brian Torwelle
Erin Zeltner

Quality Control Technicians
Laura Albert
John Greenough
Angel Perez

Proofreading and Indexing
TECHBOOKS Production Services

Cover Image
Anthony Bunyan

This book is dedicated to my son, Mark. I love you, Poopie.

Foreword

Since about 1991, when Microsoft first released Windows 3.0 with Multimedia Extensions — and with it introduced the first digital-media-and-player features to the Windows PC — I have been enamored with digital media (as I suspect most of you have). In the early '90s, sound cards and CD-ROM drives were rare; even if you were among the lucky few to have a "Multimedia PC," you put up with tinny music, horrible synthesized sound, and (even worse) the IRQ and DMA Rodeo of trying to set up your hardware.

A lot has changed in the past decade. Sound cards are capable of reproducing 5.1- or even 6.1-channel surround sound; most of us would be hard-pressed to tell the difference between a synthesized orchestra out of our PCs and the real thing. Sound cards and PCs finally live up to the term "Plug and Play." The subcategory of "Multimedia PC" has disappeared; it's assumed that *any* new PC you buy these days will have the latest and greatest digital-media playback features — and (in a growing trend) support for creating your own audio CDs and home movies.

When Paul asked me to write the foreword to his book, I was flattered. I wasn't sure I was the right person until I started recalling my own experiences with digital media. When I first joined Microsoft, I began my career in the Developer Tools Division. I was fascinated by application development and three-tier application design; but in my spare time, my interest in digital media (and in the promise of compressed music formats such as MP3) was growing. In college, I had done some webcasted events using rudimentary compression — once even wiring a telephone feed into a PC sound card for a legal conference — but the unrealized potential of digital media was what I found inspiring. I was learning to rip my music into the MP3 format, and was creating simple, server-side Web apps so I could listen to my music library whether I was at work or home. The big problem I had was bandwidth — at decent quality levels, my MP3s were still too big for my fledgling DSL connection to handle.

One Saturday afternoon in 1998, that all changed. I discovered a project being worked on at Microsoft Research and the newly formed "Streaming Media Division." It was called "MS Audio." I downloaded a utility and converted one of my uncompressed .WAV files into this new format and I was astounded. I could barely tell the difference between that raw .WAV file and the compressed version that was *half* the size of MP3. I called my then-fiancée in and had her listen to the file. She couldn't tell the difference, either. It was then I realized that Microsoft was getting it right — that a digital-media revolution was about to begin, and significant investment was driving an effort to bring digital media to mainstream consumers. Two months later, I joined what is now the Windows Digital Media Division at Microsoft.

In the span of just a few years, the use of digital media has become one of the top activities that consumers enjoy with their PCs. Consumers are sharing home videos, listening to thousands of Internet radio stations around the world, and discovering a new level of personalized music with cheaper and easier access to Audio CD burning. As for the fledgling .WMA format, it's now supported in every major portable music player, every major PC-based media player or jukebox, and even some in-car devices and home digital audio receivers for playback in the living room. Like countless others, I have discovered a new passion — home-movie creation with Windows Movie Maker (which Microsoft first introduced in Windows Me). For my wedding, I even used Movie Maker to create a slideshow with music that summed up the years that my wife and I grew up apart, and then what we looked forward to together. We played it at the rehearsal dinner; family members went away with a keepsake — a burned CD containing the video. I received many phone calls from family and friends wanting to know how I did it, and how they could do it themselves. My answer today is simple: Windows XP.

When we first started thinking about what digital media in Windows XP would look like, we started with how users *want* to use their PCs, not how they *actually* use them today. We wanted Windows XP to be the best operating system for digital media and entertainment — and built it that way from the ground up. We discovered, very early on, that users don't think in terms of applications, they think in terms of *experiences* or *activities*. The new system had to make the capture, editing, and sharing of home movies a nearly effortless experience. CD burning needed to be easier. We wanted to make digital video so simple that you'd never have to leave full-screen view if you wanted to jump to a new chapter in a DVD, streamed, or downloadable movie — and we wanted quality so good that you could barely see the difference.

Sometimes I get asked by the press why I would want to work at Microsoft (or, more specifically, in digital media). For me, it's a kick to get up every morning knowing that what I work on today will be used by a new family in San Francisco, CA to share the first movie of their newborn child with distant relatives — or by a college student in Tulsa, OK to create a custom CD to play in his or her car — or a musician in London to share a new creation with others. And the best part of it is knowing that I'm just one of hundreds of others here on the Windows XP team who get up and go to work with the same vision.

I hope you enjoy this book the way I have — and urge you to try out the new digital-media experiences in Windows XP for yourself.

Sean Alexander

Technical Product Manager

Microsoft Corporation

Preface

*G*reat Digital Media with Windows XP is your end-to-end solution for discovering the digital-media experiences in Windows XP — exclusively available in a portable, wood-based format we call a *book*. It is possible that, within our lifetimes, this venerable artifact may go the way of DOS, the Soviet Union, and rotary telephones — but in the meantime, here it is and I hope you enjoy it.

Welcome Back to the Future

In the summer of 2000, our friends Dave and Debbie had a christening for their son Ritchie, and I dutifully drove out to the church with my wife Stephanie and our son Mark, then two years old. Mark was nice enough to fall asleep in the car, so I parked it under a tree, and my wife went inside to make a showing at the christening. I stayed outside with Mark, wished I had thought to bring a laptop, and proceeded to do what anyone would, barring any other distraction.

I thought.

I thought about how things were going, where I was, where things were headed. I won't bore you with the details of most of it, but I had been going over a variety of book deals at the time and decided to take stock of the situation. At the time, I was contracted to write a couple of really boring books about technical topics like *COM+* and *Active Server Pages,* but there was something about these titles that just didn't seem right. Sitting there under the shade of a big tree, watching my son sleep, it finally dawned on me what was wrong.

I didn't *want* to write these books. They were technical, they were boring, and no one was going to read them. Most problematic, I wouldn't have fun writing them at all. So I decided then and there that when I got home, I'd call up the publishing companies and explain to them why both projects should be canceled. And I did just that: Thankfully, I never needed to write either one of them.

In the meantime, I wanted to write something *fun*. Something that people — real people — could be excited about. Not just geeks, programmers, or IT professionals. Real people: My dad or that young couple across the street with a new baby. People who didn't use a computer for the sake of using a computer, but did so when it could help them get something done — preferably something fun.

It had to be digital media. Right then, with Mark snoring away beside me, I plotted my family's transition to digital media and decided that I would write about it. We would ditch the SLR camera and slow scanner and get a digital camera. I would record my hundreds of audio CDs onto the hard drive in MP3 format and lock those CDs away in the cellar (like valuable backups) next. And we would get a digital camcorder and archive our home movies on the computer, with the eventual goal of recording them on DVD. It was all coming together, right there, under the tree.

I thought about who to contact about doing a digital-media book. You have to sort of imagine what it was like at the time: Microsoft was getting ready to release Windows Millennium Edition (Windows Me), the first version of Windows that would include integrated digital-media solutions. It was fairly obvious at the time, however, that Windows Me wasn't going to be a gangbuster release, and I didn't expect anyone to be too interested in a Windows Me book. In the end, I decided it would have to be Windows-based, but not Windows-Me-specific.

The christening finally ended and, almost simultaneously, Mark woke up. But by then, my mind was set: I would write this book. I would write something fun. I would have fun doing it, and people would have fun reading it because it would open them up to possibilities they had perhaps never considered. On the way back to Dave's house, I excitedly explained my grand plan to Stephanie, and she nodded along politely as you might expect. (She's cute like that.) Then she asked how much this was all going to cost.

A week later, the two companies that suddenly found themselves sans books from me were not particularly excited about taking me on for something completely different. I don't blame them, but I think they missed the boat on a popular trend. In the meantime, things were heating up with my day job at *Windows 2000 Magazine*, and I ended up spending the rest of the year being pretty busy traveling and writing. But I bought a digital camera as promised and took it halfway around the world, literally, to Israel, on a business trip I will never forget. It took months to record all my CDs onto the computer, and by the time I was done, I had literally destroyed one drive in the process. And we finally got a nice digital camcorder, which Mark insists be used so he can see himself in the side-mounted LCD display.

Months later, at LinuxWorld 2001 in New York (of all places), I ran into Deborah Williams Cauley, who had been bugging me for months to write some kind of a book. We sat down and I finally told her about my ideas for a digital media title and how I thought the then-beta "Whistler" project (which became Windows XP) would be a perfect subject, because of its integrated (and surprisingly powerful) digital-media experiences. "Write up a TOC," she said. "Let's make this happen."

And happen it did. My first book in two years.

A couple of stories about the writing process for this book: Because of my continuous travel schedule, much of this book was written on airplanes, trains, and in hotel rooms all over the United States. This required me to cart around a bizarre variety of hardware, including portable music devices, USB video splitters, FireWire-equipped camcorders, and a Pocket PC, among other things. I can only imagine what hotel house cleaning thought of me.

My favorite form of travel is train, and fortunately I get to go this route fairly often: On Amtrak between Boston and New York you can often get a table and really spread out, and I travel this route at least once a month, every month. On one trip to New York — for the Office XP launch in late May 2001, I believe — I was sitting at a table on the train across from a woman who was painting watercolors and eating a granola/yogurt mixture that actually looked pretty good. I unpacked a monstrous Dell laptop with integrated FireWire, a Canon digital camcorder, various USB and FireWire cables, and proceeded to record, edit, and produce a digital video. The woman across from me was extremely curious about what I was doing and kept looking up to catch a glimpse of the setup. Finally, she couldn't stand it anymore.

"Sorry, but do you mind if I ask you what you're doing?" she asked.

And I replied "I'm capturing video from the camera, editing it on the computer, adding titles and background music, and then I'm going to save it back to the computer. When I can afford one, I'm going to buy a DVD recorder so I can record versions of this for my parents and other relatives." Or something like that.

She took this in for a few seconds, clearly amazed and not fully comprehending what it was that I had said. And then she said something that will probably stick with me forever.

"You must have a wonderful life."

She was met by a blank stare. How do you answer that? I'm not sure that I ever did, to be honest, but I do remember fumbling over an appropriate response. I sort of took this stuff for granted, in a way. But I think this underscores how liberating and exciting this technology can be. How fun it is. And, frankly, how much of it can be had fairly cheaply. We live in a time of great riches when it comes to technology. It's time we had some fun with it.

And I want you to have a wonderful life, too. Think of this book as the tour guide.

How to Read This Book (Don't Skip This Part!)

You don't have to read this book from beginning to end, in order, unless you really want to. There are plenty of cross-references for more information, so if you decide to skip around, you won't be penalized for it.

Some sections, of course, include chapters that build on each other. If you don't know how to play videos in Windows Media Player for Windows XP (MPXP), for example, you probably shouldn't dive straight into digital-video creation. But you may feel like you're up on digital photography, and decide to skip ahead to digital music first. That's fine, as long as you promise to go back eventually and read the whole thing: Windows XP makes its treasure-trove of functionality easy to discover, but a lot of the really dazzling stuff is still buried and unobvious. Even if you think you're an expert, I recommend taking the time to go through each section to see what's up. You might be surprised.

A Little about This Book's Structure

This book is divided into four parts; each part contains a different number of chapters. (You'd think I would have organized this a bit more logically, but sometimes a book takes on a life of its own. [It's not my fault. Honest.]) Here's what you can expect to see as you progress through this book.

Part I: A Picture is Worth a Thousand Words

In Part I, you learn about the digital-photography features in Windows XP, such as the new and improved My Pictures folder, the buff Scanner and Camera Wizard, and some help with installing digital-imaging hardware. We also take a look at the process of acquiring digital photographs from scanners and digital cameras.

Part II: Music to Your Ears

This part shows you how to play, organize, and record digital audio. You learn about the cool new Media Player for Windows XP (MPXP), the new and improved My Music folder, features for copying audio CDs, and ways to make your own "mix" CDs and backup data CDs.

Part III: Baby, You're a Movie Star

This part explores the world of digital movies. You get a look at digital-movie playback — including DVDs — in Media Player for Windows XP, as well as some tips on video management, home moviemaking, and the new version of Windows Movie Maker (which you can use to record, edit, and compose your own movies).

Part IV: Working with the Outside World

Part IV briefs you on the digital-media features in Windows XP that extend beyond your PC; these include the Internet-and-digital-media integration features in Internet Explorer and MSN Explorer. Then you check out some twenty-first-century gadgets (such as Pocket PCs and portable audio devices) that you can use to take digital media with you.

Appendixes? Not here.

This book concludes with zero (yes, 0) appendixes. I felt that this was an important enough feature to point out, since most technical books are full of appendixes listing things like API calls, video modes, and other miscellanea. This book is supposed to be fun, thus, no appendixes.

CD-ROM? Nope.

This book also contains zero (0) CD-ROMs, or *coasters*. You'd lose it anyway, and I wasn't in the mood to make something that was going to be obsolete the second you opened it up. So in lieu of the AOL strategy, I decided to include a . . .

Web site? You bet.

This book contains exactly one (1) Web site. Well, it doesn't actually *contain* a Web site, because you'd probably lose that, too. But it does have a complementary Web site available at www.xpdigitalmedia.com. This way, you can stay up to date on this, and we don't have to kill any more trees to make it happen. (It's what the Washington Conservatory might call a "win-win" situation.) The *Great Digital Media with Windows XP* Web site includes links to digital media news stories, information about Windows XP updates, and other information related to digital media and this book. Check it out!

Icons Used in This Book

This book contains a few icons to help point out important information to you. As you see these, make sure you take note of them:

This icon is the equivalent of a "power up" in your favorite video game. It gives you the information you need to take it to the next level. In this case, the next level is digital-media *mastery:* By the time you're done with this book, you should be able to turn off all that excess UI stuff and still get work done efficiently. You will become *uber-geek* and rise to a higher level of existence (patent pending).

This icon gives you information that could cause planning, implementation, or functionality problems. I use these only when necessary, so do pay attention to them.

This icon points the way to useful information in other locations in the book. In general, this is required because of the slipshod nature in which most books are created, but the reality is that most topics are hard to explain in a linear fashion. (And frankly, those that aren't are often boring anyway.)

This icon gives you some additional information about the subject at hand.

 This is a piece of friendly advice, like "don't feed the animals," or "don't give out your credit card information over Windows Messenger."

Acknowledgments

I would like to thank Debra Williams Cauley for putting up with two years of uncertainty: We finally made a book! Thanks also to Amanda Munz Peterson for dealing gracefully with perpetual delays and constant changes: It's hard writing about a topic this complicated during its development, and of course other projects (and real life) get in the way. Amanda was a trouper, though I suspect I cut off years of her life. Sorry.

Special thanks to Microsoft's Sean Alexander for putting up with my boneheaded questions. Sean is a digital-media maven who puts me to shame: I bow before his greatness.

Very special thanks, of course, to my wife, Stephanie and my son, Mark, who gave up precious time so I could get this book finished. It sounds trite, but this kind of project could never be completed without a sacrifice or two from family, and I owe mine big-time. Plus, Mark will never live down all those pictures and home movies I put on the Web. (I can't wait until I meet his first prom date.)

Contents at a Glance

Contents

Part I: A Picture Is Worth a Thousand Words   1

Introduction

Windows XP is the latest Microsoft operating system for *individuals* — that is, it's designed for real people, not for servers or embedded systems. It is the company's most impressive upgrade in over five years, and the realization of a long-standing dream to unite the code-bases of the venerable DOS/Windows family with NT, Microsoft's high-end solution for businesses.

In this introduction, I'd like to provide a quick look at Windows XP. I'm starting with where it fits into the overall history of Windows, a product line that's been in development for almost twenty years. If you haven't yet upgraded to Windows XP, this introduction may convince you that doing so is a great idea. If you are already running Windows XP, then congratulations: You made the right choice. No doubt about it.

A Short History of Microsoft Windows

The story of Windows begins with the first IBM Personal Computer (PC), which was released in October 1981. At the time, Windows wasn't even a gleam in Bill Gates' eye, but the release of the first PC is important because it ushered in the notion of Microsoft as an operating system supplier. The IBM PC shipped with PC-DOS 1.0 (which Microsoft first called DOS and then MS-DOS), and though two other OS options (CPM/86 and p-System) were later added, it was Microsoft's DOS product that captured the minds and wallets of millions of PC customers. And as the IBM PC roared into instant success, so too did Microsoft.

Windows is born

DOS, being a cryptic command-line operating system, made the need for a friendly, graphics-based interface glaringly obvious. Thus Microsoft began work on something called *Interface Manager*, which was to be a graphical environment that ran on top of DOS; even at this early stage, Microsoft realized that compatibility with the successful products of the past (in this case, DOS) was the key to continued success. Interface Manager was later renamed Windows and Microsoft *announced* the product at Fall Comdex in 1983, just two months before Apple released its graphically oriented Macintosh product.

Two years later, Microsoft finally *released* Windows 1.0, setting the stage for later scheduling embarrassments. The new product bombed big time: Compared to the elegant Mac OS, Windows was a hack, and it was an ugly hack. On-screen windows could not overlap, but could only be tiled. It was a step up from DOS, but only a small one.

A few other uninspiring releases followed. In December 1987, Microsoft released Windows 2.0, which finally featured overlapping windows and compatibility with Intel's 80286 microprocessor, giving it access to a then-heady 1MB of RAM (Windows 1.0 was limited to 640K). Windows 2.0 was later split into two separate products, Windows/286 and Windows/386, the latter of which provided support for Intel's 80386; this version could use "virtual machines" for DOS applications, protecting these from each other for the first time.

OS/2: Successor to DOS?

During the 1980s, however, Windows wasn't selling and few developers bothered writing applications that took advantage of its special features. For this reason (and to protect its important relationship with IBM), Microsoft began co-developing another follow-up to DOS, this time with IBM's help. It was called OS/2 (get it?). OS/2 would be a 16-bit operating system like DOS, providing a graphical interface called Presentation Manager (PM), memory protection, and other advanced features.

Though the project had the backing of an industry giant (IBM) and the de facto OS maker (Microsoft), OS/2 never really took off. The first version lacked the promised graphic interface, and had higher-level hardware requirements than DOS. Only in October 1988 did Presentation Manager finally arrive — but (as with Windows) users stayed away in droves. Sadly, this trend would continue throughout the history of OS/2, which evolved into an elegant, if often overlooked, product.

Windows reborn

Meanwhile, at Microsoft, only a handful of engineers remained at work specifically on Windows. But these engineers came up with something fairly elegant, a feature that was designed also for the next version of OS/2. They created a version of Windows that could safely multitask 16-bit graphical applications as well as DOS apps. (In other words, it could protect the applications from each other.) This version of Windows was given the green light internally, assigned many more developers, and was finally released in May 1990 as Windows 3.0.

And then something unexpected happened. Windows 3.0 became an immediate success, selling over 1 million units a month by the end of the year. IBM, sensing that Microsoft had secretly shafted OS/2, began discussions which eventually led to the breakup of the two companies' relationship, with IBM handling OS/2 on its own after that and Microsoft going forward with Windows. For Microsoft, the choice became easy after the release of Windows 3.0; until that time it had been unclear which environment they should back. The little GUI replacement for DOS had come into its own.

Windows 3.0 was followed two years later by Windows 3.1, which sold even better than its predecessor, cementing the Windows dominance that we're now so inured to. Windows 3.1 added new font technology, support for Object Linking and Embedding (OLE), and other tweaks. For the next decade, Windows reigned supreme over the computing landscape.

Microsoft moves upmarket with Windows NT

Meanwhile, Microsoft realized that its 16-bit DOS/Windows products were reaching the technological end of the line; the company began looking for ways to enter the 32-bit market initiated by the Intel 80386 chip. Two options emerged. First, in the late 1980s, Microsoft hired the architect of Digital's VMS operating system, Dave Cutler. Cutler was charged with making a next-generation 32-bit operating system, which was immediately named NT, for "New Technology." First designed as a successor to OS/2, NT was eventually renamed to Windows NT and overhauled to look like Windows 3.0. But Windows NT had nothing in common with Windows technically — only the user interface looked like Windows. But Microsoft also designed the underlying architecture of NT to look like Windows to programmers, making it easier to port 16-bit Windows applications to the new system. And a *compatibility mode* was added so 16-bit Windows apps would actually run under NT (albeit slowly).

Windows NT took five years to come to market. Its initial release in May 1993, curiously named Windows NT 3.1 to match the then-current version of Windows (3.1), didn't sell very well. NT was considered too slow and resource-greedy to be of any use to most businesses, though it was universally hailed for its robustness and stability.

For the next few years, Microsoft continued to improve Windows NT, with two releases that increased the speed of the system, and cross-platform releases that allowed the OS to run on a variety of 32-bit chips from vendors other than Intel. Though these other versions of NT were eventually cancelled, their development would make it easier for Microsoft to one day transform NT to the 64-bit platforms of the future.

Meanwhile, the DOS/Windows team wasn't sitting still either. In 1992 and 1993, Microsoft released two network-savvy versions of Windows, under the moniker Windows for Workgroups, that quietly incorporated a number of features that were planned for a hybrid 16/32-bit system code-named Chicago, due for release in the mid-1990s. These features included a file-system access capability that could bypass DOS entirely, further enhancing speed and stability. Though most users were unaware of the stealth feature set in Windows for Workgroups, that product closely resembled an upcoming version of Windows that would one day take the world by storm.

Media event of the decade: Windows 95 is released

In August 1995, Microsoft finally released version 4.0 of Windows ("Chicago") and sold it as Windows 95. An instant success, Windows 95 set new standards for marketing, sales, and mindshare. Windows 95 was (at least partially) a 32-bit operating system that used largely the same programming interfaces as Windows NT while preserving compatibility with the DOS/Windows past. It presented a beautiful new user interface that made Windows 3.*x* (and NT) appear sickly by comparison. It supported long file names, 32-bit applications, and Plug and Play hardware (a standard designed to take some of the drudgery out of upgrading your PC with new components).

By that Christmas, Windows 95 had sold tens of millions of units at retail, an unheard-of record for software that was generally acquired only with a new PC. Windows 95 was the first retail success for Windows, a feat that has yet to be duplicated by subsequent upgrades.

On the NT front, Microsoft prepped a version of its high-end 32-bit system that used the new user interface found in Windows 95; it would also run the same applications. Released in July 1996 as Windows NT 4.0, the product achieved success far above any previous version of NT, which took the product into new markets. Within a few years, NT had secured the top spot as the corporate standard for desktop and server operating systems.

Sequels are never as successful

Following the blockbuster release of Windows 95 and the successful (but more subdued) launch of Windows NT 4.0, Microsoft set about to meld the two OSes into a single, cohesive product. The company began by plotting yearly upgrades to Windows 95, which would allow PC makers to include support for new hardware. The first few of these releases were available with new PCs as OEM Service Releases (OSRs), which fixed bugs, added small features, and added that important hardware support. Retail buyers of Windows 95 were stuck, however, with the initial (unenhanced) version released in 1995.

After a few years of OSR releases, however, Microsoft finally began development of a Windows product that would follow Windows 95 into retail stores. Eventually sold as Windows 98, this product became infamous for its hybrid user interface — which melded the classic Explorer from Windows 95 with Internet Explorer 4 (IE 4), the company's Web browser. The public generally perceived Windows 98 (then at the heart of a government investigation into Microsoft business practices) as a lackluster upgrade since most of its features were available for free download for Windows 95 users — but it sold well and eventually became the desktop OS standard.

In 1999, the company released an even less exciting upgrade called Windows 98 Second Edition (SE), which added a new and improved version of Internet Explorer and a feature called Internet Connection Sharing (ICS), that allowed users to easily share one Internet connection between two or more PCs.

At about this time, development of Windows NT 5.0 was heating up as well; Microsoft began promising that the new NT release would bring with it the long-promised melding of the NT and Windows 9x product lines. Unfortunately, that never happened.

Potholes on the road to unity

A couple of problems occurred during the development of Windows NT 5.0. First, Microsoft wanted that release of NT to feature the same hardware and software compatibility as Windows 98, so a number of new technologies had to be grafted onto NT — which wasn't designed with this sort of feature in mind. Secondly, NT 5.0 had to scale up and out to a wider range of (more sophisticated) servers than Windows NT 4.0 did — thus its directory-services feature had to be upgraded significantly to compete with similar products from Novell and others. And Microsoft had corporate-oriented features it wanted to add. In the end, everything but the kitchen sink was added to the NT 5.0 feature set.

As the years dragged on — 1997, 1998, 1999 — something had to give. Finally, Microsoft decided that Windows NT 5.0 (confusingly renamed "Windows 2000," which made it seem like an upgrade to Windows 98, not NT) would *not* include a version for consumers and would instead be marketed solely to businesses as the next NT. With the naming decision public, however, they stuck with the name Windows 2000 — and finally released the new Windows version in early 2000.

Despite the long gestation (and analysts' fears that Windows 2000 wouldn't make it to market), the product was an immediate and obvious success. Windows 2000 featured support for Plug and Play, DirectX, USB, AGP, and many other advances that had previously been the province of Windows 9*x* only. It lacked that one crucial feature — application and device compatibility for consumer products — that would have allowed it to be sold to the consumer-oriented Windows 9*x* market. But it quickly sold millions of units as businesses began the rapid process of upgrading from NT to Windows 2000. Although the new release made a smaller media splash than had 95, Windows 2000 was a technical success under the surface. Microsoft could, and did, build a future on it.

Pro and consumer versions part company: Windows Me

Meanwhile, the Consumer Windows team was left without a product for 2000, so a team began working on the specifications for a new Windows 9*x* product, code-named Millennium, which was given the green light in early 1999. Millennium was eventually released as Windows Millennium Edition (Windows Me) in mid-2000. Although it sold well through new PC bundlings, the product was a marketing disaster for Microsoft because of incompatibilities and bad press.

The problem was that there wasn't much that could be done with the 15-year-old base upon which Windows Me rested. Microsoft removed an older piece of code called Real Mode DOS (this had been around in one form or another since 1983) and added some stability features such as System Restore and System File Protection. But many users experienced wild incompatibilities with Windows Me, giving it a black eye from which the product never really recovered from.

However, Microsoft did get one thing very right with Windows Me. Sensing that users wanted to more closely integrate digital media technologies such as digital photos, music, and movies into their PCs, Microsoft added a number of features to Windows Me that made these technologies easier to work with. Windows Me included Windows Media Player 7 (MP7) — the company's first integrated all-in-one streaming player and media jukebox — and Windows Movie Maker (WMM) 1.0, which let users make simple home movies. Though overlooked by many users, Windows Me was setting the stage for the future for consumers.

Whistler, Blackcomb, and .NET

That future was a product called Whistler, which would be based on the Windows 2000 Engine (or *kernel*) and offer all the digital-media features of Windows Me while fulfilling the hardware and software compatibility that never happened with the original release of Windows 2000. Whistler eventually came to market as Windows XP; server versions of the product are marketed as the Windows .NET Server Family. (A follow-up to Windows XP, currently known as Blackcomb, is being created.) And of course, the company is transitioning to a Web services-based future it calls .NET ("dot net"). It never ends.

But in the meantime, we've got Windows XP. It's arguably the best release of Windows since Windows 95; take a look and judge for yourself.

Why Windows XP?

Microsoft had a number of goals for Windows XP — and though this book is ostensibly about digital-media integration, the realization of these goals will affect everyone who upgrades to Windows XP. First, Windows XP is designed to be equally applicable for home and business users, and for new users and power users alike. This sounds like a rather lofty promise, but it's been largely realized in Windows XP.

Microsoft likes to say that it used to integrate *applications* (such as IE and Windows Media Player) in the Windows environment, but now it integrates *experiences* with Windows XP. (In fact, XP actually stands for *experience,* if you're curious.) While this sounds like a bit of marketingspeak, it's actually not that far off the mark. Windows XP features an entirely new task-based user interface that "bubbles" features up to the user in clear and easy-to-use ways. This book is all about those experiences, many of which revolve around digital-media technologies.

Windows XP was also designed to be easy to set up (or *deploy*, as corporate administrators would say) and use. Though the User Interface (UI) looks all new, anyone used to Windows 95 or newer versions should be comfortable enough to get right in and get to work. Like previous versions of Windows, XP is tightly integrated with the Internet. It is compatible with your games and other applications. Windows XP makes it easier to get help if you have a problem, and solve those problems without making a lengthy or expensive phone call.

Best of all, Windows XP finally melds the reliability and scalability of Windows NT/2000 with the application-and-hardware compatibility of Windows 98. It's designed to be the best of both worlds; unlike Windows Me, it succeeds and then some.

Core Windows XP Technologies

Under the hood, Windows XP is based on a new version of the Windows NT kernel, which is now dubbed the *Windows Engine* in this release. The Windows Engine ensures that Windows XP is the most dependable, intelligent, and well-connected operating system you can use today.

Additionally, the Windows architecture has been rebuilt so the user interface can be completely overhauled more easily. The new Windows XP user interface — which was code-named *Luna* during development — features two default visual styles: Windows XP and Windows Classic. The default Windows XP style (shown in Figure 1) is brand new, providing users with a gorgeous new look and feel that's best seen on modern high-resolution displays. Windows Classic looks a lot like Windows 2000 or 98, as shown in Figure 2.

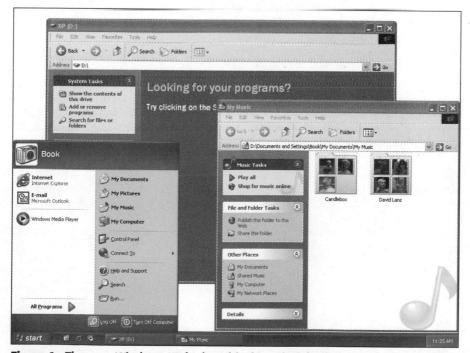

Figure 1: The new Windows XP look and feel is colorful, vibrant, and designed for high resolutions.

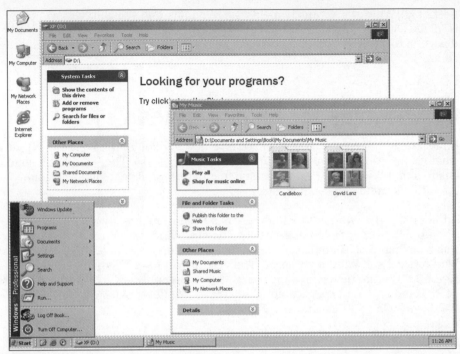

Figure 2: For compatibility, Microsoft is also including the Classic theme so users can make Windows XP look like Windows 2000/Me.

The Windows XP visual style offers subtly curving window borders, rich colors, and a three-dimensional shading effect that really sets it apart from previous versions of Windows. More importantly, its task-based Explorer windows (shown in Figure 3) help users (whether new or experienced) get at functionality more easily, without having to hunt and peck through multiple folders, looking for the right place.

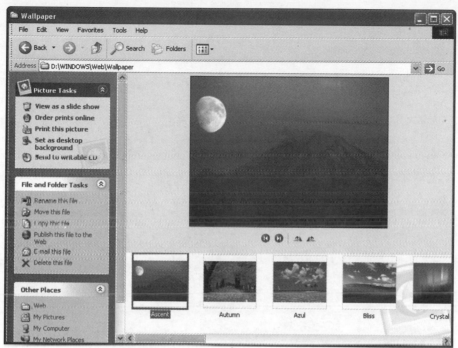

Figure 3: Task-based Explorer windows help you get work done without hunting around for options. Note the Picture Tasks in the left Web view pane.

The new Control Panel (shown in Figure 4) is a good example of the XP design approach. In Windows 2000, the Control Panel consisted of a large, alphabetized group of icons. In Windows XP, this has been replaced by a categorized Web-like window that displays common, frequently used tasks, with cross-links to related locations. The Control Panel groups are simple, logical, and easily navigated, making it easier to find tools and perform tasks. More subtly, dialog boxes have been enhanced to do away with the "OK" and "Cancel" choices of the past. When you want to change your password, for example, the dialog box has a button clearly labeled *Change my password*.

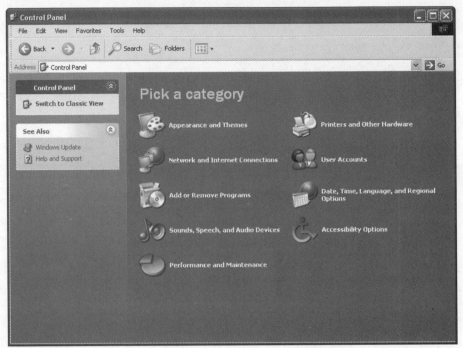

Figure 4: In Windows XP, the Control Panel has been upgraded with a categorized presentation.

Navigating through files and folders, it's obvious that a lot of work has been done to give you an immediate and clear understanding of what you're looking at. Image files are displayed as thumbnails; you can see, at a glance, what each file contains. Special shell folders such as My Pictures and My Music supply special views that bubble up the appropriate functionality: The My Pictures folder, for example (shown in Figure 5), offers up choices to view a slideshow or print photos from the Internet.

For users with LCD displays — common on laptops, of course, but becoming more common on desktop machines as well — a new technology called ClearType effectively triples the horizontal resolution of the screen, making text much more readable.

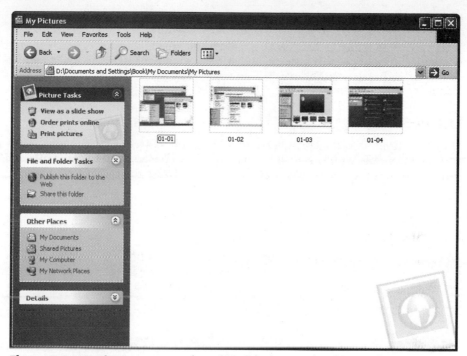

Figure 5: In My Pictures, you can launch a slideshow, order prints online, or print pictures using a nice wizard.

New User Experiences

In Windows XP, Microsoft has integrated a number of user experiences, which let you easily take advantage of your PC in ways that used to require tons of third-party applications. Some of the more critical new experiences include the following:

Music

Windows XP makes it easy to copy music CDs to your computer, create personalized music libraries, and copy music to portable audio devices. You can even make your own audio "mix" CDs.

Pictures

Users with scanners can easily copy their traditional photographs onto the computer, and digital camera users can download images quickly and easily. In either case, you can edit, view, and share those photographs with other users via the Internet.

Video

You can record family events on an analog or digital camcorder, copy them to the computer with low-cost hardware, and edit those movies into short films you can share with others (whether over the Internet or by using a Pocket PC device).

Games

Windows XP utilizes the latest version of Microsoft's DirectX multimedia libraries and is compatible with the most popular Windows-based games on the planet. You can play games online and easily add gaming hardware to your system without having to go through complex setup procedures.

Mobile use

Windows XP lets mobile users work anywhere and link back to the office and network-based files upon return. Windows XP supports the latest power-management technologies, ensuring that your laptop stays up and running as long as possible.

Home Edition Versus Professional Edition

Don't be surprised if the two different versions of Windows XP generate some confusion among users. Windows XP Home Edition ("Home") and Windows XP Professional Edition ("Pro") are slightly different. In short, Pro is a superset of Home; that means it has everything that's in Home, plus some other unique features.

Features for home users

Windows XP Home Edition is designed as an upgrade for most Windows 98 and Windows Me users, so it includes features that are comparable to those releases. For example, Home offers the following features:

✦ Improved software (application) and hardware compatibility when compared to Windows 2000 Professional.

✦ Simplified security model.

✦ Simplified logon featuring new "welcome" screen.

✦ Fast user-switching so multiple users can be logged on to the system simultaneously.

✦ A new "Windows XP" user interface ("visual style"), featuring context-sensitive Web views.

✦ Enhanced support for digital media (including movies, pictures, and music).

✦ DirectX 8.x multimedia libraries for gaming and multimedia.

Features for experienced users

Windows XP Professional (Pro) is a logical upgrade for business users running Windows NT 4.0 Workstation or Windows 2000 Professional. But Pro isn't just for corporate drones. Instead, Pro is also targeted at power users, programmers, and any other individual that wants to get more out of their PC. The following features are unique to Pro—that is, they are *not* present in Windows XP Home Edition:

Power user

✦ **Remote Desktop.** All versions of Windows XP (including Home Edition) support *Remote Assistance*, which is an assisted support technology that allows a help desk or system administrator to remotely connect to a client desktop for troubleshooting purposes. But only Pro supports the new Remote Desktop feature, which is a single-session version of Terminal Services with two obvious uses: mobile professionals who need to remotely access their corporate desktop and remote administration of clients on a network. You can access a Windows XP Remote Desktop from any OS that supports a Terminal Services client (such as Windows 98).

✦ **Multiprocessor support.** Windows XP Pro supports up to two microprocessors, while Home Edition supports only one.

✦ **Backup and Automated System Recovery (ASR).** In a somewhat controversial move, Microsoft has removed the Backup utility from Windows XP Home Edition, though a less-capable version can optionally be installed from the Home Edition CD-ROM. The reason for this probably has to do with the integration of Microsoft's new Automated System Recovery (ASR) tool into Backup. ASR can help a system recover from a catastrophic error (such as one that renders the system unbootable). ASR-enabled backups can be triggered from Setup, which means you can return your system to its previous state even if the hard drive dies and must be replaced.

 Caution

Unlike consumer-oriented features such as System Restore, ASR is *not* automatic. It must be enabled manually from within the Backup utility in Windows XP.

✦ **Dynamic Disk Support.** Windows XP Professional (like its Windows 2000 equivalent) supports dynamic disks, a more capable way of using hard drives than that available in Windows 9*x*/Me, but Home Edition does not (instead, HE supports only the standard Simple Disk type, which is compatible with Windows 9*x*/Me). Dynamic disks are not usable with any OS other than Windows 2000 or Windows XP, and they cannot be used on portable computers. Likewise, Home Edition does not include the Logical Disk Manager.

✦ **Fax.** Home Edition has no integrated fax functionality.

✦ **Internet Information Services/Personal Web Server.** Home Edition does not include the IIS Web server found in Pro.

Security

✦ **Encrypting File System.** Windows XP Professional supports the Encrypting File System (EFS), which allows you to encrypt individual files or folders for local security (EFS is not enabled over a network). EFS-protected files and folders allow users to protect sensitive documents from other users.

✦ **File-level access control.** Administrator can limit access to certain network resources, such as servers, directories, and files using access control lists. Only Windows XP Professional supports file-level access control, mostly because this feature is typically implemented through Group Policy Objects, which are also not available in Home Edition.

✦ **C2 certification.** Microsoft will attempt to have Windows XP Professional certified with the "C2" security designation, a largely irrelevant status for most end users, but one which will not be afforded to Home Edition.

Management

Because Home Edition is not designed to handle the heavy-duty missions assigned to business software, its system-management features are more modest than those of Pro. The following areas of comparison should clarify the contrast between versions:

✦ **Domain membership.** Home Edition cannot be used to log on to an Active Directory domain. For obvious reasons, the Domain Wizard is also missing in Home Edition.

✦ **Group Policy.** Home Edition cannot be used to log on to an Active Directory domain. Thus, Group Policy (whereby applications, network resources, and operating systems are administered for domain users) is not supported either.

✦ **Windows Media Player management and deployment features.** Using group policies or Active Directory, you can now standardize your media player deployments. For example, you can customize the look, features, and network settings of Media Player for Windows XP, and even limit access to consumer features.

✦ **IntelliMirror.** Microsoft gathers a wide range of semi-related technologies for managing change and configuration under the IntelliMirror umbrella — and none of these features are supported in the consumer-oriented Home Edition. IntelliMirror capabilities include user-data management; central management of software installation, repair, updating, and removal; user-settings management; and Remote Installation Services (RIS), with which administrators can remotely install the OS on client systems.

✦ **Roaming profiles.** This feature allows users to log on to any computer in an Active Directory network and automatically receive their customized settings. It is not available in Home Edition, which cannot log on to an Active Directory network.

Corporate deployment

✦ **Multilanguage support.** Only Windows XP Professional is available in a MultiLanguage version and supports multiple languages in a single installation.

✦ **Sysprep support.** Windows XP Pro supports the System Preparation (Sysprep) utility; Home Edition does not.

✦ **Remote Installation Services (RIS) support.** See the IntelliMirror heading in the previous section; Home Edition does not support RIS deployments.

64-bit edition

Microsoft has prepared a special 64-bit version of Windows XP for Itanium systems which is functionally identical to the 32-bit Professional Edition; Home Edition will remain limited to 32-bit Pentium systems.

Networking features

✦ The user interface for IPSecurity (IPSec)

✦ SNMP

✦ Simple TCP/IP services

✦ SAP Agent

✦ Client Service for NetWare

✦ Network Monitor

✦ Multiple Roaming feature

User-interface features

Windows XP Home Edition has some different default settings that affect the user interface. For example, Guest logon is activated by default in Home, but left turned off in Pro. The feature that allows the taskbar to move is turned off by default in Home, but turned on in Pro. Other user interface features are present in Pro but not Home; these include client-side caching and the Administrative Tools option on the Start menu.

Other notes on Home and Pro Editions

Home Edition will support upgrades from Windows 98, 98 SE, and Millennium Edition (Me), but not from Windows 95, NT 4.0 Workstation, or Windows 2000 Professional. You can upgrade from Windows 98, 98 SE, Millennium Edition (Me), Windows NT 4.0, or Windows 2000 Professional to Windows XP Professional. Interestingly, you can also upgrade from Windows XP Home Edition to Windows XP Professional Edition.

Deciding which edition to buy is simple: Peruse the above list and decide whether you can live without any of the high-end business features. If you can't, then you're going to want Professional. But either edition will work fine for the purposes of this book. The examples used here are *not* limited to Pro-specific features.

Requirements and Recommendations of Windows XP

Speaking of this book, I'd like to discuss a few realistic expectations. Digital media integration is going to require a little work on your part (fortunately, Microsoft has made those tasks pretty easy in XP). The process, however, is also going to require a little cash outlay.

If you want to copy audio CD music to your PC, for example, you're going to need a CD-ROM drive, which are fairly common, but you're also going to need a lot of hard drive space as digital audio can take up a lot of space. If you want to copy music to a Walkman-like digital audio device, then you're going to have to spend a couple of hundred bucks on one of these devices. Or several hundred dollars on a Pocket PC device. Likewise, movie and video integration can be expensive. DVD drives are fairly common these days, but if you want to copy video onto your system, you need a camcorder or other video device, plus a way to get that recorded imagery into your system. Hardware interfaces start at only $50, but can quickly jump into the hundreds of dollars, depending on the system.

Okay, you knew all this. And of course, you don't have to bite this all off at once. Chances are you have some audio CDs lying around, so you can begin there. And though a digital camera may be in the distant future, scanners are cheap, and you can use one to get your traditional photographs into the system. How you progress is up to you.

Given this information, I've compiled a list of the hardware you're likely to want if you're after what I call the "full meal deal"—all that Windows XP has to offer for digital-media integration. This list includes notes about why you might want each device; you can pick and choose as you go. (And of course, I make specific recommendations throughout the book.)

What you need

Just to run Windows XP, Microsoft says you'll need the following hardware:

- ✦ **CPU:** 233 MHz minimum, 300+ MHz recommended
- ✦ **RAM:** 64 MB minimum, 128+ MB recommended
- ✦ **Hard drive space:** 1.5 GB minimum

Okay, that doesn't look too bad. Until you realize that it's completely unrealistic (that is, too small and too slow), especially if you want to take advantage of digital media. My recommendations for readers of this book are as follows:

- ✦ **CPU:** 500 MHz or higher
- ✦ **RAM:** 256 MB or more
- ✦ **Hard drive space:** 20 GB or more

Don't be discouraged by this list. RAM and hard drives are *extremely* cheap these days, and there's little reason to not take advantage of this fact. Windows XP will take advantage of whatever hardware you can throw at it. I recommend letting it do so.

What you want (if you don't have it already)

Okay, we've dispensed with the bare minimums. To best take advantage of Windows XP and this book, you'll want at least a few of the following.

- ✦ **CD-type drive:** One CD-RW, one DVD, or one combo CD-RW/DVD drive.
- ✦ **Video card:** 3D accelerated with at least 32MB of RAM.
- ✦ **Display monitor:** A 19-inch (or larger) CRT or a 15-inch (or larger) LCD monitor capable of at least 1024 x 768 resolution with 24- or 32-bit color. Media files such as photos and videos demand the best you can give.
- ✦ **Sound card:** Any will do, but something that supports four speakers and/or digital sound is preferable.
- ✦ **Speakers:** Two speakers with a subwoofer should be considered a bare minimum for any digital music buff.
- ✦ **Portable audio device:** A SonicBlue Rio 600, 800 or Volt, Iomega HipZip, Compaq PA-1, or related device will let you take your digital music on the road. Look for one that supports both Windows Media Audio (WMA) and MP3 for the most flexibility.
- ✦ **Pocket PC device:** Really a miniature PC with a touchscreen, the Pocket PCs can fill a surprising number of roles for digital media buffs. You can display photographs, show home videos, and listen to digital audio, all in a device that can be used for word processing and personal information management to boot.
- ✦ **Camcorder:** Analog (8mm, VHS, or VHS-C typically) will work, but digital (Digital-8 or Mini-DV) is better. If you just want to experiment, hook up your VHS video player or component DVD player.
- ✦ **USB-based video input:** Windows XP ships with Windows Movie Maker, which is limited to 320 x 240 video capture through USB; but a cheap USB-based video input device will work just fine and let you get your feet wet inexpensively.

✦ **PCI/IEEE 1394-based video input:** If you've got a digital camcorder, go with a PCI card or 1394-based solution, which will give you higher resolutions approaching DVD quality and programmable controls in Windows Movie Maker. 1394 is also referred to as "FireWire" and "iLink."

✦ **Scanner:** No digital camera? Scan your existing photos with a USB-based or FireWire-based scanner. Good USB scanners are available for well under $100.

✦ **Digital camera:** These days you can get a nice 2.1- or 3-megapixel (MPX) digital camera for less than $500 and the quality will shock and amaze you. Online photo services even let you get traditional prints.

✦ **Digital audio receiver:** SonicBlue Rio and PC makers (such as Dell Computer and Gateway) sell component devices that let you pipe your PC-based digital audio through your stereo system using your home's built-in phone jacks. It's a nice way to leverage your PC-based music collection in the living room or den.

I cover each of these hardware devices in more detail in the appropriate places in the book. Your mission, should you decide to accept it: Dig into what you want to know, and have some fun. It's your PC!

A Picture Is Worth a Thousand Words

P A R T

I

◆　◆　◆　◆

In This Part

Chapter 1
Managing Photos
and Images

Chapter 2
Using a Scanner with
Windows XP

Chapter 3
Using a Digital
Camera with
Windows XP

◆　◆　◆　◆

Working with digital photographs and other images is probably one of the first things you'll want to try in Windows XP, and it's arguably the least expensive. If you're using a standard point-and-click or SLR camera, you can move your prints onto a personal computer (PC) using a cheap scanner, but this approach is time-consuming. If you can afford it, a digital camera offers you stunning quality and easy PC connectivity. Plus, you can order prints from a digital camera using online photo services or print them yourself using an inexpensive ink jet printer. This section examines all the Windows XP features and techniques available for working with digital images.

Managing Photos and Images

If you consider the various "experiences" that Microsoft has built into Windows XP, the ability to easily work with digital photos and other images has to be one of the most exciting. Over the past few years, digital photography has been one of the fastest growing segments of consumer electronics. Even professional photographers are beginning to turn to digital photography as the perfect solution for many tasks — but this capability has many advantages for the average user as well. Those on the fence don't have to decide now; Windows XP works equally well with traditional photos, using a scanner, and digital photos.

Whichever way you acquire your images, the goal is to get them on the computer. From there you can manage your photographs and archive them, view, edit and print them, and share them with others, via e-mail or the Web. Once your photographs are in digital format — stored on your computer — the sky is the limit.

This chapter takes a look at the digital photo management tasks that are common to both scanners and digital cameras. In other words, no matter how you acquire your images, the management issues are the same. You can organize your images with the My Pictures folder, view images and perform simple editing tasks with the built-in Preview applet, and edit images with Microsoft Paint. And new to Windows XP is a Photo Printing Wizard that can have you printing professional-looking prints in no time.

Subsequent chapters in this section cover the issues specific to scanners and digital cameras.

Managing Images with My Pictures

In Windows 95, Microsoft introduced the My Documents folder as the default save location for all documents. In earlier

Windows versions (believe it or not), most applications automatically saved documents in either the WINDOWS folder or the root of the C: drive. But we've come to take the My Documents folder for granted over the past few days, and all modern Windows programs use this location for their documents and other data files.

From a technical standpoint, My Documents is a special shell folder. It has a physical location on the hard drive (C:\My Documents in Windows 9x/Me, but C:\Documents and Settings\[*Your user name*]\My Documents in Windows XP/2000; Windows NT had a similar location under C:\Winnt\Profiles) — but it also has a location in the shell hierarchy. You can see this by opening Windows Explorer or by opening My Computer and turning on Folders view (View ⇨ Folders). For each user, the top of the shell is marked by the My Documents folder, as shown in Figure 1-1. Other items in the top level of the shell hierarchy include My Computer, My Network Places (Network Neighborhood in previous Windows versions), and the Recycle Bin.

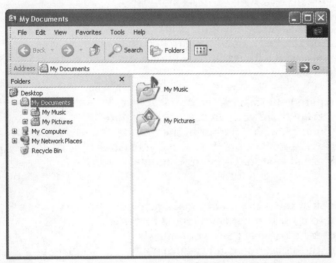

Figure 1-1: In Explorer view, you can see the shell hierarchy.

In Windows XP, Microsoft has elevated two other folders to "special shell folder" status. These include My Music (designed to manage and organize digital music files) and My Pictures (which does the same for digital photographs and other images). Both My Music and My Pictures are located inside the My Documents folder by default, though you can change this if you desire. But because they are special shell folders that you may want to access frequently, both My Music and My Pictures are also available directly from the Start menu, as shown in Figure 1-2. For more about My Music, see Chapter 6; but for now, the My Pictures folder has center stage.

Figure 1-2: In the Start menu, you can see special shell folders on the right side.

My Pictures is designed as the central repository for all your digital still images, be they digital photographs or other images. As you discover in the next two chapters, Microsoft has built wizards into Windows XP that can automatically store images obtained from digital cameras and scanners into this folder or sub-folders within this folder. But since we can't assume that you've acquired any images yet, let's grab a few sample images before proceeding.

Navigate to the C:\WINDOWS\Web\Wallpaper folder (or its equivalent; If you installed Windows XP to the D: drive, for example, then this folder resides at C:\WINDOWS\Web\Wallpaper). In here, you'll see a number of images files, which can be used to decorate your desktop. But we can also use them to see how the My Pictures folder can work; so copy them (copy, not move) over to the My Pictures folder.

Viewing photos and images

By default, the My Pictures folder (Figure 1-3) shows files in Thumbnails view, which shows a small preview of each image in lieu of normal icons.

You can view an individual image by double-clicking its icon. This launches the Image Preview applet, shown in Figure 1-4, a decent image viewing application that comes free with XP.

Figure 1-3: Thumbnails view provides a small image in place of an icon.

Figure 1-4: Image Preview provides simple viewing and image manipulation options.

Getting image file metadata

You can also obtain special information about an image or other file types—called *metadata*—by moving the mouse pointer over its icon without clicking (a maneuver known as a *mouseover*). When you do so with an image file, a tooltip window appears next to the mouse cursor and displays the dimensions of the image in pixels (800x 600, for example), the type of image (such as Bitmap, JPEG, or GIF, among others), and its size on the disk (typically in kilobytes, though larger images might actually be measured in megabytes). This feature is shown in Figure 1-5.

Figure 1-5: To get metadata for any file, simply move the mouse pointer over its icon.

Getting more information

To find out more information about an image, you can look at that image's *Properties sheet*. You do this by selecting it and choosing File ➪ Properties. (Alternatively, you can right-click an image and choose Properties from the pop-up menu that appears). The Properties sheet has two panes, General and Summary. By default, the Summary pane appears (in Simple view), as shown in Figure 1-6.

You can get even more information by clicking the Advanced button. This displays the Advanced view, shown in Figure 1-7.

Figure 1-6: The Summary pane of an image's Properties sheet displays basic information about that file.

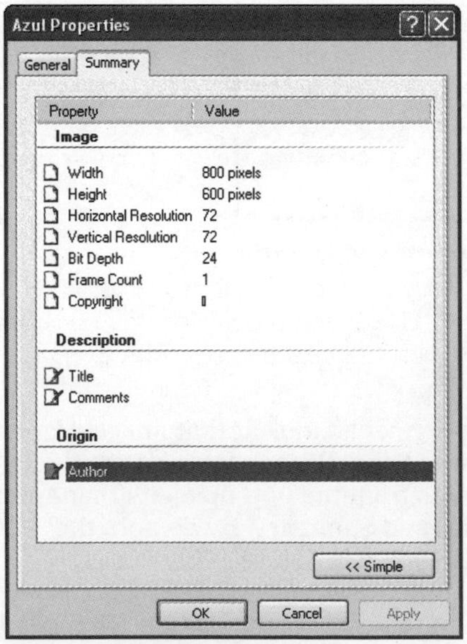

Figure 1-7: In the Advanced view, more metadata is exposed.

What's interesting about this information is that some of it can be edited. You can't change the width or height, obviously, but you can add a title, an author, or some comments if you'd like. To do so, click the area to the right of the Title, Comments, or Author field, respectively, and type in an appropriate value. Then click OK to close the dialog box and save this information — known as *metadata* — as part of the file.

Changing metadata for multiple files

Let's say you've got a directory full of image files and you'd like to add author information to every one of them. Sure, you could manually get the properties to each file, one at a time, and add the author info to each file's Properties sheet. But there's a faster way: Simple select all the files in the folder that you'd like to change, right-click, and choose Properties. Now you'll see a properties sheet that is applicable to all the files. Now, you can change the Title, Comments, and Author's field for each file, all at the same time.

Using subfolders to manage My Pictures

From an organizational standpoint, a single My Pictures folder only works if you're not dealing with a large number of images. For example, if you think you're going to be scanning in a lot of traditional photographs (as described in the next chapter) or taking advantage of digital photography (see Chapter 3), you have to start thinking about organizational issues.

The simplest solution is to use subfolders, which you can create directly inside My Pictures. So you might create a *Wallpaper* folder, and drag all those wallpaper images we've been working with in there, rather than leave them in the root My Pictures folder. As you scan in photographs or copy photographs from a digital camera, you could use subfolders that represent specific dates, events, or other logical groupings. It's up to you.

One cool feature of Windows XP: When you copy images into a folder and are viewing that folder with Thumbnails view, the folder icon changes to display up to four thumbnails, as shown in Figure 1-8. This lets you tell what's in a folder at a glance (especially useful when you've got a lot of images and subfolders to manage).

Figure 1-8: Folder thumbnails are new to XP, and they help you quickly determine what's contained within.

Customizing Image Folders

The My Pictures folder — and to a greater extent, the subfolders it contains — can be customized in many ways that make image files more enjoyable or efficient to work with. You can customize the way folders and folder icons look, use the Details section of the Web pane to see metadata and thumbnails quickly, view slide shows of folder contents, and display individual image files as your desktop image. This section examines these possibilities.

Using Folder views

If you open the My Picture folder, or a subfolder that contains images, it shows the contents of that folder in one of several view styles. By default, My Pictures defaults to Thumbnails view, but other views are possible; a discussion of each is coming up.

Filmstrip view

When you create a subfolder under My Pictures and populate it with image files, Windows Explorer uses Filmstrip view by default. This view, shown in Figure 1-9, renders a preview of the currently selected image in the top of the right pane of the window, while displaying the folder contents as a single row of thumbnails along the bottom of the window, in a manner similar to a filmstrip. As you select each icon along the bottom, the upper image changes to display the contents of the newly selected image file. This preview image is accompanied by a subset of the image controls found in the Image Preview applet (details come later in this chapter). These buttons let you move to the previous and next images, and rotate the image both clockwise and counterclockwise.

Figure 1-9: Filmstrip view provides an image preview right in the window.

Thumbnails view

Thumbnails view, as described previously, displays each image icon as a thumbnail of the contained image. This makes it easy to identify each file at a glance, but thumbnails can be slow to render if you have too many images in the folder.

Tip

To change the view style manually, select the View menu and then one of the following: Filmstrip, Thumbnail, Tiles, Icons, List, or Details. Most of these choices should be familiar to you if you've worked with previous versions of Windows, but they're described below just in case. Note that Filmstrip and Tiles are new to XP; Thumbnails has been significantly updated since Windows 2000 and Windows Me.

Tiles view

As the default view in upper-level shell folders such as My Computer and My Network Places, Tiles view shows a standard icon and file name alongside other metadata that's related to the current folder view options. For example, in the My Documents window, shown in Figure 1-10, icons are shown arranged by name, so the metadata displays the name of the document, the type of document (Microsoft Word Document, for example), and the size, in Kilobytes. If you change the way the icons are arranged, the metadata display can change as well.

Figure 1-10: Tiles view provides metadata about each file.

Icons view

If you've been using Windows for a while, Icons view is probably familiar; it's the default view style used by every release of Windows since Windows 98. Icons view (formerly called Large Icons) displays simple, large icons with no metadata information. Figure 1-11 shows an example.

Figure 1-11: Icon view is analogous to Large Icons in previous versions of Windows.

Note   The Small Icons view style was removed from Windows XP; this view style was present in Windows 95 through Windows Me, Windows NT 4.0, and Windows 2000. Microsoft says that Small Icons view was removed because so few people used it.

List view

Suitable for folders with numerous files, List view offers smaller icons that automatically sort themselves by filename, which is convenient. List view is shown in Figure 1-12.

Details view

Details view is another holdover from the early days, offering a columnar view of file and folder information, with sections for metadata information such as file size, type, last date modified, and so on. The column for which the folder is sorted is now highlighted, a subtle new feature in Windows XP. This can be seen in Figure 1-13.

Figure 1-12: List view is the way to go if you're dealing with a folder that contains many files.

Given these folder views, it's likely that Filmstrip and Thumbnails fit the bill for most image folders. If you like the preview mode of Filmstrip, stick with that (I find it obtrusive and hard to work with, personally). Otherwise, use Thumbnail. If you find that folder rendering is glacially slow, however—probably because you've got dozens or perhaps hundreds of images in there—then stick with one of the more traditional views. As always, it's up to you.

Customizing folder icons

In addition to the standard folder views, Windows XP also supports the concept of *folder types*, which are defined by specific *folder templates*. Folder templates are only available for standard folders, however: You can't change the folder type of the My Pictures folder, for example. But subfolders can be changed at will, another reason to stick with this form of organization.

You have two ways to change the folder type for a folder. One way is to open the folder you'd like to change, right-click an empty area of the window, and choose *Customize this folder*. Alternatively, you can select a folder icon, right-click, choose *Properties*, and then navigate to the *Customize* page. Either way, you'll be presented with the Customize Folder view, as shown in Figure 1-14.

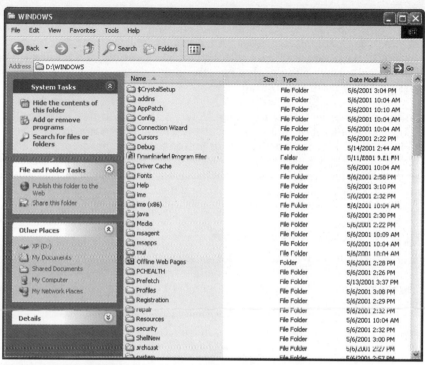

Figure 1-13: Details view has been enhanced with color so you can more easily tell which column the folder is sorted by.

Figure 1-14: You can customize individual folders using the Customize tab.

You can see a number of choices listed in the top drop-down list, including a few that are appropriate for image folders: *Documents (for any file type)*, *Pictures (best for many files)*, and *Photo Album (best for fewer files)*. The Documents choice is sort of a standard boilerplate for folders that can contain a variety of document types — but if you're dealing with a folder that contains only images, one of the other two choices is probably more appropriate.

In the Folder pictures section of this page, you can also determine whether the folder icon displays a set of thumbnails while in Thumbnails view, or a picture of your choosing. Click the Choose Picture button to pick a picture if you like.

If you're not using Thumbnails view, you can choose to change the icon of the folder instead. This is accomplished by clicking the Change Icon button.

Using the Details Web view

In the Web pane of the My Pictures folder and its subfolders, there is a Details section that is hidden by default, but you might find it of use, especially if you're not using Thumbnails or Filmstrip view. Open My Pictures or any other folder that contains image files to see how it works.

First, you have to unhide the Details section, which is accomplished by clicking the double down-arrow icon, as shown in Figure 1-15.

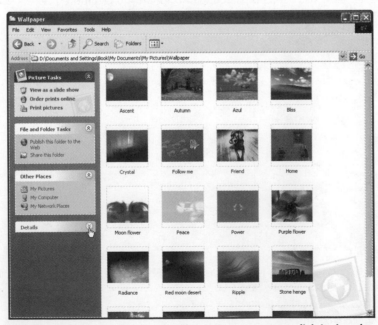

Figure 1-15: To display the Details section, you must click its header.

If no file in the folder is selected, you see detailed information about the folder, including its icon image (typically containing thumbnail images), its name, and the date and time it was last modified. This is shown in Figure 1-16.

Figure 1-16: If no file is selected, the Details option provides information about the entire folder.

If you select a file in the folder, the Details section changes to give you information about that file, as shown in Figure 1-17. Detailed information includes file name and type, dimensions, size, and the date and time it was last modified. Note that this information can be obtained by placing the mouse pointer over the icon for each file (as described previously), but you might find this method a bit easier.

You can also select multiple files. Doing so diminishes the amount of information shown in the Details section. Now it displays only the number of files selected and the total amount of disk space occupied by these files.

Tip

Why bother with the Details section of the Web view, when you can get image previews using Thumbnail view? Well, if you've got enough files in a folder, you may choose to use a different view style, such as List view, because Thumbnail view is actually pretty slow when you have a lot of files. When using List view, you can move from image to image and still get a quick thumbnail preview (albeit in the Web view) by unhiding the Details section.

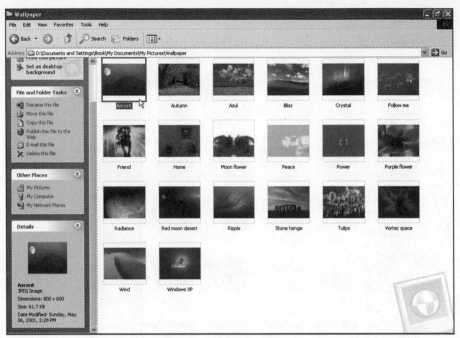

Figure 1-17: When a file is selected, Details provides a thumbnail when appropriate and other metadata.

Cool Picture Tasks: Slide Show and Desktop Background

In the upper part of the Web view for any folder containing an image is a section called Picture Tasks. This section looks at some of the options in this section throughout the remainder of this chapter, but two worth mentioning now are *View as a slide show* and *Set as desktop background*.

The option labeled *View as a slide show* launches the Slide Show application, which runs full screen and offers an automated, screensaver-like animation of all the images in the current folder. If you just click this option, the screen goes blank and the images in the folder appears, one at time, for about five seconds each. But you can control how the slide show acts as well. Move the mouse while the slideshow is running and a small toolbar appears in the upper-right corner of the screen, as shown in Figure 1-18.

This toolbar lets you start or pause the slide show, manually navigate to the previous or next image in the slide show, or stop the slide show (which closes the application). The buttons are drawn to resemble VCR controls, so their use is pretty obvious.

Figure 1-18: The slide show feature lets you view all the images in a folder.

Using a slide show as a screensaver

Many slide shows would make for a nice screensaver, so it might come as no surprise that Microsoft built this feature into the OS as well (those engineers at Microsoft — they seem to think of everything).

Here's how you enable this feature.

1. Open Display Properties (the quickest way is to right-click an empty spot on the desktop and choose *Properties*) and navigate to the Screen Saver tab.

2. In the Screen saver drop-down list box, choose My Pictures Slideshow.

3. Click Settings to display the Screen Saver Options dialog box, as shown in Figure 1-19. In this dialog box, you can determine how often the pictures change and other options. But the important one lets you choose which folder to use for the slide show. Click the Browse button to choose a folder. Also, be sure to play with the other options a bit: You can use transition effects and choose stretch smaller images, among other options. Click OK when you're done setting options.

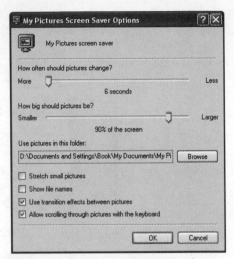

Figure 1-19: You can determine the behavior of your slide show screensaver with the Screen Saver Options dialog box.

4. In the Display Properties dialog box, click Preview to test your creation. As needed, return to the Options dialog box to tweak the options until you're happy with it. Note that moving the mouse or pressing a key during the preview will end the preview.

5. Click OK to close the Display Properties dialog box.

Using an image as a desktop background

The Display Properties dialog box has always made it possible to display a certain image as the desktop background, but this required you to launch the dialog box and then find the image. In Windows XP, you can do the reverse: When you find an image you like, you can tell Windows to use it as the desktop background. To do so, simply find an image you like and then click *Set as desktop background* from the *Picture Tasks* section of that folder's Web view.

It doesn't get any easier than that!

Looking Closer at the Image Preview Applet

Earlier in this chapter, we looked at the Image Preview applet very quickly, but there's more to this built-in tool than simple image viewing. Image Preview also performs a variety of other commonly needed image management tasks, including:

✦ **Image navigation** — Once you open an image with Image Preview, it is possible to navigate through all the images in the same folder by clicking the Previous Image and Next Image buttons in the Image Preview toolbar, which is located at the bottom of the window, as shown in Figure 1-20.

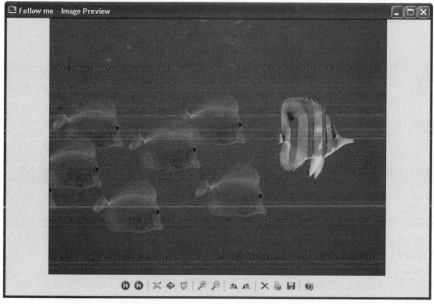

Figure 1-20: The Image Preview applet offers simple editing tools and viewing options.

✦ **Change the image preview size** — You can choose to show the selected image in its actual size or in a size that best fits the Image Preview window (which is resizable); you do this by clicking the Actual Size and Best Fit buttons, respectively.

✦ **Zoom in and out** — Using the Zoom In and Zoom Out buttons, you can increase and decrease the magnification level of the previewed image.

✦ **Rotate the image** — You can rotate the current image, clockwise or counterclockwise, in 90 degree increments, by clicking the Rotate Clockwise and Rotate Counterclockwise buttons. One caveat: When you do this, the actual image is changed (!) so be careful when using these options.

✦ **Delete an image** — Click the Delete button and (poof!) it's gone. You can restore it from the Recycle Bin if you're system is set up that way, but be careful with this option as well.

✦ **Print** — Click the Print button and the Photo Printing Wizard launches. We'll discuss this option more closely later in this chapter.

✦ **Copy the image**—If you click the Copy To button, which looks curiously like a Save icon, you can do the equivalent of a Save As and save that file, with a new name, and in a new location if desired.

✦ **Get help**—Click the Help button (or press F1) to view the Image Preview help file.

So what can't this little beauty do? Well, it can't edit image files. Fortunately, Microsoft supplies a simple Paint program, described in the next section, which offers some basic editing functionality. But you're going to want more than this if you're editing digital photographs or scanned photographs. Commercial image editing programs, like Adobe's excellent *Photoshop Elements* or *Microsoft Picture It!* are designed to overcome this limitations with such features as red-eye removal and more. I recommend a commercial package for anyone that needs more than just the basic tools offered in Image Preview and Paint. You can find reviews of such programs on the Web site for this book: www.xpdigitalmedia.com.

If you're a professional graphics artist, you're probably familiar with the TIFF file format, which is popular in this market. But TIFF files are also used often with computer-based faxes, so Microsoft has beefed up Image Preview to provide additional features when a TIFF image is displayed. This includes a capability to annotate TIFF images with text and simple drawings. TIFF files are generally enormous—because they are not compressed like JPEG and GIF images—and they tend to be of much higher quality.

To annotate a TIFF image, open one in Image Preview (they open in Image Preview by default), and you'll notice a number of new toolbar options, as shown in Figure 1-21.

Figure 1-21: You can annotate TIFF images in Image Preview.

Describing all these options is a bit beyond the scope of this book (and arguably of limited usefulness beyond faxes), but it's documented in Image Preview help and is fairly similar to how any other image editor works. If you do make annotations in a TIFF image and attempt to move to the next or previous image, or close Image Preview all together, the application warns you and ask whether you'd like to save it first.

And, if you're interested in finding a TIFF image to experiment with, the Microsoft Paint program (see the next section) offers the capability to open a Bitmap or JPEG image (among others) and save it as a TIFF. We'll look at some of Paint's other basic features next.

Editing Images with Paint

Microsoft Paint isn't the most elegant application in the world; in fact, it's barely changed since the days of Windows 3.1. But over the years, Microsoft has improved this often overlooked application (slowly but surely); you may find that it does a good percentage of what you need. And because it's free, you can't argue about the price.

In Windows 95, 98, NT 4.0, and 2000, Microsoft Paint was the application that opened when you double-clicked a bitmap file, but in Windows Me and XP, this procedure has changed: Image Preview loads instead. If you want to open an image file with Paint, select its icon under My Computer and then choose File ⇨ Edit (or, right-click the icon and choose Edit from the pop-up menu). Either way, Paint opens; maximize the window if necessary and your screen should resemble Figure 1-22.

Paint is a fairly simple image-editing program, with a toolbox for frequently used image editing tools, and a color box for selecting foreground and background color. Paint can be used to flip or rotate images, and this feature works a bit more elegantly than the similar feature in Image Preview. You can stretch and skew an image, but it doesn't do a very good job of this, and this is a typical area where a third party application such as Photoshop Elements really makes a difference. Paint can also invert the colors of an image, which gives an interesting (if rarely needed) negative effect.

And of course, Paint can be used to add text, paint in various ways, draw shapes, and cut and paste between images. And that's about it. But it works as advertised, and it's nice to have in a pinch. Again, commercial photo-editing applications offer many more photo-specific tools; shop around for prices and features.

Figure 1-22: Microsoft Paint is the perennial favorite.

Printing Photos with the Photo Printing Wizard

One amazing new feature in Windows XP is the Photo Printing Wizard, which is designed to take advantage of the fact that low-cost inkjet printers are now available that can print photo-quality and near photo-quality prints. The Photo Printing Wizard allows you to determine how you'll print your photos, and it includes templates for all the most common photo sizes. So if you want a sheet of wallet-sized prints, or 3 × 5s, or whatever, this wizard makes it easy. Let's take a look.

You can launch the Photo Printing Wizard in a variety of ways. If you select a single image icon, you can click the Picture Task labeled *Print this picture*; select a group of pictures, or no pictures at all, and the *Print picture* option is available. Either way, the Photo Printing Wizard starts up, as shown in Figure 1-23.

In the next page of the wizard, you can select which images you'd like to print. You can select all the images in the current folder (the default), or choose Clear All and then manually select the image or images you want, as shown in Figure 1-24.

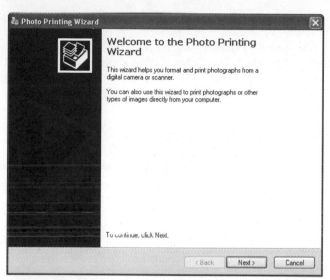

Figure 1-23: The Photo Printing Wizard is one of the coolest digital image tools in Windows XP.

Figure 1-24: You can easily choose which images you'd like to print.

In the next page, *Printing Options*, you can select the printer you'd like to use and any applicable printing preferences. If you have only one printer, you can pretty much skip over this step, but if you've got two or more, this is where you can select the correct one (hopefully, a nice color inkjet with photo-realistic printing capabilities).

The next page is where things get exciting. In *Layout Selection*, you can choose the type of photo layout you'd like, as shown in Figure 1-25. As you scroll down the list of available layouts, the Print preview pane changes to show you a preview of how the selected images look when printed. The Contact Sheet layout lets you print up to 45 thumbnails to a page which is perfect for printing numerous small images in a manner similar to the preview prints most photo printing services now offer.

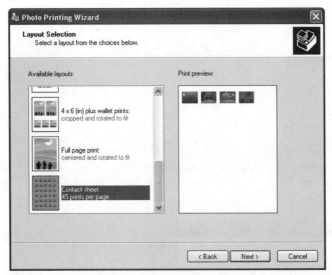

Figure 1-25: The Photo Printing Wizard offers a number of nice layouts that let you choose the way your photos print.

In the next step, your photos are printed; then you can close the wizard.

Ordering Prints Online

If you don't have a high-quality color printer, or simply want to create enough prints that a printer would be too slow or expensive, you can also order prints over the Internet. And as usual, this feature is built right into the shell. Previously, you'd have to manually navigate to online photo services with a Web browser, upload your photos, and then make an order. Now, it's a simple, step-by-step wizard.

To order prints online, click the *Order prints online* task in the *Picture Tasks* section of the Web view for a folder containing images you'd like printed. (What else would it be called?) This launches the *Online Print Ordering Wizard*, which lets you choose between online printing companies such as Ofoto and Kodak, as shown in Figure 1-26. Microsoft tells me that other companies will be added over time as well.

After you've chosen the online printing company (this example uses Ofoto, though the process will be similar for other services), the wizard downloads the mini-Web pages specific to that service. In the case of Ofoto, you are prompted to log on to the service next, or to create a new account (as shown in Figure 1-27).

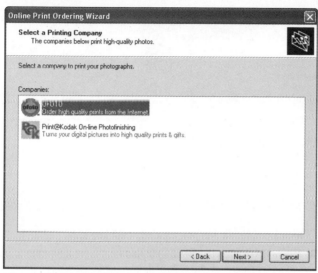

Figure 1-26: Online photo-printing services let you obtain prints from your digital photos.

Figure 1-27: The Ofoto logon process, now in wizard form

At this point, the online printing service offers some way for you to create an order. In the case of Ofoto, this consists of choosing the quantity you want of each sized print, as shown in Figure 1-28. The size you can choose for your prints depends on the quality of the original images. That is, an unedited picture taken with a 2MP camera (for example) lets you order prints up to 8" × 10" in size.

Figure 1-28: For each photo selected, you can choose one or print sizes.

Next, you choose shipping information and the type of shipping you'd like. Shipping costs are determined by geographical area and the type of shipping you choose. Finally, you can enter credit card information and finalize the order.

Note   The exact path taken by the wizard can vary, depending on the service you choose. And (of course) each service will probably update its wizard over time as well.

Sharing Photos with Others

Online photo services such as Ofoto and Kodak offer photo sharing functionality on their Web sites, but it's also possible to share photos with others in more generic ways. And with Windows XP, you can share photos over the Internet as well as locally, on your own system, with other users.

Sharing photos on the Internet

To share photos on the Internet, you have two choices: Web and e-mail. You can use the Web Publishing Wizard, which is built into Windows XP, to publish photos to the Web. To start the wizard, open a folder of images you'd like to share or select an image or group of images. Then select one of the following options from the File and

Folder Tasks section of the Web pane: *Publish this folder to the Web, Publish this file to the Web,* or *Publish the selected items to the Web* (what you see is determined by which files, if any, are selected).

Regardless, in the first stage of the wizard, you can choose an online service provider, such as MSN or Xdrive, where you'd like to store your files (We'll use MSN for this example). This is shown in Figure 1-29.

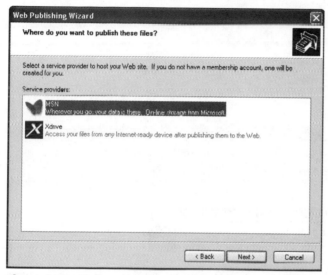

Figure 1-29: Online storage providers such as MSN and Xdrive can be used to archive data on the Web.

You may be required to log on at this point, although the Passport feature in Windows XP can be used to automate this process. Then, you'll be asked to choose where you'd like to store your files at the online service. Typically, you are given a certain amount of space at the service, and you can create your own directory structure on the service. MSN has a nice feature where you automatically resize images when they're uploaded, as seen in Figure 1-30.

Then, the images are uploaded. This could take time based on the size and number of images and the speed of your connection. In Figure 1-31, you can see the progress of the upload.

When the wizard completes, you are given a Web address (what the geeky guys call a URL) that displays the contents of the online folder that contains the images you uploaded. Such a folder is shown in Figure 1-32. You can click any image name to display it in the browser.

MSN, Xdrive, and other online storage locations offer a number of file management capabilities. Once you've uploaded files to one of these services, you can delete, rename, copy, or move them, and add other files.

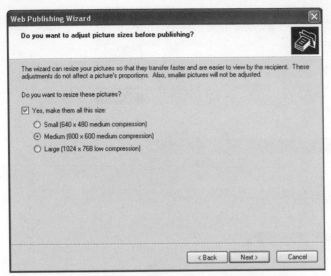

Figure 1-30: MSN allows you to automatically resize images before they are uploading, saving space and time.

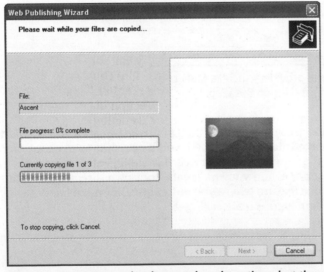

Figure 1-31: Image uploads can take a long time, but the Web Publishing Wizard keeps you up to date during the transfer.

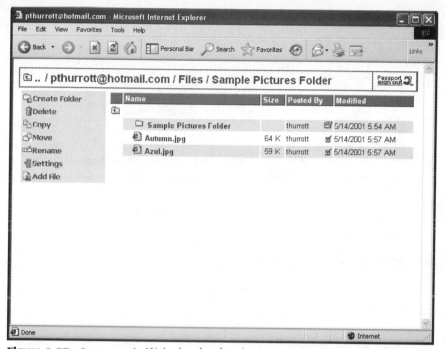

Figure 1-32: An example Web site that has had content uploaded from Windows XP

You can also share photos via e-mail, and this capability has some interesting resizing options. Again, you can share a file or group of files (but not an entire folder, oddly) as needed and then click the appropriate choice (either *E-mail this file* or *E-mail the selected items*) in the File and Folder Tasks section of the Web view to get started. This time, there's no wizard. Instead, a cool little dialog box (Send Pictures via E-mail, shown in Figure 1-33) lets you resize the shared images on the fly — a valuable option, especially when you're working with high-quality images, which can often be quite large. It's unlikely you'll want to send multi-megabyte files via e-mail.

Select the option titled *Make all my pictures smaller* if you want to resize the image(s) to 800 × 600 (any images smaller than 800 × 600 are not resized). However, you can click the *Show more options* link to fine-tune this and choose other resize options, like those shown in Figure 1-34.

At this point, a new e-mail message is created, using your default e-mail program (typically Hotmail, Outlook Express, MSN Explorer, or perhaps Outlook if you've installed Office) with a subject of *E-mailing: [image name(s)]* and the selected images included as attachments. The body text has been filled in with a message reading *Your files are attached and ready to send with this message*, as shown in Figure 1-35, but you can change this as you like. You'll have to add a recipient to the *To* line as well.

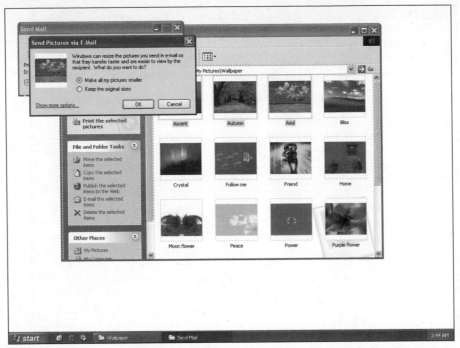

Figure 1-33: When you send image files via e-mail, you can shrink the pictures automatically.

Figure 1-34: You can fine-tune the way that Windows XP shrinks images before uploading them.

Sharing photos at home

Internet sharing is nice, but for many people, a more localized solution fits the bill. If you're using the fast user switching feature in Windows XP to share a single PC with more than one user, you can place images in a special shared location that all users can access. Or, if you've got a home network with two or more PCs, you can create a shared folder that other users can access from across the network. We'll look at both of these choices in this section.

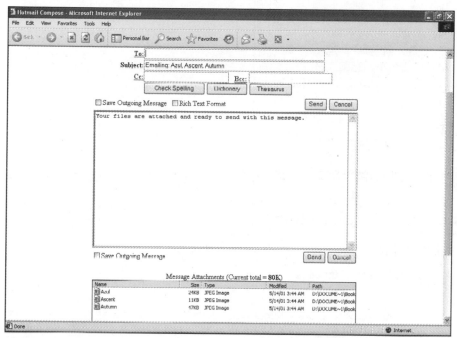

Figure 1-35: A sample e-mail with attached images, shown in Hotmail

Sharing photos on the same PC

To share photos with other users on the same PC, you can utilize a special shared folder — Shared Pictures. If you navigate to your My Pictures folder, which is designed solely for your own use (every user has his or her own My Pictures folder), you see a link in the Other Places section of the Web view pane called Shared Pictures. This is actually a folder (which resides at C:\Documents and Settings\All Users\My Documents\My Pictures by default) that's designed to be accessible to all users. So if you want to make images available to everyone, simply copy them there.

Sharing photos on a home network

Sharing photos on a home network is almost as easy: Simply navigate to the folder you'd like to share, right-click its icon, and choose Sharing and Security. Doing so opens the Properties dialog box for that folder, with the Sharing tab displayed (as shown in Figure 1-36). To share the folder, simply check the option titled *Share this folder on the network* and check *Allow other users to change my files* if you'd like that option to be enabled. Note that you might need to run the Home Networking Wizard before this option is made available.

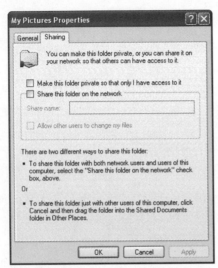

Figure 1-36: To share a folder, simply set up a share and determine whether users can alter any of the files it contains.

Tip   If you attempt to share a folder and haven't enabled sharing yet, XP will prompt you to run the Networking Setup Wizard to ensure that your system is properly configured. Once the wizard is complete, you'll be able to share that folder.

When you check the option to share the folder, a *share name* is created. This is the name other users see when they navigate to their My Network Places folder. So (for example) if you create a share called *My Pictures*, then users browsing the network see a share named *My Pictures*.

✦   ✦   ✦

Using a Scanner with Windows XP

Although it'd be convenient for Microsoft (and book writers too, come to think of it) if everyone would simply drop what they're doing and move on to the "next big thing," the reality is that most technology advances come in slow, measured steps. So it is with digital imaging. Because digital cameras are dropping in price and rising in sophistication, it's only a matter of time before traditional film is relegated to the scrap heap of history. But with "throw-away" 35mm cameras filling the checkout aisles of every convenience store on the planet, it's clear that film has a long life left. These things happen; they just take time.

But so many film-based photo prints exist on this planet that it would take generations to digitize them all anyway. Since the dawn of the personal computer, there have been many attempts at making it easy to take a film print or negative, digitize it, and get it into a computer in a form that can be manipulated, edited, and shared. The most successful of these is the scanner.

Scanners are generally available in flatbed form and (as with all technology) the price has really come down over time. Early, expensive models used to use SCSI technology, primarily with Macintosh computers; the more proletarian IBM-compatibles eventually settled on parallel port versions that were as slow and cumbersome as the systems that utilized them. Finally, both Macintosh and Windows PCs settled on the USB standard for scanners, which gave these products true Plug and Play (PnP) capabilities (plug it into the computer and it basically just works) and a mass market audience. Prices fell, features improved, and life was good.

This chapter looks at how Windows XP interacts with modern scanners.

Looking at Scanners

In general terms, a scanner is an imaging device that attaches to your computer through a *Universal Serial Bus* (USB) port, though models are just now appearing that support higher-speed IEEE-1394 (known as FireWire in Mac circles) and USB 2.0 connections as well. The first USB ports were designed by Intel Corporation in the mid-1990s to help PCs support the addition of high-speed peripherals — and to offer a faster alternative to the pokey older port types (such as parallel, serial, and proprietary game ports).

Examining USB

Although a special version of Windows 95 had been created for PC makers so they could offer USB support, USB didn't really become popular until the release of Windows 98 (the first mass-market retail operating system to support the technology). Of course, Apple Computer would like to take credit for the success of USB. That company claims that its iMac computer was the machine that ushered in the era of USB. Poppycock: Microsoft sold more copies of Windows 98 in a month than Apple sold iMacs in its first year of availability. And most USB peripherals are designed for Windows, not the Mac.

Regardless of the history, USB was and still is a huge success. Thousands of USB-compatible peripherals are on the market — including mice, keyboards, speakers, digital cameras, scanners, portable audio devices, Pocket PC devices, CD-RW and DVD drives, and networking adapters. When USB was first made available, its bus speed (about 10 Mbps for you techie types) was considered excellent, especially when compared to the parallel and serial ports on most legacy machines. But USB has other advantages: You can (theoretically, at least) daisy chain up to 127 USB devices on a single USB port, which opened a market for USB *hubs*, special hardware devices that split a single USB port into multiple ports. There's just one problem: Any given USB port has an upper speed limit of 10 Mbps period — so each device you add drains bandwidth. Some high-bandwidth devices (such as scanners and digital cameras) work best if they have one dedicated USB port per device. Realistically, however, most USB ports have to deal with no more than a handful of USB devices.

Two solutions currently exist for the bandwidth problem. The first is something of a stop-gap: In addition to USB hubs, USB cards are available; each card offers four or five independent ports, and each port has a full 10 Mb of bandwidth. (I'm using one of these on my desktop machine as I write this.) The other solution is USB 2.0 (just now coming on the scene) — USB 2.0 is a specification for the next generation of USB devices. Fortunately, USB 2.0 is backward-compatible with all of today's USB devices. But devices actually designed for USB 2.0 can use up to 480 Mbps of bandwidth — a huge increase over USB 1.*x*. Look for the newest digital cameras, hard drives, and other high-speed devices to take advantage of USB 2.0.

And then there's FireWire, which was designed by Apple Computer, though PC makers are marketing the technology under a variety of names (Sony calls its implementation iLink, for example). FireWire has been relatively successful, with most compatible products falling into the digital camera and external hard drive arenas. And because FireWire is fast (400 Mbps), it's fast enough for a few years yet. FireWire proponents tell me that a much faster version will be available soon (but that's probably true of just about any technology these days).

Exploring scanners and USB

Most scanners you pick up these days are USB-based; they feature a flatbed design that lets you scan, or *image*, paper-based pictures and text. Although other types of scanners are available—such as handheld versions that are good for smaller images—flatbed scanners are more useful, and they are relatively cheap and readily available. The differences between models comes down to two factors (detailed in the next section):

✦ **Size of the scanning bed.** Some are fine for 8.5 × 11-inch paper (and only that size); other models offer larger sizes.

✦ **Degree of resolution.** This is another term for the possible quality of images scanned with the device.

Choosing a Scanner for Windows XP

When purchasing a scanner for use with Windows XP, the first step is to make sure that it's a compatible, USB-based, Plug-and-Play version. These types of scanners will auto-install in Windows XP and give you access to the wonderful new *Windows Image Acquisition* (WIA) technology that's available in this OS. WIA makes imaging devices like scanners easier to control so you can acquire images without all the fuss and bother.

Beyond that, key considerations include price, color depth, resolution, and speed. Scanners can be purchased for under $100 (sometimes well under $100), but the prices can also creep quickly up, even into the thousands. Often, you get what you pay for; most scanners offer at least 300 dpi (dots per inch) resolution and 32-bit color—but both of these terms require some explanation.

Thinking about scanner resolution

Let's say you want to scan in a 4 × 6-inch photograph using a flatbed scanner. If you scan at 300 dpi, the resulting on-screen image measures approximately 1800 × 1200 pixels. That's because 300 dots (pixels) per vertical width of 6 inches is 1800, and 300 dots (pixels) per horizontal width of 4 inches is 1200. An 1800 × 1200 image is pretty big, considering that most modern Windows desktops are only 1024 × 768 (and for purposes of illustration, a 2.1 Megapixel digital camera can shoot high-quality images at 1792 × 1200 resolution). In JPEG format, such an image would take up only 275K or so of disk space, which isn't so bad. But JPEG is a compressed, or *lossy* format (that is, it loses some of the image data to achieve smaller file sizes). An uncompressed bitmap of this same image would take up about 12 megabytes (MB). A fax-friendly TIFF image would occupy a whopping 20MB of space. It adds up quickly.

Given this problem—and the fact that some scanners can get resolutions of 500 dpi and higher—the resulting file sizes would be even more gigantic if you scanned photos at the maximum possible resolution. The point here is that resolution itself is not the only factor to consider; take into account what it is that you're trying to achieve. If you want high-quality archives of your most important photos, then high resolution is probably the way to go. But if you want to publish images on the Web, a more reasonable (and yes, less costly) 150 dpi scanner might be a better deal. Likewise, any scanner should be capable of scanning at rates *lower than its maximum:* A 300-dpi scanner can scan at 100 or 150 dpi, for example.

As with many things in life, a compromise — in this case, between quality/size and speed/convenience — is probably the most practical approach. I recommend 150 dpi for images intended for use on the Web; even then you may want to resize them down a bit.

Understanding color depth

Color depth is measured in bits, in the same way that your desktop's color depth is measured in bits. 8-bit color gives you 256 possible colors; 16-bit nets approximately 65,000 colors. The next step up, 24-bit color, provides millions of colors, and is sometimes called *true color*. But scanners can do better than that: 32-bit color is basically 24-bit color with an 8-bit alpha channel (for transparency). In other words, it provides 16 million possible colors. And some scanner makers are pushing something called "36-bit color," which is the technological equivalent of a guitar amp going to 11. 36-bit scanners tend to have different horizontal and vertical resolutions — these are typically the scanners you see that have 1200×600 dpi resolution.

The good news is that you're never going to run into a modern scanner that doesn't support at least 24-bit color, which is the minimum you'll want for photographs. And since Windows XP completely automates this process, you're not going to have to worry about color depth after you've bought the scanner. Windows XP *always* uses the highest possible color depth when scanning.

Installing and Detecting a Scanner

Once you've purchased the scanner, it's time to bring it home, unpack it, and set it up. This involves plugging in two cables — the power cable, which (of course) goes into a power outlet, and the USB cable, which should be given a dedicated USB port. (In other words, don't plug it into a USB hub unless you're positive that the other devices on there won't be used while you're scanning). The setup isn't difficult.

Now it's moment-of-truth time. Make sure you've removed any plastic or cardboard pieces that don't belong in the scanner and, with Windows XP running, turn on the scanner. Depending on the model you bought, you could experience some churning and bubbling, on the part of the scanner: Lights blink, sounds emerge, that kind of thing. It's all perfectly normal.

Because it happens very quickly, you really need pay attention to the screen to see when Windows XP detects the scanner. Unlike previous versions of Windows, you aren't prompted for the Windows CD-ROM or any drivers. Instead, a small yellow balloon appears in the lower right of the screen, labeled *Found New Hardware.* Initially, it detects the scanner simply as *USB Device,* as shown in Figure 2-1.

Figure 2-1: In the first phase of the new hardware detection, only the type of device is detected...

But after a short few seconds that changes to read the actual name of the device, such as *Scanmaker X6u* (as shown in Figure 2-2). Then the bubble disappears and you're left wondering what happened.

Figure 2-2: ...And then the exact type of hardware is identified.

What happened is one of those subtle small things in Windows XP that really sets it apart from its predecessors: You're literally done installing the scanner at this point. *Everything* should be this easy!

To test that the scanner was properly installed, you should see evidence of its existence in a few locations. If you open My Computer, you should see an icon for the scanner listed under a new group called *Scanners and Cameras.* This is shown in Figure 2-3.

You can also open Control Panel and navigate to the *Printers and Other Hardware* category to start the Scanners and Cameras applet, which displays any related devices inside the shell window. This is shown in Figure 2-4.

The next section shows how to scan a photograph. (About time, right?)

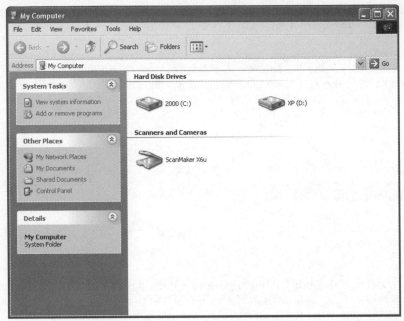

Figure 2-3: When you install a new scanner in Windows XP, it shows up as a shell object in My Computer.

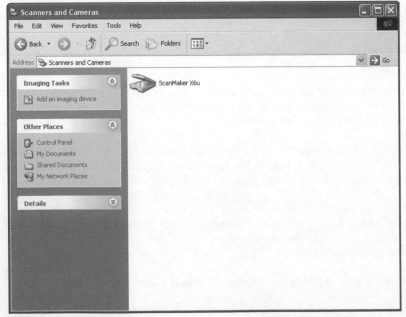

Figure 2-4: You can also access the scanner from the Scanners and Cameras applet, available in Control Panel.

Acquiring Images with a Scanner

Acquiring images from a scanner is almost as simple as the installation procedure. First, place a photograph on the scanner and check the documentation for your particular piece of hardware to see exactly how this process works. (That's usually good practice anyway.)

When you have the photograph lined up correctly and you're ready, double-click the scanner icon in My Computer (or the one in Control Panel). This launches the Scanner and Camera Wizard, shown in Figure 2-5, which identifies the hardware device to which it is attached. Note that this wizard is generic to a variety of imaging devices — for example, it works with digital cameras as well — but its behavior depends on the capabilities of the device you are currently using.

Figure 2-5: The Camera and Scanner Wizard provides a friendly front-end to the Windows Image Acquisition technologies in Windows XP.

Choosing scanning preferences

In the first phase of the wizard, you are presented with a number of scanning preferences, such as those shown in Figure 2-6. First is the picture type, which can be:

✦ Color

✦ Grayscale

✦ Black-and-white picture or text

✦ Custom

The first three of these choices probably seem obvious, but the custom option deserves some discussion.

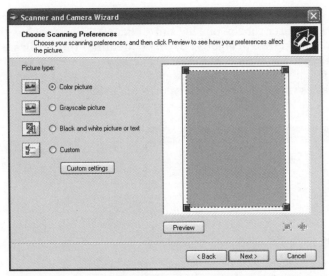

Figure 2-6: In the first phase of the wizard, you choose general scanning preferences.

If you click the *Custom settings* button, an Advanced Properties dialog box for the scanner is displayed, shown in Figure 2-7. This lets you alter appearance preferences, such as the brightness and contrast, the resolution (in dpi) and the picture type (color, grayscale, or black-and-white). The resolution defaults to 150 dpi, but you can change it according to the capabilities of your device. Therefore, the Custom settings choice is required if you plan to scan at any resolution setting other than the default 150 dpi.

On the right side of the Choose Scanning Preferences step of the Scanner and Camera Wizard is a preview pane that allows you to preview the photograph before it is scanned. It's a good idea to do this by clicking the Preview button (as shown in Figure 2-8) because the wizard is designed to auto-select an area that matches the dimensions of the photograph you are scanning. Although the wizard usually gets this right, nothing is perfect, so Microsoft lets you manually adjust the area to be scanned as well.

You adjust the area manually by selecting the guidelines in the preview pane and dragging them until they enclose the area you'd like to scan, as shown in Figure 2-9.

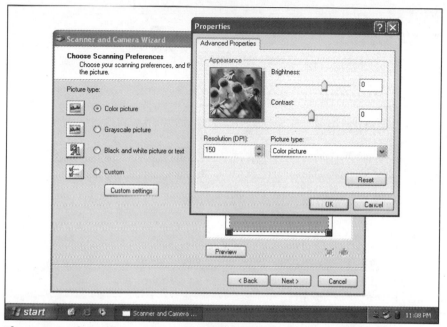

Figure 2-7: The Advanced Properties dialog box allows you to determine the scan resolution, as well as the brightness and contrast.

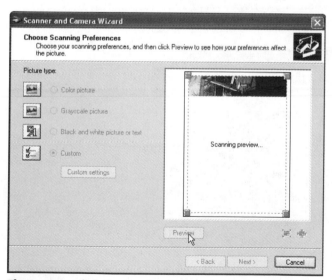

Figure 2-8: Click the Preview button to preview your scanned image and have the wizard auto-select the area to scan.

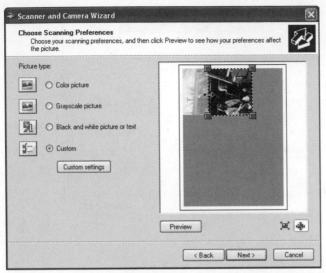

Figure 2-9: You can resize the area to be scanned with the guidelines in the preview pane.

You can also enlarge the selection area so it occupies as much space in the preview pane as possible; this makes it easier to manually edit the area you'd like to scan. You do this by clicking the small Enlarge icon below the preview area, as shown in Figure 2-10.

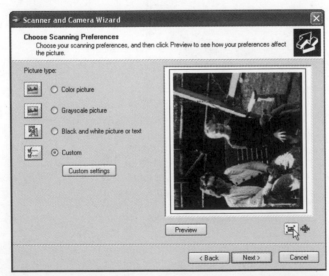

Figure 2-10: Enlarge the scanned area to occupy the entire preview pane.

Alternatively, you can click the *Show the entire image* button to go back to the normal full view and re-edit the selection area if you want.

Whichever method you chose, click Next to continue.

Choosing the picture name and destination

In the next page, shown in Figure 2-11, you can select a name for the scanned image, its destination folder, and the file format in which it is saved.

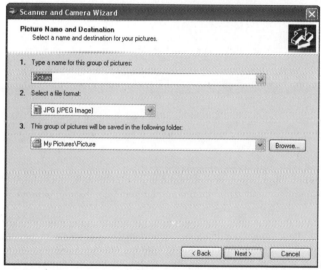

Figure 2-11: You can choose a name for the scanned image, a file format, and a destination folder where it is saved.

The first step is to choose a name for the image. Note that when you do this, the destination folder in Step 3 is automatically changed so a folder with the same name is created under My Pictures (as shown in Figure 2-12). Thus, if you want to save the scanned image as *Test*, the wizard auto-creates a folder named Test that sits inside My Pictures. You can change this arrangement if you like (in fact, I recommend it). Automatic creation of folders makes sense if you're using a digital camera or have a number of images to download at once. For the most part, however, you probably don't need a new folder for every image you scan in. Sometimes the user really *is* smarter than the machine.

We've briefly discussed a few image-file formats previously, and by the time you hit Step 2 of this dialog box, you'd better be up to speed. The Scanner and Camera Wizard can save images in JPEG (the default), Bitmap, TIFF, or PNG format (but not GIF, which is limited to 256 colors). The format you choose is a balancing act between practicality and personal preference: JPEG and PNG feature small file sizes but they use lossy compression; images saved in these formats can have *artifacts* (extraneous graphical "junk" that results from compression) and other possible problems. Bitmap and TIFF images, conversely, create humongous files, but their compression-free images have clearer detail and no visual artifacts.

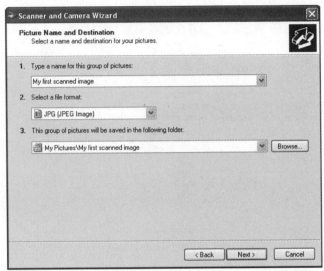

Figure 2-12: When you enter a filename, the destination folder is automatically generated.

I tend to scan images in BMP format and then convert copies of these large master images into smaller JPEGs when I want to use them on the Web or send them via e-mail. (For details on the relative advantages of these formats, see Chapter 1.)

Tip   Remember: You don't have to accept the default destination folder that the wizard gives you in Step 3. Feel free to change the destination to fit your needs.

Scanning the picture

In the next page of the wizard, the actual scanning occurs — a hands-off affair, as shown in Figure 2-13. A picture progress bar keeps you up to date during the process (which should only take a few seconds at 150 dpi, maybe more if you're using higher resolution).

Printing online or integrating with the Internet

The next page of the wizard is a feature that was added rather late in the Windows XP beta cycle, and it's an unwelcome addition in many ways, though I understand what Microsoft was trying to achieve. In this page, shown in Figure 2-14, you're given the option to publish the photo you've scanned to a Web site, order prints of the image from a photo-printing Web site (a curious choice for a photograph you just scanned), or to just skip out and continue. Thankfully, this last choice (artfully labeled *No, thanks*) is the default.

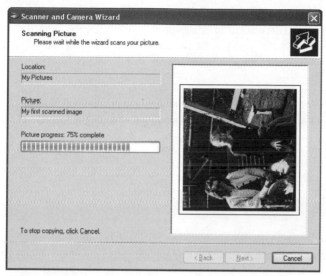

Figure 2-13: During scanning, a progress bar keeps you up to date, but the process only takes a few seconds.

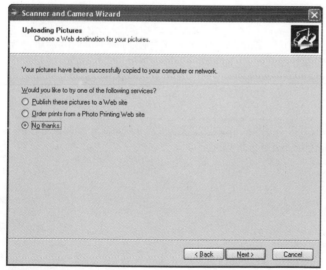

Figure 2-14: The wizard allows provides access to other wizards for uploading your scanned image to a Web site or online photo printing service.

If you choose to publish this picture to a Web site, you are connected with the Web Publishing Wizard. Choosing to print a photo to a Web site also connects you to the Online Print Ordering Wizard. For the time being, choose the option labeled *No, thanks*.

When you choose *No, thanks*, the wizard is completed. And when you close the wizard, the folder containing the image you scanned opens, showing the image highlighted (as shown in Figure 2-15). That's helpful if you save the file to a folder that contains many images.

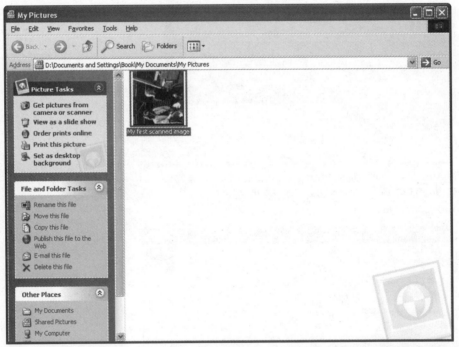

Figure 2-15: When the scan is complete, the wizard will close, and the destination folder appears with the new image highlighted.

✦   ✦   ✦

Using a Digital Camera with Windows XP

Using a scanner to obtain photographs digitally is nice, especially when you've got a wide library of prints and you'd like to get them into the computer. But scanning photographs is a slow, virtually never-ending process. If you intend to continually archive your photographs digitally, you have to manually scan them in, one at a time, each time you get a roll of film back from the drugstore or photo printing service. Other alternatives exist (such as Photo CDs and services that scan negatives) but a simpler (and arguably more efficient) solution is simply to purchase a digital camera. Digital cameras are cheap and surprisingly powerful these days, and (in my opinion) it's only a matter of time before they completely replace film-based cameras.

In the meantime, you may find that a digital camera can fulfill just about all your photography needs, unless you're a professional photographer. But for weekend birthday parties and trips to Europe, nothing beats the convenience of a digital camera, especially if your ultimate goal is to share your snapshots with others.

If you'll pardon the not-so-smooth transition from one sell job to another, it should also come as no surprise that Windows XP was designed to work well with digital cameras. The Scanner and Camera Wizard you saw in the previous chapter is actually limited when used with a scanner, but it comes to life when you attach a digital camera.

This chapter looks at some general issues regarding these wonderful devices and the ways they interact with Windows XP. If you're like me, you may discover that the combination of a good digital camera and Windows XP is just too good to resist.

Acquiring a Digital Camera

In the world of film-based photography, there is precious little to worry about, choice-wise. Aside from some Polaroid holdouts, today's low-end point-and-click cameras and disposable cameras have standardized to 35mm film. When you move to a digital camera, however, you have number of issues to deal with. Although I can't possibly hope to cover every topic related to digital photography, it's definitely advisable to at least think about some of the following issues. But in the end, what we're primarily concerned with here is how a digital camera interacts with Windows XP.

Megapixel? What's a megapixel?

Like any other digital media device, digital cameras support varying resolutions, which directly affects the quality of the pictures you're going to take. So this will probably be the feature you're primarily worried about, once you get over the sticker shock. Unfortunately, the digital camera world settled on a mouth-filling term — *megapixels* (MP) — to define picture quality, where one megapixel is the same as million total pixels. So a 2MP camera can output at least 2 million pixels-worth of resolution (as a comparison, a 1024×768 screen uses 786,432 pixels). And the higher the resolution (excuse me, the more megapixels), the higher the quality of the image.

But high quality, as always, brings with it a price. The higher the resolution, the more disk space each image takes up — and even today, most digital cameras use storage media with a pretty small capacity. You have two possible ways to make allowance for the problem: Use lower (but still acceptable) resolution when you take pictures, or purchase higher-capacity storage media (see the later section on media types for details).

The camera I'm currently using is a Kodak DC290 — a fine (even recommended) device that supports 2.1MP. However, that degree of resolution is the maximum possible with this (or any other) 2.1MP camera. Kodak, like many consumer electronic companies, would like to spare consumers the rigor of understanding complex subjects such as file types and resolution. So they designate the possible image-quality levels as Uncompressed, Best, Better, and Good (note that "uncompressed" is better than "best"). An *uncompressed* image is stored in TIFF format and takes up over 6MB of space on the disk (which means I can store just five of these images on a single 32 MB memory card), at a resolution of 1792×1200 (if you do the math, it's just over 2.1 *million* pixels). The image quality is beautiful, and doesn't suffer from compression-related artifacts. But 6MB files are hard to work with, even on a powerful PC.

When I choose the "Best" setting, the resolution remains steady at 1792×1200. But now the camera just saves in JPEG format, which is (technically) a "lossy" type of compression. These images take up a little bit more than 500K, however, so I can store 45 of them on a single memory card, which is far more acceptable. And 2.1MP images are good for prints as large as 8×10 inches if I want to have them printed at a photo service (3MP is good for prints as large as 11×17 inches).

Over time, look for the price of memory cards to drop, even as capacities increase (128 MB and 256 MB cards are now becoming common). But also keep in mind that camera capabilities will grow. As with many other computer capabilities, consumers wind up in sort of a perpetual "hamster wheel" of upgrades.

Media types

Speaking of memory cards, another key consideration is the type (and of course, size) of the storage that your camera will use. These days, most digital cameras utilize a storage format called CompactFlash (CF), which comes in various sizes from 4MB up to 256MB and beyond. Other formats include SmartMedia and Memory-Stick (a Sony format, which is mostly limited to Sony cameras). Some cameras even utilize high-capacity floppy disks or recordable CDs, though this is less common. Most of these cards, including CF, resemble small cartridges; they have no moving parts, which is battery-friendly.

In the previous section, I mentioned getting 45 images on a single memory card. In this case, the memory card is a 32MB CompactFlash storage card; I generally bring two of these along when I want to take pictures. Fortunately, 128MB cards are getting cheaper; you may want to review your options if you're in the market for a new camera. Most current cameras still use relatively skimpy memory cards (my Kodak's card is 16MB).

In any event, there's little reason to choose a camera because of the media format it uses. One possible exception is the MemoryStick, which is proprietary to Sony. If you need to buy additional cards or adapters (such as PC drives that work with the media directly), you're stuck with Sony. Fortunately, Sony generally makes great imaging equipment; just keep the memory-card issue in mind.

"Techie" camera features

As digital cameras increase in complexity and gain more professional features, look for some "bells and whistles" from the 35mm world to creep in — for example, adjustable shutter speed, exposure, and so on. As with the traditional film-photography market, however, most digital cameras today are the point-and-click variety. You should be able to pick one up, turn it on, perhaps switch between wide-angle and telephoto, and then snap a photo; that's how 99 percent of the world uses a camera, regardless of format.

But digital cameras offer other unique features that aren't found in most 35mm cameras. Many offer a digital view screen on the back so you can see the scene you're photographing without having to look through a viewfinder. You can delete images immediately and preview images you've already taken before you load them onto a PC. Some cameras can even shoot short (admittedly poor-quality) movies, limited mostly by the size of the memory card you're using.

Connection type

When digital cameras first came on the market, many of them connected to the computer via the *serial port,* a low-speed legacy port (once used with certain ancient types of printers and mice) that doesn't even exist on many modern PCs. It will probably be hard to get this wrong, but just in case, be sure you're getting a camera that connects to the computer using a USB cable. USB is fast and it's Plug and Play compatible, meaning that you can plug and unplug your camera on the fly without needing to reboot your system.

No doubt the upcoming generation of cameras will work with higher-speed interfaces such as FireWire (IEEE 1394) and USB 2.0. Such ports are fine for your connection, of course, but just say no to serial.

Tip   Be sure you're getting a camera that connects to the computer using a USB cable. USB is fast *and* Plug and Play-compatible; you can plug and unplug your camera on the fly without having to reboot your system.

Battery type

Unfortunately, digital cameras burn through batteries like they're going out of style. Most work with standard AA batteries, but also accept rechargeable, AA-sized Ni-MH batteries (which last a lot longer). My advice: Get two or more sets of the Ni-MH rechargeable batteries and bring along a charger while on vacation. Your camera will keep working and you won't miss any important shots.

Digital cameras in the real world

A few final observations gleaned from over a year of traveling with a digital camera:

✦ **Always carry spare batteries.** The aforementioned battery issue is the number one problem you're likely to have when you're on a trip, so be sure to bring spares.

✦ **Try a disc reader for photo transfer.** Companies (such as SanDisk) sell inexpensive USB-based readers that you can attach to your computer so you can plug in a memory card and transfer photos without draining the batteries in the camera.

✦ **Bring a laptop on your trip if you've got the room.** You can use it to download images off the camera's memory card each day, dramatically increasing your photo storage capacity. (Besides, you want to bring your entire digital music collection with you while you're on the road, right?)

Detecting a Camera in Windows XP

If you went through the chapter about scanners, you may have been surprised by how quickly and easily you can add such a device to a Windows XP-based system. Well, a digital camera is no different.

The details of the hardware connection depend on your particular system; in general, the camera connects to the PC with a USB cable. When you turn on the camera, a small hardware-detection bubble-help window appears in the lower-right corner of the screen, announcing the name of the device it found (*Kodak DC290 Digital Camera* in my case) as shown in Figure 3-1.

Figure 3-1: A digital camera is automatically detected by the system.

Then the bubble changes (Figure 3-2) to read *Your new hardware is installed and ready to use.* And that's literally all there is to it. At this point, the Scanner and Camera Wizard begins.

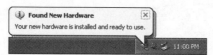

Figure 3-2: And that's all there is to it — no driver disk required, no request for the XP CD-ROM.

Tip   As with a scanner, you can also access a digital camera from the My Computer window.

Acquiring Images from a Digital Camera

When using a digital camera, the opening page of the Scanner and Camera Wizard has an interesting hyperlink, which is labeled as for *advanced users only* (a detailed look at it comes later in this chapter). For now, click Next to see an easy way to get pictures from a digital camera.

Using the Wizard

In the Choose Pictures to Copy step (Figure 3-3), you can preview the images stored on your camera and choose which ones you'd like to download to your PC. Each image is shown as a thumbnail so you can see them before they download. By default,

they're all selected, so they all download unless you choose otherwise. In this page, you can choose to unselect all the images (Clear All), select all the images (an option cunningly named Select All), or you can pick and select (or deselect) individual images.

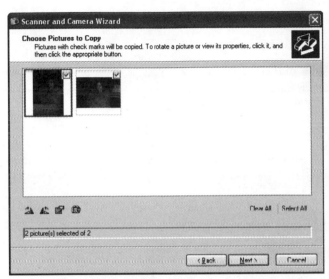

Figure 3-3: In the first stage of the Scanner and Camera Wizard, you can choose which pictures to download and perform simple actions on those pictures.

But wait, there's more. You can highlight individual images; while they're still in the camera, you can use a small toolbar to rotate them clockwise or counter-clockwise. (You can find the toolbar sitting below the thumbnail preview area, as shown in Figure 3-4.)

You can also bring up a Properties window for any individual image by clicking the Properties button. This window, shown in Figure 3-5, will show you when the photograph was taken, what the file format is, and how much space it takes up on the memory card.

Curiously, you can also use this dialog box to tell the camera to take a picture (provided this feature is supported by your camera). Simply click the *Take a picture* button (shown in Figure 3-6), and the camera snaps a photo — and, after a slight delay, adds that new picture to the selection of photos copied to the PC.

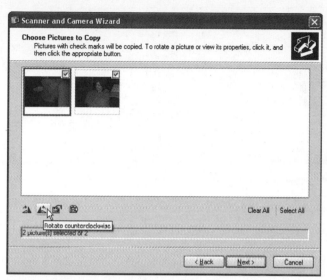

Figure 3-4: Before you download an image, you can rotate it.

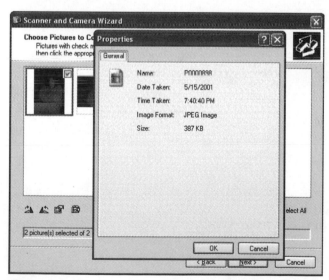

Figure 3-5: The Properties window for an image still on a camera.

Figure 3-6: By clicking this button, you can actually take a picture with the camera currently connected to the system.

When you're ready to copy the selected photos to the PC, click Next and move to the Picture Name and Destination page, shown in Figure 3-7.

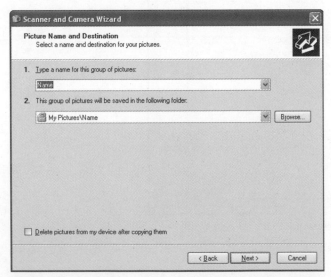

Figure 3-7: The Picture Name and Destination page gives you a chance to choose where the photos are downloaded and what to call them.

Tip This feature is more useful for a Web camera, which is a USB device that connects directly to your system but offers no local storage media; when you want to take a still image with such a camera, you could use this wizard to do so.

This process is similar to adding images to your computer from a scanner, with some interesting camera-specific differences. First, you can choose the name given to the *group* of photos being copied from the camera; a scanner can acquire only one image at a time. The name you give to this group forms the basis for each file-name created as the photos are copied. So the first photo in the collection is saved as *Name 001.jpg*, the second as *Name 002.jpg*, and so on.

Thus, if you're importing photos from your son's birthday party, you might name the group of photos *Just hanging around*. When you do so, the destination folder changes to match the new name, as shown in Figure 3-8. By default, the Scanner and Camera Wizard saves your photos to a subfolder under My Pictures.

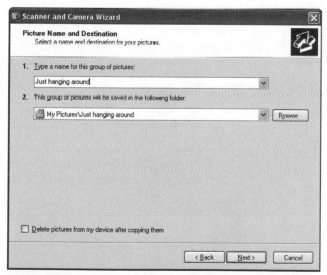

Figure 3-8: Changing the name of the picture group will also change the name of the destination folder to match.

Another interesting new feature that's specific to digital cameras is the quick delete: You can automatically delete all the images from the camera after they're copied to the PC, which "empties" the camera storage card so you can use it again. To do so, just check the option shown in Figure 3-9.

Once you click Next, the photos are copied to the destination you've chosen (Figure 3-10). This happens rather quickly, especially if you're used to using a scanner.

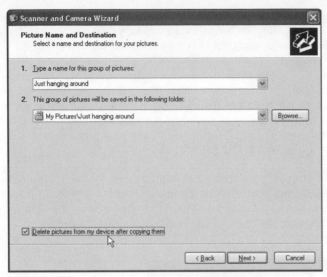

Figure 3-9: You can instruct the Wizard to delete the images on the camera after the download is complete.

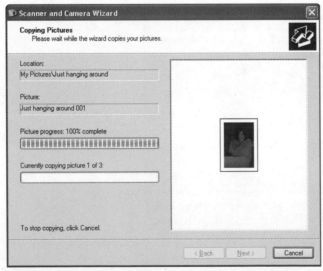

Figure 3-10: Copying pictures from the camera to the computer is quick — the fewer the images, the quicker the process.

If you requested that the wizard delete the photos after the copy process is completed, this happens next, as shown in Figure 3-11.

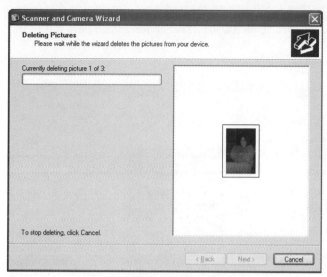

Figure 3-11: If you've chosen to delete the images, this phase occurs after they are copied to the hard drive.

Next, the wizard presents the following set of options:

✦ Publish the pictures to a Web site

✦ Order prints from a photo-printing Web site

✦ Skip this whole rigmarole and move on

(Thankfully, the default is to move on—if you're interested in those other two options, refer to Chapter 1). At this point, the wizard has finished its task; Windows XP opens the directory that contains the images you just copied, as shown in Figure 3-12.

Obtaining images the advanced way

If you're not interested in that namby-pamby wizard stuff, Windows XP allows you to access your camera as if it were a (small) hard drive. When you connect your camera and The Scanner and Camera Wizard and the *advanced users only* appears, choose this option, and watch as an Explorer window opens, displaying the contents of your camera (as in Figure 3-13).

You copy, move, or delete files from your digital camera just as you would any files on your hard drive. Of course, you have to create a destination folder manually before you can copy the images to your PC. And you don't get the automatic image-renaming provided by the wizard; instead, the camera auto-numbers each image for you.

This window, however, does offer a civilized touch—the Camera Tasks section of the Web pane. Here you find options you can use to relaunch the Scanner and

Camera Wizard, take a new picture, get information about the camera, or delete all the pictures from the camera. This feature takes some of the pain out of the non-wizard approach.

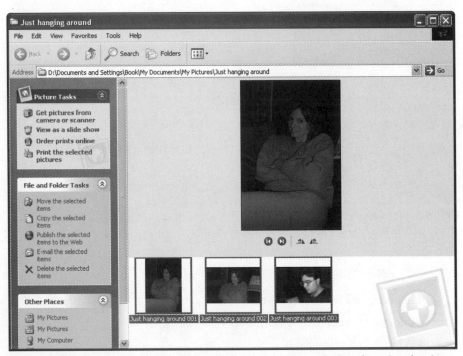

Figure 3-12: The group of downloaded pictures, presented after the wizard quits.

Getting camera information

One of these options is new: Clicking the option labeled *Show camera properties* displays the Properties dialog box for the camera, as shown in Figure 3-14. (Or you can right-click the camera icon in My Computer, choose Properties, and get the same result.)

This window contains a wealth of information about the camera. In the general tab, you can discover how much of the memory card's capacity is used up, the flash mode, the battery level, and the current time, as reported by the camera (note that the availability of this information will differ from camera to camera). It will also contain the current picture size setting and a button to test the camera. When you click this, a short diagnostic test is run.

The Properties dialog box also contains an Events tab (details coming up shortly), and a Color Management tab (shown in Figure 3-15) that displays the color profiles associated with the camera. A hardware device that inputs or outputs color from the system uses a *color profile* to tell Windows XP what its capabilities are so the operating system can accurately and consistently correct the color—a feature of great importance for the publishing industry. As professional color devices (such as cameras, scanners, inkjet printers, and the like) come down in price, this consistency is increasingly important for home users as well. At least it's not something you generally have to deal with manually.

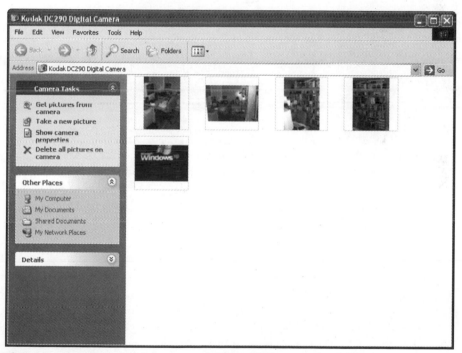

Figure 3-13: You can navigate your camera as if it were a hard drive, using standard shell skills to copy, move, and delete images.

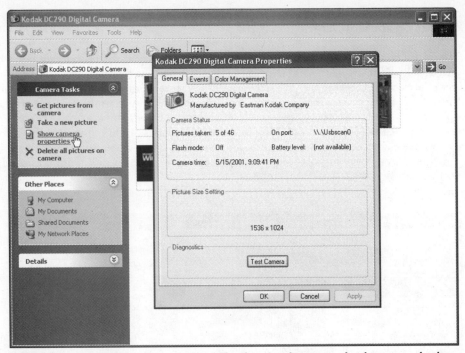

Figure 3-14: The Camera Properties dialog box is where you check to see whether the camera is working correctly (and get other vital information).

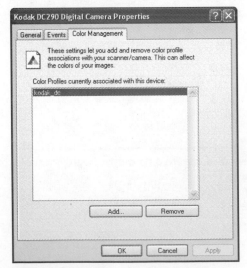

Figure 3-15: Each color device that's attached to an XP system has an associated color profile.

Managing a Digital Camera in Windows XP

The Events tab of the digital camera Properties dialog box exposes some powerful and exciting functionality. With this tab (shown in Figure 3-16), you can determine how your camera responds to certain events—for example, when it is first connected. What you can do is choose an event, and then decide how the camera responds (You can find your range of possible responses in the Actions section.)

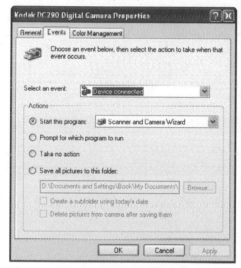

Figure 3-16: From the Events tab, you can determine what Windows XP does when you connect a camera.

By default, Windows XP is set up to launch the Scanner and Camera Wizard when it detects that the camera is connected. So the action titled *Start this program* is selected. If you'd prefer to launch a different program—such as Microsoft Word, Adobe Photoshop Elements, or any application registered with the system as imaging-compatible—you can choose the program from a drop-down list (shown in Figure 3-17).

You can also tell the system to prompt you with a small dialog box whenever the camera is connected. In the case shown in Figure 3-18, the system offers you a choice of applications to run when you plug in the camera.

A third option, *Take no action*, means you can forego responding to a connection event. You might choose this option if you prefer to use the camera like a hard drive.

Figure 3-17: In the drop-down list, you can choose which application to run when a camera is connected.

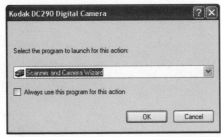

Figure 3-18: If you choose to be prompted when a camera is connected, you will see this dialog box, which lets you choose an application to interact with the camera.

The final option automatically saves pictures to the hard drive when the camera connects — and this option is wonderfully thought out. You can create a subfolder under My Pictures (using the current date) and then delete all the pictures from the camera if you so choose. In, delete, and out. No muss, no fuss. If you choose this option and reconnect your camera, the photos are copied over (as shown in Figure 3-19). Then a shell window opens to display the pictures, as shown in Figure 3-20.

Figure 3-19: If you're the automation type, you can tell Windows XP to automatically copy all the pictures off the camera when it's connected.

Figure 3-20: When this automatic copy is complete, the images appear in a standard Explorer window.

✦   ✦   ✦

Music to Your Ears

Every Windows XP digital-media experience is exciting in its own way, but none is as thorough in this new OS as that of digital music. This part looks at Media Player for Windows XP (the latest version of Windows Media Player) and ways to organize and manage digital music on your PC. Here you can explore the process of copying music from audio CDs to the PC, creating your own audio "mix" CDs, and backing up vital information on data CDs.

Playing Digital Music

Available exclusively in Windows XP, Media Player for
Windows XP (MPXP) is the sequel to the industry's first
all-in-one media player, Microsoft Windows Media Player 7
(MP7). The all-in-one design means that MPXP is conceivably
the only program you'll need for listening to music and other
audio, watching movies, recording music and video, managing
locally stored media, listening to Internet radio stations,
moving music to portable digital audio devices, and creating
audio CDs. In the past, much of this functionality was scat-
tered among separate products from a variety of vendors.
Microsoft decided to create a single program that does it all —
and triggered the development of various similar products
from its competitors. And now Media Player for Windows XP
builds on the basic design behind MP7, incorporating changes
based on extensive usability studies and customer requests.

That's all well and good from a marketing perspective. To you,
the user, the latest Windows Media Player is arguably the first
all-in-one player that's worth your attention. Before MPXP,
even the people who actually used Microsoft's player would
often turn to other tools for a variety of reasons. With a few
exceptions (such as the file-format incompatibilities mentioned at the end of this chapter) that is no longer an issue.
You can now use MPXP as an "end-to-end" product suitable
for just about any task you may have for your audio or video
media. So in this way, MPXP really does deliver. In this chapter, we look at the player and see how it interacts with the
Internet, CD audio, and locally stored music files. If you've
harbored any sort of anti-Microsoft feelings regarding their
endless integration strategies, MPXP may just turn you
around. It's that good.

Windows Media Player for Windows XP

Windows Media Player for Windows XP, is the literal centerpiece of the Windows XP digital-media experience. With this player, you can

✦ Listen to audio files stored on music CDs, your system, and the Internet.

✦ Copy music from music CDs to your system.

✦ Organize audio and video media that is stored on your system.

✦ View DVD movies (requires a DVD drive and appropriate "codec" software).

✦ Listen to radio stations over the Internet.

✦ Find new music and video content on the Internet.

✦ Copy audio and video media from your system to a portable device, such as a Pocket PC or portable digital audio player.

✦ Create personalized "mix" audio CDs (requires a CD-R or CD-RW drive).

✦ Personalize your digital-media experience with the player's customizable user interface, visualizations, and skins.

To make this all possible, Windows Media Player for Windows XP presents an updated interface that's based on the Windows XP visual style that's used as the default user interface for the OS. Windows Media Player for Windows XP is highly customizable, with various UI elements, such as the menu bar and taskbar, that can be hidden, and a resizable Full mode window that can shed its boxy outline to take on a rounded, more organic look, as shown in Figure 4-1. This means that you can resize the full-size Windows Media Player window as you see fit (as shown in Figure 4-2), without having to switch to Skin mode.

Windows Media Player for Windows XP also offers a variety of *skins* — graphical arrangements of controls that give you even more control over the size and look of the player (at the expense of some esoteric functionality). Windows XP comes with several skins, such as the one in Figure 4-3; many more are available for download from the Web.

The next chapter takes a closer look at ways to customize Full mode and Skin mode.

Launching Media Player for Windows XP

Are you having problems finding the player? Well, fear not: Windows Media Player for Windows XP can be started in a variety of ways. It appears as an icon in the Start Menu when you first use Windows XP (though that introductory icon may disappear over time if you start launching and using other icons). If you don't see a Windows Media Player icon in your Start Menu, then open the More Programs item in the Start Menu to display the Programs menu. You should see a Windows Media Player shortcut there as well, as shown in Figure 4-4.

Figure 4-1: Windows Media Player for Windows XP in "Full mode," where all of its features are available.

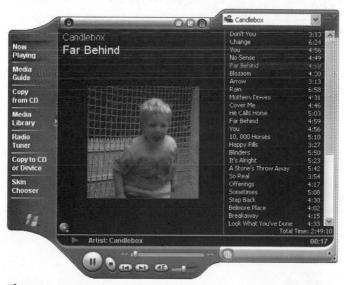

Figure 4-2: New in MPXP is the capability to resize and configure the Full mode.

Figure 4-3: A sample "skin," which generally provides the most commonly used functionality in a smaller package.

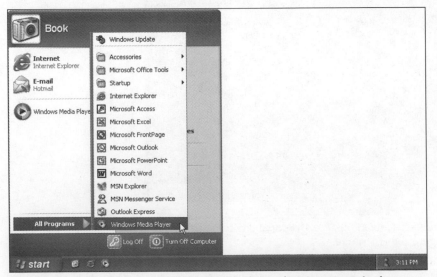

Figure 4-4: A shortcut for Windows Media Player always appears in the Programs menu, but you may have one in the Start Menu as well.

You may want to place shortcuts to Windows Media Player for Windows XP on your desktop. This is fairly easy to do, and gives you ways to start Windows Media Player for Windows XP from a variety of locations that won't change, as the Start Menu does.

To create a shortcut on your desktop, open the Start Menu and expand the More Programs item to display the Programs menu. Right-click Windows Media Player and drag it to an empty area of the desktop. When the pop-up menu appears, choose Copy Here.

Closing Windows Media Player for Windows XP

When you're done using Windows Media Player for Windows XP, you can close its window and recover any resources that it's using. You do so as you would for any Windows application: You can click the Close Windows button in the player's title bar or choose File ➪ Exit. But because MPXP can be customized in so many ways, these two options may not be available. Fortunately, there are still many ways to close the player.

If the menu and window title bars are not visible, the player sprouts new Minimize and Close buttons, as shown in Figure 4-5. You can click the small Close button to close the player.

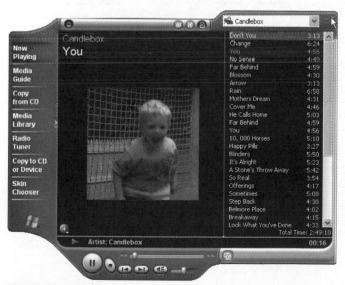

Figure 4-5: When the title bar and menu is hidden, the Windows Media Player window sprouts new Minimize and Close buttons.

Another special situation is when the player is in Skin mode. Each skin should supply a Close button, which resembles an *x* character. The size, exact shape, and location of the Close button depends on the skin, so you may have to look hard to find it.

Power users can close Windows Media Player two other ways, both of which work in both Full and Skin mode. Right-click the Windows Media Player button in the taskbar and choose Close from the pop-menu that appears. After making sure that Windows Media Player for Windows XP is the currently selected application, press Alt+F4 to close the window.

Using the Media Guide

We live in a connected world, and Windows Media Player for Windows XP reflects that with its Media Guide, which aggregates digital media content from a variety of Web sites into a central place that's easy to navigate and use. Best of all, it changes every day, providing you with a constantly updated look at the latest music, movie trailers, radio stations, and other similar content, as shown in Figure 4-6.

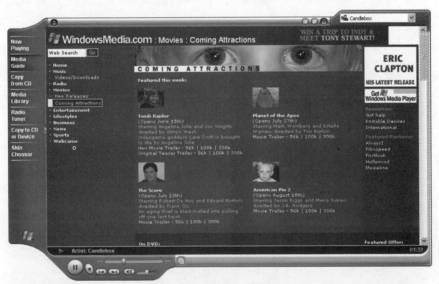

Figure 4-6: The Media Guide provides Web-based music, movie, and radio content that's updated daily.

Basically a Web site that's piped into MPXP, the Media Guide is (obviously) accessible only if you're connected to the Internet. Microsoft has it set up to display by default when the player starts, but if you turn off that function or want to view it manually, select the Media Guide taskbar button; and you'll be there in no time.

Unsurprisingly, you navigate the Media Guide just as you would a Web site: You can click hyperlinks to view new pages, and the page scrolls if there's more information than can be seen inside the window. If you find the navigational controls in MPXP limiting (there's no standard Back, Forward, Refresh, or Stop buttons, for example), you can actually load the content up in Internet Explorer as well. Simply navigate to the Windows Media Web site (www.windowsmedia.com) with IE.

It's curious that Microsoft didn't think to add Web browser buttons to the Media Guide, but most of this navigational functionality is available in the Media Guide if you know the keyboard commands. You can press Alt+left arrow for Back, Alt+right arrow (or Backspace) for Forward, Esc for Stop, and F5 for Refresh. This makes the Media Guide convenient to use while you're in MPXP; you don't have to open a separate browser window. If you attempt to use one of these keyboard commands and it doesn't work, select an empty portion of the Media Guide with the mouse and try again. Sometimes you may find that the selection has changed from what was in the window, and the keyboard commands don't work.

Also note that the Media Guide is only available in Full mode: You cannot access it while in Skin mode.

Listening to Music

Okay, if you've been trying out features as you read, then probably you can start and stop Windows Media Player for Windows XP and navigate around the Web-based Media Guide. As you may have guessed, however, this is only the tip of the iceberg, so don't start patting yourself on the back quite yet. One of the more common tasks you may want to accomplish is to play some music or other audio with the player. The next two sections examine the ways you can do so.

Playing audio CDs

Many people have pretty extensive audio CD collections, which began replacing cassette tapes in the late 1980s. Audio CDs offer high-clarity, digital sound, and come in a pretty convenient form factor (corporate-speak for "they're flat"). A decade after they first became popular, CDs are now everywhere: in portable players, cars, homes, and yes, computers. So it's no surprise that people often sit down at a computer, throw in an audio CD, and get to work.

If you do that in Windows XP, Windows Media Player starts (if it isn't already running) and begins playing the CD, as shown in Figure 4-7. If you're connected to the Internet, you should see the name of the CD listed in the Playlist drop-down list box, and the song listing displayed in the Playlist. Depending on how MPXP is configured, it probably starts playing a cool graphical visualization in the main window.

Figure 4-7: When you insert an audio CD, MPXP starts up, loads the song list, and starts playing.

Of course, for a variety of reasons, you may not see any of this. You may be running MPXP in Skin mode, for example. This isn't a problem: MPXP can play audio CDs in Skin mode.

But maybe your computer isn't set up to automatically play audio CDs when they're inserted. If you insert an audio CD in a CD, CD-R, CD-RW, or DVD drive attached to your computer, and nothing happens — that is, MPXP doesn't launch and start playing the CD — then you can fix this, unless it's configured the way you want it. If this is the case, you can manually start Windows Media Player. Choose the CD icon from the top of the Playlist drop-down list box, and the music begins playing automatically (You may also want to click the Now Playing button on the MPXP taskbar to display the playlist and visualizations).

To ensure that your system is set up to play audio CDs automatically, you have two choices: either do some spelunking in the Windows Registry (not recommended) or use a tool such as Microsoft's excellent TweakUI to ensure that your audio CDs autoplay when inserted. You can find TweakUI — and instructions for using it — on the Web site for this book at www.xpdigitalmedia.com

With the rise in popularity of CD-RW and DVD drives these days, there's one other interesting possibility that may cause you some problems: What happens when you have two or more CD-type devices? Glad you asked.

Working with multiple CD-type devices

Fortunately, Windows Media Player for Windows XP is savvy to the notion that you may have more than one CD-type device. In fact, it works with whatever CD-type devices you have. CD content is shown at the top of the Playlist drop-down list box, so if you open it up and scroll to the top of the list, you see whatever CD devices you have installed, as shown in Figure 4-8. An empty CD device is listed as *Please insert a Disc*, whereas audio CDs show up with their names intact, if you're connected to the Internet. So If you insert Sting's *Brand New Day* CD, for example, the Playlist drop-down list box displays *Brand New Day* next to a CD icon.

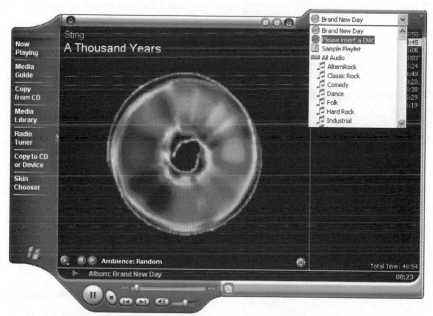

Figure 4-8: The MPXP Playlist drop-down list box displays any CD devices you have installed.

Audio CDs and the Internet

This reliance on the Internet isn't meant to keep you tethered to your Internet connection. Microsoft programmed MPXP this way because there are third party services out there who do a great job of maintaining lists of CD albums, along with all the songs they contain. The service used by MPXP is called the All Music Guide (AMG), which also maintains databases for videos, DVDs, and video games (indeed, MPXP connects to their DVD database as well). The difference between AMG and other audio CD databases such as the more well-known CDDB is crucial: AMG's list is maintained by a list of professionals who meticulously check their album lists against the actual CDs. This means that AMG's lists are the most accurate. The rival CDDB service uses a first-come-first-served system in which users are allowed to type in album lists and upload them to the service. This results in numerous spelling errors, style differences, and other problems. You can find out more about the AMG service on their Web site (www.allmusic.com).

But fear not, you can still play audio CDs without an Internet connection. Simply insert the CD and it plays as usual. The only difference is that it's listed as Unknown CD in the Playlist drop-down list box and none of the song titles are automatically filled out. But the CD plays normally.

Working with High-Definition CDs

In addition to playing the standard audio CDs, Windows Media Player for Windows XP can also play High-Definition CDs (HDCDs), which offer improved fidelity over their more widely available cousins. HDCDs are still pretty rare, but there are over 5000 titles available, many of which are of interest to audiophiles. But hundreds of these titles are mainstream, pop, and rock music CDs, so you never know. As with regular audio CDs, expect the price to come down over time; you may soon see them available in a retail store near you. Whatever happens, MPXP will be ready.

Playing digital audio files

In addition to audio CDs, many users like to play digital audio files that are stored locally on their computer. These files can take many forms, such as older WAV ("wave") and MIDI format files, and newer MP3 and Windows Media Audio (WMA) format files. Digital audio files contain music or other audio content that you can listen to just as you may listen to music on audio CDs. The only difference — as far as playback is concerned — is that the music is typically stored on your hard drive rather than on an audio CD.

A quick overview of HDCD

HDCD is a patented process that improves on the fidelity of normal audio CDs while preserving musical information that is normally lost during the analog-to-digital recording process. According to Microsoft, HDCD provides more dynamic range, a more focused 3D sound stage, and natural musical and vocal timbre for the full body, depth, and emotion of the original performance.

HDCD-encoded CDs can be played on standard CD players — including the one in your PC — but the best experience is only achieved through the use of HDCD-equipped CD players. For more information, head on over to the HDCD Web site (www.hdcd.com), which also provides a way to purchase these discs online.

In fact, for convenience, many users want to copy all or part of their audio CD library to their hard drives. This is covered in Chapter 7. But if you have a number of appropriate digital audio files on your system already the next section is especially relevant.

Scanning your system for audio files

Although it's possible to navigate around your system in My Computer and find audio files, Windows Media Player for Windows XP includes a search feature that scans your system automatically for media.

To access this feature, choose Tool ➪ Search for Media Files (you can also launch this function by pressing F3 at any time while using MPXP). This brings up the cunningly titled Search for Media Files dialog box (shown in Figure 4-9), which contains a variety of user interface elements that should be obvious to most users. Notable are the Advanced button (which reveals advanced search options for skipping certain kinds of digital media files) and the Browse button (which lets you forego an entire system search and navigate to a specific location). The Browse button's direct approach is useful if you have already created a number of files yourself and stored them somewhere specific; it saves having Search waste time on the rest of the hard drive.

Figure 4-9: The Search for Media Files dialog box finds any digital media files on your system.

However you tinker with the options, eventually you have to click Search and go for it. This brings up another dialog box—confusingly, *also* titled Search for Media Files—that displays a progress bar while it searches. If you don't touch any of the search options, and haven't created any audio files yourself (again, see Chapter 7 for how to do this), the search should end relatively quickly and only find a handful of files. So where are they? To find them, first you have to close the two dialog boxes (select Close, and then select Close again).

Well, unless you already have some decent digital audio on your system—most likely WMA or MP3 files—you're probably not going to find much. The player should find some sample files that are associated with Windows Movie Maker or the Pinball game, for example, and of course Windows Media Player comes with sample audio files. To see these sample files, switch to the Media Library by clicking the Media Library option on the MPXP taskbar. More about the Media Library in Chapter 7; for now, expand the All Audio tree in the left pane of the Media Library to select (first) Audio and then All Audio. Figure 4-10 shows what to look for.

Figure 4-10: The Media Library displays all media files you have registered with Windows Media Player for Windows XP.

Playing digital audio

You can double-click media files in the Media Library to play them individually, but you can also tell the Media Library to play groups of songs in specific groups, such as All Audio, songs from particular albums, songs by particular artists, or songs in a particular genre. This functionality is especially useful when copying music from an audio CD. Only then does this feature really start to make sense.

Cross-Reference   For more information on copying music from an audio CD, see Chapter 7.

Plugging into Internet Radio Stations

In addition to audio CDs and digital audio files, Windows Media Player for Windows XP can also be used to playback music on Internet radio stations. Obviously, you'll need an Internet connection for this feature; not quite as obviously, the faster the better: A broadband Internet connection, such as that provided by a cable modem, works better than a dial-up account for this feature. But even a standard 56K modem should do the trick; Internet radio stations aren't particularly bandwidth-heavy. You just want to be sure not to overload that wimpy little modem (if that's what you're stuck with).

In any case, an *Internet radio station* is exactly what it sounds like — a radio station that broadcasts over the Internet rather than the airwaves. That's not *strictly* true: Many Internet radio stations are simply Internet versions of existing radio stations, such that you can listen to your favorite Boston radio station (for example) in Sri Lanka. (Assuming you can get online).

Windows Media Player for Windows XP offers a Radio Tuner option on its task-bar, which loads up the Windows Media Internet Radio Directory, as shown in Figure 4-11. This interface allows you to choose between preset radio stations—Microsoft's "Featured" list, and your own "My Presets" list, where you can save favorite stations—and a search function that lets you find Internet radio stations.

Figure 4-11: The MPXP Radio Tuner gets you in tune with Internet radio stations.

Using presets

If you just want to test the feature that receives Internet radio stations, you can choose from Microsoft's list of Featured presets. Simply choose Featured from the Presets drop-down list box and then choose from the items on Microsoft's list—which includes the House of Blues, National Public Radio (NPR), BBC World, MSNBC, Jazz 102.2 FM, and others (it's eclectic). Double-click the station you'd like to hear and it should eventually play; the speed is based on that of your connection. MPXP *buffers* the content coming from the station, storing several seconds of audio before it begins playing. This way, the player is always "behind" by a few seconds, but it can compensate for slowness in the connection (or for a low-quality connection that peaks and spikes).

What you see when you do connect is based on the station. Many of the Internet radio stations spawn an Internet Explorer window that provides a link to that station's Web site. This can be closed or viewed as desired. Some stations actual switch the player into the Now Playing view and display information about the currently playing song, as shown in Figure 4-12.

Figure 4-12: Some Internet radio stations, such as cablemusic.com's Hot 100, display information about the current song in the Now Playing box.

Many stations don't display much at all. It all depends on the station.

Editing presets

Microsoft's list is a good start, but it's likely that you're going to want to work with your own list of presets. Of course, you'll have to make one first. You can edit the Presets lists by clicking the Edit button next to the Presets drop-down list box; this spawns the Edit Presets List — Web Page Dialog window, as shown in Figure 4-13. This dialog box allows you to edit and delete existing preset lists (but annoyingly, you can't delete Microsoft's Featured list). And you create a new list if you see fit. Or just use the pre-built (but empty) My Presets if you like.

One nice feature of this dialog box is the *Create local station list* option: To see a list of local radio stations, type in your ZIP code and hit Add. If you're living in exile, you can type in the ZIP code of your old home and listen to that favorite station you thought you'd never hear again. Once you're done, exit the dialog box and choose the ZIP code list (it may be called something like *85016 Stations*, where *85016* was the ZIP code I entered). MPXP will populate the presets list with whatever stations are available, as shown in Figure 4-14. As always, double-click a station you want to hear, sit back, and enjoy it.

Figure 4-13: You can edit the Internet radio stations preset lists, adding your own lists and auto-generating a list of stations based on your ZIP code.

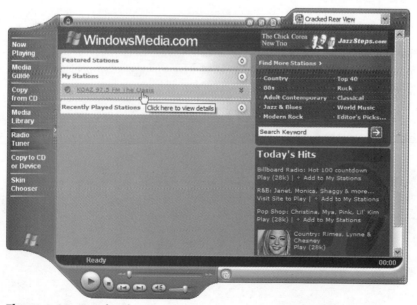

Figure 4-14: Your local station list is auto-populated with radio stations in your particular ZIP code.

There's one little problem with the ZIP code list you make this way: There's no way to make multiple lists. If you go back and change the ZIP code, it overwrites your existing ZIP code list, rather than make a new one. That's lame. Hopefully, a future version of WMP will let you rename preset lists, or add multiple ZIP code lists so this doesn't happen. In the meantime, there is a way to find the radio stations you really want, but you have to go through the search function first. Coming right up.

Searching for Internet radio stations

If you want to find Internet radio stations, Windows Media Player for Windows XP offers extensive search functionality. The Station Finder area of the Radio Tuner allows you to search by format, band, language, location, call sign, frequency, or keyword, using the Find By drop-down list box. And most of these options trigger the display of either a second list box or a text box.

For example: Suppose you want to see all the radio stations that are available in Massachusetts. You would open the Find By drop-down list box and choose Location. This displays the Select Location list box, where you can choose United States. Doing so, in turn, displays the Select State list box, where you can choose Massachusetts. And then, finally, a list of Massachusetts-based Internet radio stations appears, as shown in Figure 4-15.

Figure 4-15: The Search function lets you find Internet radio stations using a variety of criteria.

If you receive a long list, you can sort the list by the categories found in the column headings at the top of the list; if you want to sort by format, for example, click the Format header. And so on.

Adding a found station to a Presets list

After you've found that perfect station, you can add it to a Presets list. First (from the Presets drop-down list), select the list you'd like to add the station to. Then select the station in the right pane of the player, where the Found list appears. Doing so enables the <<< button, which allows you to copy a station from the Found list into the Presets list. Just click the <<< button to make it happen, as shown in Figure 4-16.

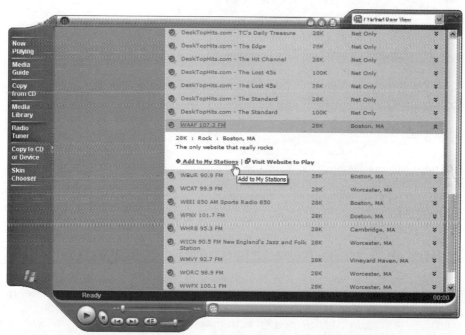

Figure 4-16: Copying a found station to a presets list is as easy as clicking a button.

Now that station will be available whenever you need it. (Barring online glitches, of course.)

Removing a station from a Presets list

Conversely, you can remove a station from a Presets list (but not from the pre-built Featured list) by selecting it in the Presets list pane and clicking the >>> button. Be careful when you do this, however: There's no confirmation; once you click the button, the station is deleted for good.

Looking at bandwidth usage

If you're concerned about the quality of your connection, Windows Media Player can show you, on a station-by-station basis, how much bandwidth is required. Simply begin playing an Internet radio station and then choose Statistics from the View menu. This displays the Statistics dialog box (shown in Figure 4-17), which tells you the maximum amount of bandwidth that the station would require. For example, WBOS in Boston can be transmitted at up to 20.8 Kbps, which would sap about half of the bandwidth on an excellent 56K connection. But 20.8 Kbps is almost a statistical nonentity on my cable connection, which WMP lists as being greater than 1000 Kbps.

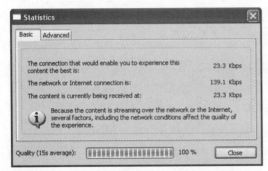

Figure 4-17: The Statistics dialog box tells you how much bandwidth the current radio station is taking up, as well as how much bandwidth you've got to spare.

Using IE 6 to browse Internet radio stations

If you're more of a Web-browser-friendly person, you may be interested to know that you can access the Windows Media Player for Windows XP Radio Tuner from the Web as well. Navigate to the Radio Tuner Web site (www.windowsmedia.com/radiotuner) and you're presented with exactly the same interface that you see in MPXP, with an additional Play button that launches MPXP.

Working with Streaming Audio Files

There's one final type of digital audio file you can play with Windows Media Player for Windows XP: Streaming files. A file that is *streamed* is delivered across the Internet and played in real time, without downloading the entire file first. In the old days, this wasn't possible: A digital media file would have to be completely down-loaded before you could begin playing it. But with streaming media, a file can be played *as it's downloaded*. That makes a huge difference in low-bandwidth environments such as the Internet.

If the streaming-media concept sounds a bit like the Internet radio stations we examined before, there's a reason: The technology is similar. The difference, however, is that streaming media deal with individual files (such as a single song), rather than a continuous source of songs (such as a radio station).

Any capability for streaming media depends totally on the quality of your Internet connection. For this reason, many sources of streaming media offer this capability at a variety of quality levels. Low-bandwidth dial-up users can choose to stream a lower-quality file; cable modem users may choose a higher-quality file that consumes more bandwidth. And of course, a similar range of quality applies to streaming video files as well as audio files.

Finding streaming audio files

Microsoft's Media Guide, discussed earlier in this chapter, is an obvious place to go for streaming media. You can load the Media Guide and navigate to the Music section (denoted by the Music tab at the top of the page), for example, and select media to stream. Though the structure and user interface of the Media Guide is likely to change over time, you'll see something similar to Figure 4-18: Various audio and video files are highlighted and available in a variety of speeds. In this example, the choices offer 56K, 100K, and even 300K. The slower-speed clips should work on just about any connection, but they are of relatively low quality. The higher-quality clips sound (or look) great, but they require a broadband connection to play correctly.

Figure 4-18: The Media Guide offers a variety of streaming media clips in a variety of quality settings.

The Media Guide also lets you find music by category or artist name while linking to record companies' Web sites that provide streaming and downloadable music.

Other streaming-media formats

Interestingly, the capability to handle streaming media is one area in which Microsoft's end-to-end approach falls short. This is because Windows Media Player for Windows XP does not support two of the most popular streaming-media formats: RealNetworks and Apple Computer. The Microsoft formats for streaming audio and video, though technically superior, currently trail those of market leader RealNetworks (RealAudio and RealVideo) in popularity. Although the Microsoft streaming-media formats far outpace number-three Apple Computer QuickTime technology in sheer number of users, QuickTime is still very popular, especially with movie studios offering trailers on the Web.

For a variety of reasons, Microsoft doesn't offer the capability to play RealNetworks or Apple formats through Windows Media Player for Windows XP. So if you want to take advantage of these formats (which are quite common on the Web), you have to download specific programs: the RealNetworks RealPlayer and Apple QuickTime. There's just no way around it, at least not until the Microsoft formats become more pervasive or WMP incorporates the technology from these other players.

RealNetworks RealPlayer

RealPlayer is available from the RealNetworks Web site (`www.real.com`) in two versions — a free basic player and a "Plus" version (which you must pay for before you can use it). Real also offers a second media application called RealJukebox, which apes the all-in-one functionality of MPXP, but it too must be purchased to obtain its full functionality.

Apple QuickTime Player

Apple Computer also offers free and "Pro" versions of its excellent QuickTime player, which doesn't offer the wide range of features in Windows Media Player, but does include some interesting streaming "channels" that Apple calls QuickTime TV.

Figure 4-19 shows both RealPlayer and QuickTime running in Windows XP. Maybe someday just one program will truly do it all.

Figure 4-19: Until Microsoft supports the Real and QuickTime formats, you'll need to download the media players from RealNetworks and Apple Computer, respectively.

✦ ✦ ✦

Configuring and Tuning Windows Media Player for Windows XP

Windows Media Player 7 was very well received by customers, but Microsoft found that its users really wanted it to be more configurable. So when development of Windows Media Player for Windows XP (Windows Media Player version 8) began, the company looked at ways to make this version more easily modifiable, giving users a more personalized experience. So the Full mode window is far more customizable than it was in MP7, there are more professional-looking skins, and the sheer number of options has skyrocketed, making MPXP one of the most configurable media players available.

In this chapter, we'll examine how you can configure and tweak Windows Media Player for Windows XP for a more personalized experience.

Customizing the Player Window in Full Mode

When you launch Windows Media Player for Windows XP, the player starts up in the mode in which it was last used. The Full Mode window presents the most options, but it can also take up a lot of space. You can resize Windows Media Player for Windows XP by using your mouse pointer to seize the grab handle in the lower-right corner of the window and moving the mouse inward (to reduce size) or outward (to increase size). By doing so, you save up to two-thirds of the space originally occupied by the player (or, if you prefer, make it larger so you have more screen real estate to work with). If the menu bar is visible, you can also maximize the Windows Media Player for Windows XP window. Note, however, that maximizing the window makes it impossible to hide the menu bar. In addition to these basic resizing options, you can also modify the Full Mode window by hiding and displaying the Taskbar, menu bar, or playlist.

Taskbar

On the left side of the player window is the Windows Media Player for Windows XP Taskbar, which presents you with one-click access to its most often-needed options. But the Taskbar takes up a lot of space; you can hide it easily enough if you don't need it. Using the Hide Taskbar button on the right side of the Taskbar, you can toggle the Taskbar on and off. This way you can still get at the player's most popular options in just two clicks. Figure 5-1 shows the two Taskbar modes.

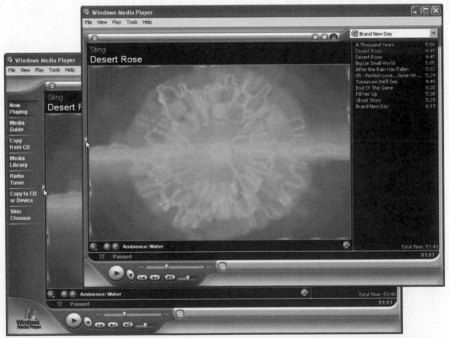

Figure 5-1: The Windows Media Player Taskbar, seen (left) and hidden (right)

You can also hide the Taskbar by choosing Full Mode Options ➪ Hide Taskbar from the View menu. To view the Taskbar once again, reselect the same option.

Menu bar

Additionally, you can choose to auto-hide the menu bar, or toggle the display of the menu bar. When the menu bar is hidden, the Windows Media Player window loses the typical boxy shape of most application windows and takes on a more rounded, organic appearance that is more visually appealing. To choose auto-hide, select View ➪ Full Mode Options ➪ Auto Hide Menu Bar (as shown in Figure 5-2). This option displays the menu bar briefly when the player starts up, but then hides it and the surrounding window frame. You can redisplay the menu while in auto-hide mode by moving the mouse pointer over the top of the window; move the mouse away again and the menu and window frame disappears once more.

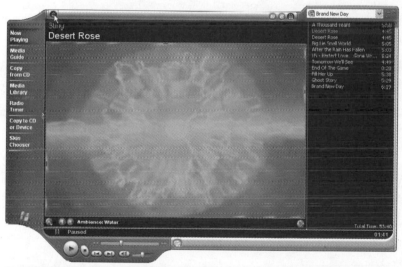

Figure 5-2: Windows Media Player allows you to determine whether the window frame and menu bar are visible.

To always hide the menu bar, choose View ➪ Full Mode Options ➪ Hide Menu Bar. In this mode, the menu and surrounding window frame does not appear unless you manually display it once again. You can do so with the Show Menu Bar button near the top of the window, as shown in Figure 5-3; you can also choose View ➪ Full Mode Options ➪ Show Menu Bar.

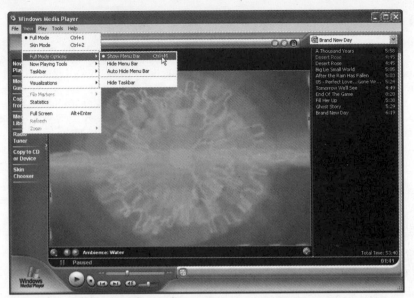

Figure 5-3: The Auto Hide Menu Bar button toggles the display of the menu bar and window frame.

By default, the menu bar is always displayed; you can return to this mode by choosing View ➪ Full Mode Options ➪ Show Menu Bar. If the menu bar is hidden, you can also click the Show Menu Bar button on the top of the window to redisplay it.

Playlist

Depending on the type of media you're playing, it might be worthwhile to display the playlist, which can be seen by default in the right of the player. But you might also want to turn this feature off to maximize the viewing area for visualizations of DVD movies. Fortunately, the playlist can be easily toggled as well, and Figure 5-4 shows the Now Playing view with *and* without the playlist. The simplest way is to click the Hide Playlist in Now Playing button, which is the rightmost of three buttons at the top of the player window. Selecting this button again makes the playlist reappear. You can also toggle the playlist by choosing View ➪ Now Playing Tools ➪ Show Playlist.

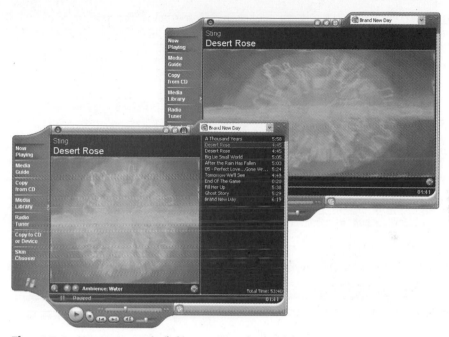

Figure 5-4: Now you see it (left), now you don't (right): MPXP with and without the playlist.

Note that you can also adjust the width of the playlist by grabbing its leftmost border with the mouse cursor and dragging it left or right. This is shown in Figure 5-5.

Figure 5-5: The Playlist can be expanded width-wise.

Combined, each of these options makes it easy to customize the Full Mode window as you see fit. In the next section, we'll take a look at some other ways in which you might actually use Windows Media Player for Windows XP.

Customizing the Player Using Skin Mode

In addition to Full Mode, Windows Media Player for Windows XP also works in a *Skin Mode*, through which you can use a variety of *skins* (custom user interfaces) to dramatically alter the look and feel of the player; an example is shown in Figure 5-6. Most skins use only a subset of the full functionality of the player, but which options are available are skin-dependent. As a rule, you see options for playing, pausing, jumping to the previous or next song, and the like. But some options, such as the visualization, graphic equalizer, or playlist displays, are only available in certain skins.

Figure 5-6: A typical Windows Media Player for Windows XP skin, which offers a smaller size than Full Mode, but with reduced functionality

Given their limitations, skins aren't meant to be used when you need to configure the player or manage your media files. Normally you use a skin when you're just playing music, such as a shuffled list of songs in a playlist, or all of the songs on a single CD. Because the skins used in Skin Mode are generally far smaller than the Full Mode display, Skin Mode is ideal when you want the player loaded but out of the way.

Choosing a skin

Choosing a skin is relatively simple, and Microsoft supplies several decent skins with Windows Media Player for Windows XP. To choose a new skin, click the Skin Chooser option in the MPXP Taskbar. The list of available skins appears (with the current selection highlighted), as shown in Figure 5-7.

There are a couple of ways to test the new skin. Double-clicking a skin name in the list automatically changes the player to Skin Mode, using that skin. You can also select a skin and then click the Apply Skin button.

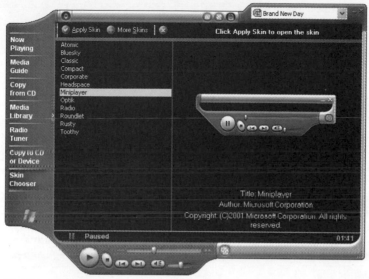

Figure 5-7: The Skin Chooser enables you to pick a skin, delete skins, and find more skins on the Internet.

Skin Gallery

The following skins are included in Windows XP Professional.

✦ Atomic

✦ Bluesky

✦ Canvas

✦ Classic

✦ Compact

✦ Corporate

✦ Goo

✦ Headspace

✦ Heart

✦ Iconic

✦ Miniplayer

✦ Optik

✦ Pyrite

- ✦ Radio
- ✦ Roundlet
- ✦ Rusty
- ✦ Splat
- ✦ Toothy
- ✦ Windows Classic
- ✦ Windows XP

Working with skins

Just because most skins visually offer a vastly reduced set of functionality when compared to Full Mode doesn't mean you can't still access at least some of the more important options. The key is the infamous right-click, which has been a staple of the Windows world since Windows 95. While in Skin Mode, right-click anywhere on the skin to access the player's right-click menu, shown in Figure 5-8.

Figure 5-8: The MPXP properties menu is available in Skin Mode so you can find options that might be hidden by the skin.

If you're into keyboard commands, you can type Ctrl+2 at any time to switch to Skin Mode. You can also press Ctrl+1 to switch to Full Mode.

Chapter 5 ✦ Configuring and Tuning Windows Media Player for Windows XP

Downloading new skins

If you'd like a wider selection of skins than those that are supplied with Windows Media Player, click the More Skins button (which appears near the top of the Skin Chooser page in Windows Media Player). Doing so spawns an Internet Explorer window, which displays the Windows Media Player Skin Gallery Web site. This site currently offers dozens of professionally designed skins, so you should be able to find something you like. But personally, I think the skins that come with the player are nicer than anything in the Skin Gallery, at least so far. (The skins that were available for Windows Media Player 7 are *particularly* bad for some reason.) Hopefully, more professional skins will appear as MPXP usage grows.

Deleting a skin

To delete a skin from the list of available skins, select that skin and then click the *Delete* button, which is curiously unlabeled. It looks like a small *X*, as shown in Figure 5-9.

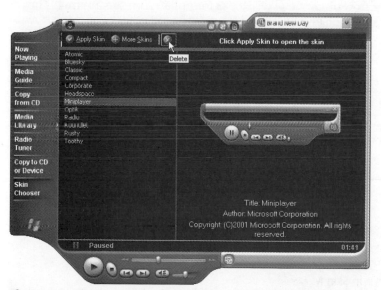

Figure 5-9: The (curiously unlabeled) Delete button enables you to delete a skin from your system.

Programming skins

If you're a programmer, you can also create your own Windows Media Player for Windows XP skins. Although this topic is somewhat beyond the scope of this book, I'll at least point you in the right direction. Microsoft maintains a Web site dedicated to this endeavor, which requires both programming and graphics arts skills, an admittedly rare combination. But if you're undaunted, head on over to the Windows Media Web site and check it out: www.windowsmedia.com.

Exercising Your Options with Windows Media Player for Windows XP

One of the huge improvements with this release of the media player is the sheer number of customizable features and options, when compared with Windows Media Player 7. This section takes a look at the Options dialog box, accessible from the MPXP *Tools* menu, where you make most configuration changes.

Setting Player options

The Player Options page, shown in Figure 5-10, is where you'll go to set up some of the more general options for Windows Media Player. The Automatic Updates section determines how often the player looks for updates on the Internet. The default is "Once a week," which should be fine for most users, unless you don't have an Internet connection. If you have a cable modem account, you might want to set it on "Once a day."

Figure 5-10: The Player options page enables you to customize updates and general player settings.

You can also determine whether the player downloads and installs *codec* updates automatically, which is the default, or whether it should notify you if a new codec becomes available. A *codec* is a data file that tells the player how to work with media types. For example, Windows Media Player comes with a codec for Windows Media Audio format, among many others. This codec allows the player to record and play audio in that format. (Obviously, this option requires you to have an Internet connection — as does the next one.)

Internet settings

The Internet settings section includes other Internet-related options. If you choose to allow Internet sites to uniquely identify your player, MPXP sends compatible Web sites a unique number that is generated by your player. This identifier doesn't betray any private information about you to the Web site, however. Instead, the identifier is used to monitor (and optionally store) the quality of your connection as you receive streaming media files. If you have a consistently strong connection, sites can optionally provide you with higher-quality streams. Conversely, if your connection drops out a lot, lower-quality streams might be substituted. If you're not interested in sites micromanaging this or are nervous about information being transmitted over the Internet, simply uncheck the option titled *Allow Internet sites to uniquely identify your Player.*

Another Internet setting, *Acquire licenses automatically*, determines whether the player automatically acquires a license for those files that require such a thing. If you uncheck this option, you are presented with a dialog box whenever you attempt to access a remote file that requires a license.

Player settings

The Player settings section includes a few basic options regarding the player itself. The first option determines whether Windows Media Player for Windows XP begins with the Media Guide displayed when you first start up the application. It is on by default, but I prefer the player to come up with whatever I was using last time, so I uncheck this option. You should also uncheck it if you are using a dial-up account; otherwise MPXP could make your system attempt an Internet connection when you launch the player. The second option determines whether the player is displayed on top of all other windows when in Skin Mode. That arrangement is probably too annoying for most people (given the size of most skins); I recommend leaving it unchecked, which is the default.

One odd option determines whether an *anchor window* is displayed when the player is in Skin mode; this is on by default. The anchor window is the small square box you might see when in Skin mode; it sits at the bottom right of the screen as shown in Figure 5-11. Microsoft added this as default because it's possible that the skin you're using doesn't offer a *Return to Full Mode* button. Although this is indeed possible, I've never actually seen a skin like this, and I find the anchor window to be annoying, so I recommend that you uncheck this option and send the anchor to a watery grave. It's also easy enough to use the right-click option and return to Full Mode that way.

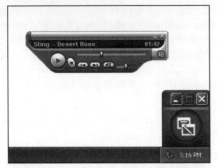

Figure 5-11: The Skin Mode Anchor window is annoying, but you can get rid of it.

If you have a screen saver configured, you can choose whether that screen saver can be activated while the player is playing music. In this day and age, PC power management features have largely rendered screen savers unnecessary but if you're still stuck on using one, this option is for you. Note that it's grayed out if you aren't using a screensaver.

The *Add items to Media Library when played* option is a crucial one, and its inclusion is a minor, but important, advance over MP7. In that player, every media file that you double-clicked was immediately added to the MP7 Media Library. This could be a problem, depending on how you use your system. Let's say you downloaded a new song and it shows up on your desktop, so you double-click it, play it in the media player, and then decide you want to keep it. So you move it into the My Music folder and then go about your business. The problem is that now MP7 has a dead link in its Media Library: It still thinks that the song is on your desktop, and it attempts to play it from there the next time you try to access that song from the player.

In Windows Media Player for Windows XP, this isn't a problem for two reasons: First of all, you could choose to not have every played song added to your Media Library. And secondly, MPXP remembers where a played file is moved when you decide to reorganize. So if you have chosen to add all played media to your Media Library, play the file from the desktop, and then move the file, MPXP remembers where you moved it and updates the location in its Media Library.

So, it's up to you. But I recommend leaving *Add items to Media Library* checked, if only because there is no easy way to otherwise add media to the Media Library without manually searching your system for new media.

However, the *Include items from removable media* option should probably remain unchecked. "Removable media" includes CDs, Pocket PC devices, and portable audio devices like the Iomega HipZip. It's unlikely that media on such devices are attached to your system permanently, so it's better to leave them out of your Media Library and avoid any nasty error messages. This option is unavailable if *Add items to Media Library when played* is unchecked.

Setting Copy Music options

The Copy Music page, shown in Figure 5-12, relates to music that's copied from Audio CDs. (This topic gets thorough coverage in Chapter 7.)

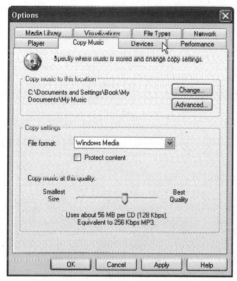

Figure 5-12: The Copy Music options page allows you to specify where music is stored on your system and change ripping options.

Setting Devices options

The Devices page, shown in Figure 5-13, allows you to configure devices that interoperate with Windows Media Player for Windows XP. Such devices include recordable and non-recordable CD devices (CD, CD-R, CD-RW, DVD, and DVD-RAM); PocketPC devices like the Compaq iPaq; and portable audio players like the Rio 800 and the Iomega HipZip.

For more about these options as they relate to CD devices, see Chapter 8; for the same about PocketPCs and portable audio devices, see Chapter 13.

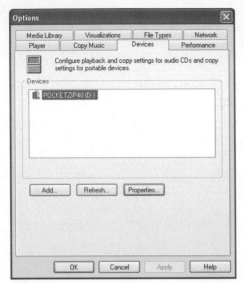

Figure 5-13: The Devices pane enables you to configure CD drives and portable devices.

Setting Performance options

The Performance page presents options related to the player's networking performance, as shown in Figure 5-14. For the most part, you can leave these options set to their defaults, but we'll take a quick look at what's here. And one of these options is particularly critical to users with advanced video-editing needs.

Connection speed

In the *Connection speed* section, you can determine whether the player automatically detects your speed—which is recommended, both by Microsoft and myself—or through a manual setting. The manual settings include such choices as 28.8-Kbps modem and 768-Kbps DSL/cable. Just leave it set to the default; there's absolutely no reason to be tinkering with something that can be far more accurately determined by the technology.

Network buffering

Like the connection speed, *network buffering* is something that's best left alone: Buffering determines how much of a streaming media file is downloaded before it begins playing. Buffering is what makes streaming media work—otherwise, network glitches and downtime would cause streaming media to stutter and skip far more often than it does. If you don't like the way buffering is working—that is, you're experiencing all kinds of skipping and pausing—you might want to set this option manually. You can enter a value of up to 60 seconds. But generally, it's best to just leave it as is.

Figure 5-14: The Performance options page is all about networking and video performance, not the general performance of the player.

Video acceleration

The *Video acceleration* option determines how the player works in full screen mode, which is generally best used for DVD movies, as explained in Chapter 9. It can be set to three options: *no video acceleration*, *some video acceleration*, or *full video acceleration*. In general, set this option to Full unless you're experiencing video-playback problems. If this happens, try moving the slider to the middle choice, *Some*. If that fails, you're probably using an older or unsupported 3D card, and you should select *None*.

Video acceleration includes an Advanced button, which launches the *Video Acceleration Settings* dialog box, shown in Figure 5-15. This dialog box enables you to set more advanced options for streaming and WMV-format video, as well as DVD video.

The Video Acceleration section enables you to determine a number of video-related features, including whether the player can go into full-screen mode while playing video files. And the DVD Video section includes an option for choosing a hardware or software decoder. Both of these options are generally best left to their defaults, as MPXP auto-detects the capabilities of your system. But if you have a hardware DVD decoder (more and more uncommon these days) and the system hasn't auto-matically detected it, this is the place to go. Changing any of these settings requires the player to be restarted.

Figure 5-15: The Video Acceleration Settings dialog box allows you to configure how video files and DVDs are played back.

The most important option here is right at the top. The Digital Video slider determines how large video can be displayed through the player. Its default setting, for some reason, is about at about the 2/3 position, meaning that you will be unable to view full-sized digital video (AVI format) at its native resolution. If you have a fairly high-end system (800 MHz or faster with at least 256 MB of RAM), then I recommend changing this to the Large setting.

Setting Media Library options

You can use the Media Library page (shown in Figure 5-16) to determine how the Media Library interacts with external programs. We'll take a closer look at the Media Library and these options in Chapter 7.

Setting Visualizations options

Visualizations are colorful, animated displays that can optionally be displayed while you're listening to music with Windows Media Player for Windows XP. Microsoft ships a number of visualizations with the player, and you can download more from the Windows Media Web site. In the Visualizations page (shown in Figure 5-17), you can add, remove, and configure individual visualizations.

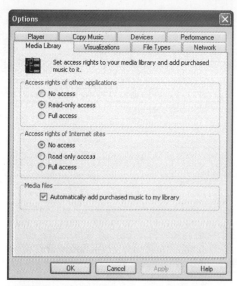

Figure 5-16: The Media Library options page enables you to configure how the Media Library interacts with external applications and Web sites.

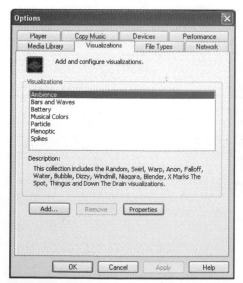

Figure 5-17: Configure visualizations from the Visualizations options page.

Adding visualizations

To add a new visualization that you've stored locally, click the Add button. Doing so presents a standard Open File dialog box that enables you to navigate to the visualization (*.DLL, oddly) that you'd like to add. However, most people don't actually have visualizations sitting around on their system, so you can navigate to the Windows Media Web site in Internet Explorer and download visualizations from there as well. Just choose Tool ➪ Download Visualizations.

Deleting visualizations

To delete a visualization, simply choose the visualization and click the *Remove* button.

Configuring visualizations

Some visualizations allow you to configure certain options. For example, you can select the Ambience visualization, click Properties and then configure its full-screen and player settings through the Properties dialog box, as shown in Figure 5-18.

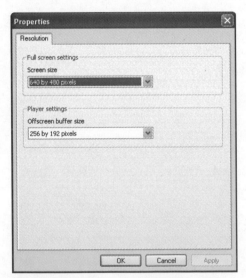

Figure 5-18: Some visualizations can be configured for full screen mode and off-screen buffer size.

The options you can configure are dependent on the visualization and some, such as Bars and Waves, don't offer any configuration at all.

Setting File Types options

The File Types page (see Figure 5-19) provides a friendly way to determine which file types are supported by the player than the normal method, which is available in the Windows Folder Options dialog box. By default, Windows Media Player for Windows XP is set up to work with all supported media types (Windows Media files, CD audio, etc.) except for DVD video. However, if you've purchased Windows XP with a new PC from Dell, IBM, or some other major PC maker, it's possible that they've configured the player for DVD playback as well. We'll discuss this in more detail in Chapter 9. Generally speaking, you can just click Select All and be done with it — unless you're using another media player (such as WINAMP) to play certain types of media files.

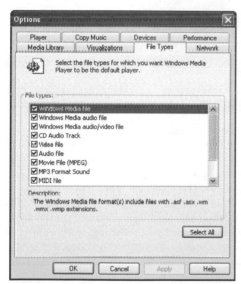

Figure 5-19: The File Types options page determines which file types are associated with the player.

Setting DVD options

The DVD page controls DVD parental control and language settings (Figure 5-20); we'll discuss this more fully in Chapter 9, but here's a shot to whet your appetite. Note that this page *only* appears if a DVD drive is attached to your system.

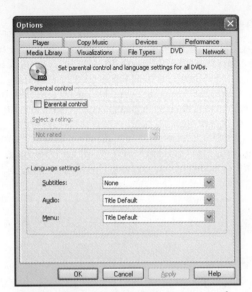

Figure 5-20: The DVD options page only provides options for parental controls and language settings.

Setting Network options

And finally, the Network page, which is curiously separate from the Performance options, determines how your player works over a network. It deals specifically with network *protocols*, which determine the rules which streaming media files must follow to interoperate between the server and your system. This is sort of a complicated subject. My advice is to simply leave all of these options set to their defaults.

The proxy settings are most often used on corporate networks, so they can be ignored as well.

Updating Windows Media Player for Windows XP

One final little tidbit about the configuration of Windows Media Player for Windows XP: You can download updates to the player over the Web. The section titled "Setting Player options" discussed how you could configure the player to automatically download player updates — new codecs, playlists, and even new security fixes. But you can manually check for new updates by selecting

Help ➪ Check for Player Updates. Doing so launches the Windows Media Component Setup dialog box, which is then populated with any available updates, giving you the option to download them all, or just the ones you want. If no new updates are available, you'll see a message to that effect, as shown in Figure 5-21.

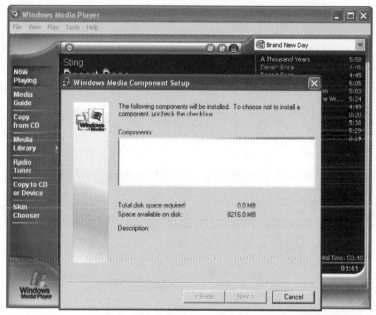

Figure 5-21: You can update Windows Media Player for Windows XP over the Internet to get the latest features and security fixes.

Generally speaking, it's probably a good idea to let the player update itself automatically. But if you hear about a new security update — possibly from my WinInfo mailing list (www.winformant.com) — this is the place to go to download the fix.

✦   ✦   ✦

Managing and Sharing Digital Music

The notion of digital music management is simple. Digital music files, like any documents, must be stored somewhere on your computer so they can be readily accessed, either by Media Player for Windows XP or by some other application. Each file has properties, or *attributes* called metadata, that describe its contents. A music file, for example, contains a song (of course), but it also contains information about that song — such as the artist, the name of the song, and the album from which it originated.

In addition to managing your digital music files, you may also want to use the Internet to share them with friends and family. Or perhaps you have a home network and would like to provide a central *share,* a source from which all computers on the network can access your digital music files. In today's increasingly connected world, such home *media servers* are becoming more common. And they're not hard to set up.

This chapter looks at these management and sharing tasks, along with the different ways you can do them in Windows XP.

Using the My Music Folder

In Windows 95, the concept of a common documents folder (dubbed My Documents) and, to a lesser extent, multiple people using the same machine, was popularized for the first time. In Windows 2000 (and its NT-based predecessors), multiple users had been part of the plan all along, so each user got his or her own My Documents folder, along with other user-specific folders for managing such things as Internet Explorer Favorites and e-mail.

Windows XP expands on this theme by elevating two folders to the same status as My Documents — My Pictures and My Music. This means that My Pictures and My Music are considered top-level shell folders in My Computer and Explorer, and they appear, by default, on the Windows XP Start menu. Microsoft elevated these folders because of the digital media focus in Windows XP — the company feels that people turn increasingly to their PCs to accomplish common tasks with digital media such as photographs and music. (This book is banking on this notion as well — I wouldn't have written it if I didn't think that this was going to be popular.)

Both My Pictures and My Music are *special shell folders* — they exhibit behavior that's different from a normal folder created on the desktop or elsewhere on your system.

 Cross-Reference   For more about My Pictures, see Chapter 1.

A look at My Music

You can access My Music directly from the Start menu, as shown in Figure 6-1. But you can also get to My Music from My Documents (under which My Music is, by default, a subfolder); a later section in this chapter covers moving one or both of these special folders. If you've ripped audio CD-based music to your system (as described in Chapter 7), you should see folders in My Music that correspond to artist names. Each folder contains one or more subfolders, which in turn represent albums by particular artists.

The folder icons in My Music are shown in the Thumbnails view by default. This allows each artist folder to display up to four thumbnail images of contained album rips. So, for example, if you've ripped four CDs by solo pianist David Lanz, you see a David Lanz folder in My Computer with four thumbnail images on it. If you only rip one CD for any particular artist, that artist's folder contains one thumbnail image. See Figure 6-2 for a variety of folder thumbnail examples.

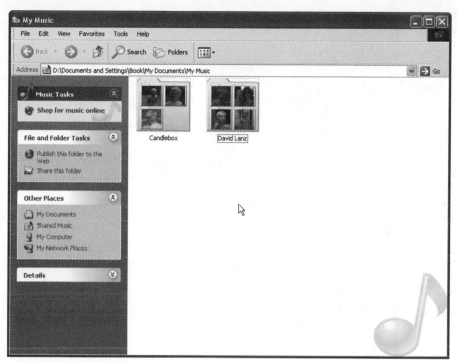

Figure 6-1: If you've ripped audio CDs, you see a number of Artist folders in My Music.

Customizing My Music folders

Each folder in Windows XP appears on-screen using a default template, and My Music is no different. But because My Music is a special folder, you cannot edit the template it uses. However, you can edit any subfolders. To do so, right-click an artist folder in the My Music window and choose Customize ➪ Properties in the resulting dialog box. By default, an artist folder uses a template called Music Artist (best for works by one artist), as shown in Figure 6-3. And generally, this is what you want for this kind of folder: By default, a Music Artist folder automatically generates thumbnails of the folders and other files it contains. If that folder contains folders that represent individual albums (as they should), you'll see the expected album art thumbnails.

Note that you should generally *not* check the box titled *Also apply this template to all subfolders*. This is because the subfolders of Music Artist folders are Music Album folders (described in the next section) that have their own special template.

Figure 6-2: Inside each Artist folder is one or more Album folders.

But you can modify the folder image if you want. Let's say you really like the album cover art for David Lanz's classic *Desert Vision* album and would prefer to have his folder display that image, rather than the automatically generated thumbnails. Look up David Lanz on All Music Guide (`www.allmusic.com`) and then search for *Desert Vision* (released in 1986). Download the album cover image, save it to the `My Music\David Lanz\Desert Vision` folder (or wherever you'd like) and then choose Properties ➪ Customize ➪ Choose Picture to display that image instead of the automatically generated thumbnail (as shown in Figure 6-4). You can also use this technique to use any image you want for any folder that's in Thumbnail view.

Tip   If you save the downloaded image as *folder.jpg,* it will *automatically* be used as the thumbnail for the folder in which it resides. This is true of any folder that's displayed in Thumbnail view.

If you're no longer fond of the customized icon view you've created, simply reopen the Properties sheet and choose Restore Default: Automatically generated, the album-cover thumbnails return.

And if you're not using Thumbnail view for some reason, you can also choose to modify the icon image that's used to display the folder. Click the Change Icon button and find an icon you'd like to use instead.

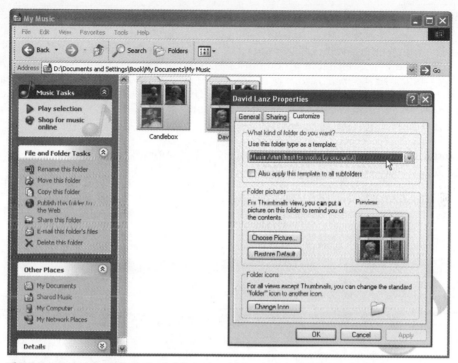

Figure 6-3: By default, Artist folders should be set up with the Music Artist folder template.

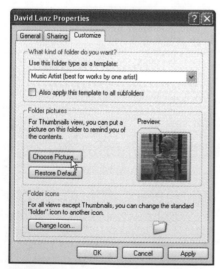

Figure 6-4: It's easy to change the image used by folder thumbnails.

Modifying Album folders

If you navigate into a Music Artist folder, you see one or more folders, each of which represents an album by that artist. So, for example, inside the David Lanz folder used in this example, a number of folders correspond to individual recordings — such as *Beloved, Bridge of Dreams,* and *Cristofori's Dream.* The name of each of these folders is the same as the name of a David Lanz album, and inside these folders you find individual Windows Media Audio (WMA) or MP3 format audio files, depending on how you ripped them.

By default, each of these folders uses the folder template titled *Music Album (best for tracks from one album),* assuming you ripped them with MPXP. If you didn't, you can change them to this template by customizing each folder and choosing this from the folder template drop-down list box, as shown in Figure 6-5.

Figure 6-5: Each album folder should be using the Music Album folder template.

If you open a Music Album folder such as *Sacred Road* (to beat my David Lanz example to death), you see one or more media files. These files each represent one song on an album, as shown in Figure 6-6, and they appear in Tiles view. Tiles view is new to Windows XP; it is a standard icon view that also displays a sampling of *metadata* (data describing the file). So, for example, a filed named `01-Dreamer's Waltz.wma` (remember that the file extension .WMA is generally hidden by default) displays two additional lines of metadata next to its icon in Tiles view: artist name (*David Lanz* in this case) and the album title (*Sacred Road*).

Figure 6-6: Album folders display files in Tiles view by default, with selected metadata shown along with the file name of each file.

More about music file metadata

But there's more metadata in each media file — to get a look at it, hover over that file with the mouse cursor, as shown in Figure 6-7. This provides information such as file name, artist, album, year, duration, type (typically Windows Media Audio file or MP3 Format Sound), bit rate, and size — all in a small yellow *tooltip* window. This information is, of course, read-only; there's no way to edit what you see in a tooltip.

Figure 6-7: A yellow tooltip window offers more metadata when you put the mouse pointer over an icon.

However, you can edit some metadata fields, either for individual media or for groups of files. To edit the metadata for an individual file, right-click that file and choose Properties and then select the Summary tab. If you don't see a window similar to that shown in Figure 6-8, click the Advanced button.

From here, you can modify the artist name, album title, year, track number, genre, or comments. Other metadata — such as license, duration, bit rate, audio sample size (in bits), number of channels (where 2 is stereo and 1 is mono), and audio sample rate — cannot be edited. You can, however, edit the metadata of the file directly, regardless of file type. For .WMA files, metadata is part of each file; for MP3 files, the ID3v2 tag gets modified. Fortunately, you never really have to worry about which is which.

Figure 6-8: The Summary tab lets you actually edit metadata, right in the shell.

Cross-Reference For an explanation of both WMA and MP3, see Chapter 7.

But you're not limited to editing one file at a time. If (for example) you want to edit the metadata for the year, for every song in a folder, just select the entire group of icons, right-click, and choose Properties. Navigate to the Summary tab again, and this time you'll see something a bit different: Items specific to a metadata file, such as track number and title, are grayed out and unavailable (as shown in Figure 6-9). But those applicable to all files — such as album title, artist, and year — are modifiable. So you can change the year (or whatever), click Apply, and be sure that you've made the change for all files in the folder — in one step.

Figure 6-9: You can edit the metadata for a group of files too.

Changing the Location of the My Music folder

Okay, now that you understand how the My Music folder works, you've probably hit on some of its limitations. If you've got a single system with a single hard drive, the default location of C:\Documents and Settings\[your user name]\My Documents\My Music is probably working out just fine. But if you have more than one hard drive, more than one system, or decided to rip your entire CD collection onto the computer, it's time to start thinking about some management issues.

Digital music files can take up a lot of space. If you're ripping CDs using .WMA format at 128 Kbps (for example), each CD will require 50 MB of space on your hard drive, give or take a few megabytes. If you've got 200 CDs, that's about one gigabyte. Now, in today's world of 30GB drives, that doesn't sound so bad. But not everyone *has* a 30GB drive; more importantly, it's not *just* music you need to worry about: Digital photographs and (even more so) digital movies take up a lot of space, too. It's worth thinking about how you're going to manage this stuff. The default location for My Music may not cut it.

How you decide to handle this depends on your particular setup and needs. But here are some options to consider. If you plan to share music with other users, you may consider ripping CDs into the Shared Music folder instead of your personal My

Music folder (this won't be an issue for single users). If you have more than one hard drive, you may consider using one of them (perhaps the bigger one) as a data drive: You could move your My Music folder to that drive and take better advantage of its size. If you have more than one system, you could map a drive locally and store your media files on the other computer. Or, if you're particularly excessive when it comes to home computers, you may even consider setting up a *media server* that would be used solely to store music, photographs, and movies. The upcoming sections consider each of these possibilities. Each has a variety of trade-offs, of course.

Before you start moving music files around your system, consider this scenario: If you've already ripped audio CDs with Windows Media Player and you later move the location of those files, WMP knows where you moved them due to its integration with the Windows XP shell. Sooner or later, however, you will probably have to wipe out the WMP Media Library database and start over. To make sure that the player knows where everything is when you start moving music files around, follow these steps:

1. Launch Windows Media Player for Windows XP.

2. Press F3 or select Tools ⇨ Search for Media Files.

3. Click Search or specify a location to search, as shown in Figure 6-10.

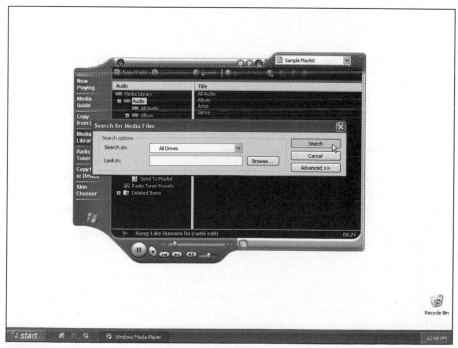

Figure 6-10: You can tell Windows Media Player where your music files are — or let it search the whole hard drive.

Cross-Reference For more about specifying a location for your music files, see Chapter 4.

Using shared music

Sucked in by the promise that Windows XP would help manage multiple users, perhaps you upgraded to this miracle of modern computing or bought a new PC. What isn't so obvious in this scenario, however, is that Windows XP provides shared folders for documents, music, and pictures — and that these are easily accessible from the shell. So while you probably want to keep your private documents away from your kids or (ahem) maybe even your spouse, it's equally likely that you wouldn't mind sharing your music with everyone in the family. This is easy enough, though Microsoft didn't make it particularly obvious.

Tip If you do want to share music, don't forget to turn off Personal/Digital Rights Management. A dialog box pops up the first time you try to rip a CD making, which makes this option more discoverable. But don't forget: If you're sharing music on a home network, turn off copy protection or it won't work.

To see what I mean, open a My Computer window and navigate to the system drive (typically C:, though mine is D:). If you haven't changed the factory defaults, you'll see the nag screen shown in Figure 6-11. Microsoft assumes you're an idiot ("Looking for your programs?" it asks, somewhat condescendingly), but I don't. Simply click the option labeled *Show the contents of this drive* to display the normal icon view. Then go into C:\Documents and Settings.

What you see there depends on the users you've set up on the system: Normally you get one folder for each of these users (Administrator, paul in Figure 6-12) and one called All Users. Old hands at Windows NT and Windows 2000 are probably familiar with the concept of *all users*; most Windows 9x/Me users (that is, most people who use Windows) aren't. This folder contains documents and settings common to all users on the system. And it's got a structure that's identical to your own Documents and Settings folder. Open it to see what I mean.

Inside C:\Documents and Settings\All Users, you find folders for the Desktop, Favorites, Shared Documents, and Start Menu. If you want an icon to appear on every user's desktop, place it in this Desktop folder. If you want an IE Favorite to appear in the Favorites menu of every user on the system, the Favorites folder is the place to go. And so on. But the Shared Documents folder works a bit differently. Shared Documents — and its subfolders, Shared Pictures and Shared Music — emulate the My Documents, My Pictures, and My Music folders that each user has. But if you place a file in Shared Documents, it won't show up in your personal My Documents folder, even as a link. Shared Documents (and Shared Pictures and Shared Music) are separate little islands in a sea of folders.

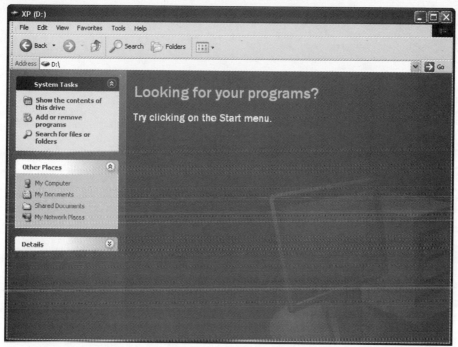

Figure 6-11: Microsoft tries to stop people from navigating around the file system.

You may want to use Shared Music as the dumping ground for all your ripped CDs (instead of the default, which is My Music). To do this, open Media Player for Windows XP and select Tools ➪ Options. On the Copy Music tab, select `C:\Documents and Settings\All Users\Shared Documents\Shared Music` as the location to which you want the music copied. And if you've already started copying music to another location (probably `C:\Documents and Settings\`[*your user name*]`\My Documents\My Music`), just move all those files and folders to the new location.

This method of organizing music files is good for families with one PC. You want your kids to be able to log on, play games, and maybe even get some schoolwork done, but you don't want them accessing your private documents (which you've marked as *private* thanks to Windows XP's security features). However, you don't mind them accessing your music. Now that it's public, they can.

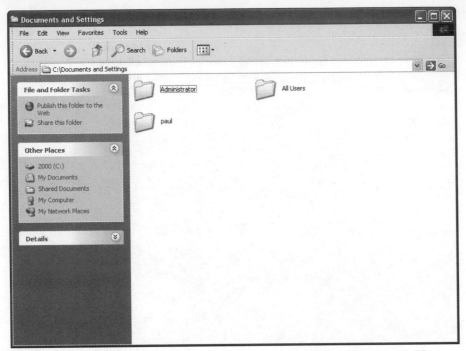

Figure 6-12: User accounts can be found in the Documents and Settings folder.

Moving the My Music folder to a new location

Okay, maybe you've got more than one hard drive and you like the idea of keeping your data separate from your OS and applications. This may seem like a Type A personality, anal-retentive kind of thing to do, but there are good reasons for it. Let's face it, Windows just up and dies occasionally, and it's nice to be able to format C: and reinstall without worrying that you just blew away your important data, such as that latest Sting CD. Although it's possible that you may never have to reinstall Windows XP, "better safe than sorry" is a good rule of thumb. Besides, imagine how well you'll sleep knowing that your data isn't on the same hard drive as Windows. (It works for me.)

For simplicity's sake, we'll assume that you've got two hard drives, C: and D:, and that Windows XP is installed on C:, perhaps along with Office and whatever other applications you have. By default, Windows XP places your documents and settings files (what was once called your *profile*) in C:\Documents and Settings\[*your user name*]\. Although moving the entire directory structure is probably possible, it's more practical to focus on moving just your documents and your My Music folder.

This type of setting is typically controlled through the Windows Registry, and yes, that chill that just ran up your spine is normal. With the Registry, you can change a number of Windows XP features, some of which are described in my Windows XP

Tips 'N' Tricks page on the Windows SuperSite (www.winsupersite.com).
Fortunately, to change the location of My Documents, you won't have to hack the
Registry. Instead, you can simply right-click My Documents on the Start Menu,
choose Properties, and then select the Move button to choose a new location. So
you may create a D:\Documents folder (or whatever) and then move My
Documents to that location, as shown in Figure 6-13.

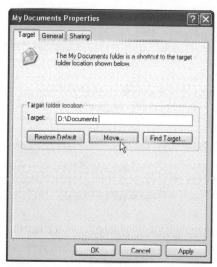

Figure 6-13: Moving My Documents
is easy: Just right-click My Documents,
choose Properties, and then tell it
where to go.

Windows XP asks you whether you want to move your existing documents to this
new location; you should probably do so, as shown in Figure 6-14. If you click "No"
for some reason, Windows XP doesn't delete your files. They just sit there in the old
location.

Figure 6-14: If you've got documents
at the old location, be sure to move
them to the new location if you move
My Documents.

Okay, so My Music probably has a similar method for changing its location, right? Not exactly. But you *can* move My Music in different ways. The easiest is drag-and-drop: Open up an Explorer window that points to where you'd like the My Music to be. Then, open a second Explorer window that displays the contents of your My Documents folder. Now, just right-click *My Music* in the My Documents window, drag it to the new location, and release. Choose Move to permanently move the folder. The folder name changes from My Music to [*User name*]'s Music (paul's Music in my case).

> **Note**   You can use the drag-and-drop method between two folder windows only. You can't drag My Music off of the Start Menu—this will only create a copy of the My Music folder.

You can also edit the Registry directly to change the location of My Music. You edit the Registry with the Registry Editor (regedit.exe), an unfriendly little program at best, but one that provides you with the interface you need to make your system sing.

Fire up the Registry Editor by choosing Start ➪ Run, typing *regedit.exe,* and then Enter. The Registry Editor, shown in Figure 6-15, allows you navigate the registry database using a standard Explorer-style interface with a tree view on the left.

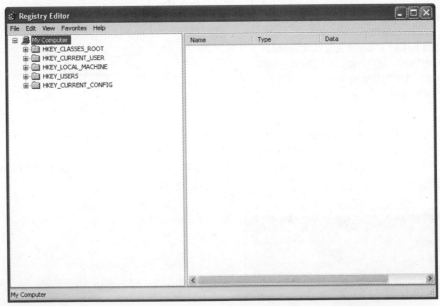

Figure 6-15: The Windows Registry is about as friendly as it looks: Not very.

You can get to the setting for My Music via the following path:

```
HKEY_CURRENT_USER\Software\Microsoft\Windows\CurrentVersion\
Explorer\Shell Folders\My Music
```

To find this location, expand HKEY_CURRENT_USER by clicking the plus sign next to it, then Software, and so on, in the left pane of the Registry Editor until you reach Shell Folders. With this location expanded, you see a list of items (or *keys,* as they're called) in the right pane, as seen in Figure 6-16.

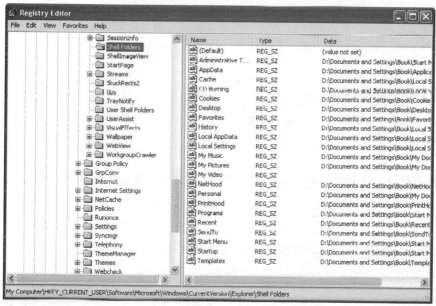

Figure 6-16: The location of the My Music folder is buried deep in the Registry.

One of these keys is named *My Music.* Double-click the key and the dialog box shown in Figure 6-17 appears; this allows you enter a new value in the *value data field.* So, for example, you may choose D:\Music or whatever strikes your fancy (make sure that location exists first, of course). Then restart the computer to make this change take place.

So if you've been following along, you may have two new folders on your big D: drive, *Documents,* for all your Word and related documents; and *Music,* for all your digital music.

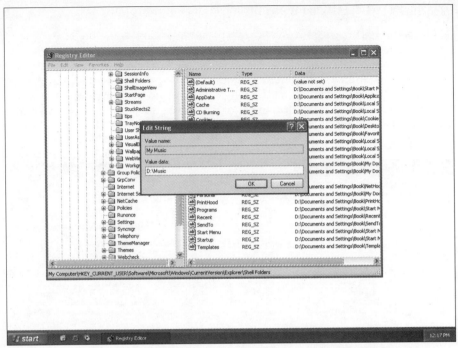

Figure 6-17: To change the location of My Music, you have to edit its Registry value.

Using other folders for digital music

If you're not interested in hacking the Registry — frankly, a healthy attitude to have — you can just ignore the My Music folder altogether and place your music wherever you want. So, for example, you may want to use D:\Music as the location for storing ripped CDs and all your other audio files.

One thing you may want to do in this instance is navigate to that folder and make sure it's set up correctly. If you're going to dump all your music files in the same folder without (for example) such amenities as subdirectories for artists and albums, you can customize the folder to use the Music template, which is "best for audio files and playlists." Or, if you choose to use the normal (and, frankly, preferred) *artist - album -* layout for song files, just make sure each folder is set up correctly for the right templates (as described earlier) so you have a folder structure that works *just like* My Music — without the hassle of moving My Music.

Another task you'll want to take care of is to ensure that Windows Media Player is set up to copy CD music to your new folder. That way, new music that's added to the system goes to the right place when it's created.

Creating a media server

Okay, suppose you're a networking god and for some reason, you've got enough computing power at home to run NORAD. These things happen, so you may as well take advantage of it: You can use one machine on your network as a *media server*, the place you store music and other media files. (Of course, such a system should have at least one *huge* hard drive on it; media files can take up a lot of space.)

Although various ways exist to accomplish this, assume (for purposes of this discussion) that you've got two machines: your daily-use machine running Windows XP and another box that's running any Windows OS. Call this other machine \\media, and that's how it appears in My Network Places.

Here's all you need to do:

1. Ensure that you can access \\media from your Windows XP box. This requires you to have user rights on that machine; the easiest way to ensure that the user account you logon with on your Windows XP machine is present as a user on \\media as well. (If \\media is a Windows 9*x*/Me box, however, this won't be required; these operating systems have almost no conception of security at all. However, using Windows 9*x*/Me for a media server is *not* recommended: The goal is for this machine to stay up and running all the time, and Windows 9*x*/Me is not very good at that.)

2. On \\media, create a directory structure to store your media files. You may create a directory called D:\Media\Music, for example, to store your music files.

3. On your Windows XP machine, choose My Computer ➪ Tool ➪ Map Network Drive.

   Doing so creates a network share by launches the Map Network Drive Wizard (Figure 6-18), allowing you to choose a drive letter and path for that network drive.

Figure 6-18: The Map Network Drive Wizard lets you easily use network resources as if they were local drives.

4. Open My Computer, and you should see a new drive called Media, listed under Network Drives on `'Media' (M:)`.

5. Copy or move all your media files to the appropriate folders in M:. For example, you may copy all your music files to `M:\Music`.

6. Now you can optionally redirect the My Music, My Pictures, and My Video folders, as described earlier. (Or not. It really doesn't matter.)

7. Start Windows Media Player and hit F3 to bring up the *Search for Media Files* dialog box. Point the *Look in* box to `M:\Music` (or wherever the share is you created), and let it search. Now your Media Library updates itself with the new location for you media files.

Tip   I use the drive letter M: for my media drive, but you can choose any available letter. In the Folder text box, either browse to the location or type it in; in our example, M: would be mapped to `\\media\Media`. Leave the *Reconnect at logon* option checked; you want this to be permanent.

You can use any PC as a media server, of course, but it's nice to have one that won't be used by a human being all day long (interactive users consume the machine's resources) but this isn't realistic for most people. My media server is actually my wife's PC. She doesn't use it that much, so it's nearly perfect for this role. And because it's my wife's PC, I'm not constantly rebuilding it and reinstalling Windows the way I am on my own PC. This tends to reduce the chance that I'll inadvertently FDISK the wrong drive and take all my own data down with it. I've been there, and it's ugly.

Using the Music Task Lists

Now that you're a music managing demon, it's time to get attuned to some of the nicer improvements in the Windows XP shell. A primary design goal for this release was to present a task-based interface that was easy to use, and Microsoft implemented this through the little-used Web view panes that you see by default in each My Computer and Explorer windows. In Windows XP, these panes are far more useful than they ever were in Windows Me or Windows 2000; though the power user in you may be tempted to turn them off as soon as you install Windows XP, bear with them a bit. Nearly everything that's available in the Web pane is also available through right-clicks and other power-user techniques — but until you know exactly *what's* available, it's a good idea to just leave the defaults in place and see what happens.

In My Music (or any other folder that uses a music-oriented folder template), you get a list of tasks appropriate for that folder's contents. So, for example, when you navigate into My Music, you see two Music Tasks listed in the folder's Web pane: Play all and Shop for music online.

Using Play all

The Play all choice is actually more sophisticated than it seems. If your My Music folder contains artist folders (which in turn contain album folders), then clicking

Play all triggers the Windows Media Player, which then plays *all* contained audio files, using whatever your player defaults were the last time you used MPXP. So, if you've got MPXP set up to shuffle songs, it plays all your music files randomly.

Tip If you've have MPXP set up to automatically add music to your Media Library when it is played, then this is also a handy way to add an audio file or several audio files to the player for later use. Just select the files, click Play all, and shut down MPXP immediately: The files don't have to play, but now they're in the Media Library.

Another interesting side-effect of this choice is that it creates a new playlist called Playlist1 by default. So when you click Play all, MPXP launches and begins playing all the audio files found under My Music. You can actually rename and save this playlist for later use if you like, though the process is far more convoluted than it should be. Here's how you do it.

1. Open My Music, select the Web pane, and click Play all. MPXP starts and begins playing the first song it finds.

2. Choose File ⇨ Export Playlist to File. In the Save As dialog box that appears (Figure 6-19), choose a name and location for the playlist (something temporary like the Desktop works fine; you'll be deleting the playlist file later).

Figure 6-19: You can export a playlist — even a temporary playlist — for later use.

3. After the playlist file is saved, choose File ➪ Import Playlist to Media Library. In the Open dialog box that appears, choose the playlist file you created earlier.

4. After some churning and bubbling, MPXP imports the playlist and displays it under My Playlists in the Media Library, as `Playlist1`.

5. Right-click Playlist1 and choose Rename. Give it an appropriate name, (such as *All of my music* or whatever), as shown in Figure 6-20.

Now, the obvious question at this point is: Why bother doing this? MPXP automatically creates a playlist, of sorts, called All Audio, which is already available in the Media Library. But, you may want to create your own for two good reasons: First, you can now edit this playlist down to cut out the songs you don't like (which is impossible with All Audio, unless you want to permanently delete them from the Media Library). Second, you can use this technique to create more personalized playlists.

Figure 6-20: Rename that playlist.

Creating better playlists with Play selection

Instead of just choosing Play all in the root of My Music, you may selectively choose music to create a playlist.

1. Open My Music and click the Folders toolbar icon to display the Folder view, as shown in Figure 6-21.

2. Expand the artist and/or album folder that contains songs you'd like to add to a playlist, as shown in Figure 6-22.

3. While holding down the Ctrl key, select one or more songs.

4. When you're done, click Folders to remove the Folder view; then click the option labeled *Play selection*.

5. Again, a new playlist is generated in MPXP, but now it contains only those audio files you selected.

6. Repeat the steps in the previous section to save your playlist.

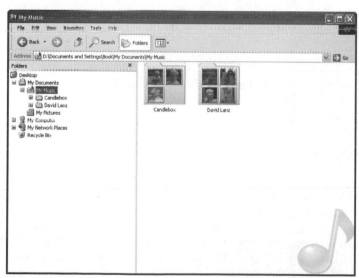

Figure 6-21: The Folders option lets you display a folder list in place of the Web view.

Play all for the power user

If you absolutely, positively cannot stand the Web view, you can still use Play all and Play selection. All you have to do is select all the folders in My Music, one or more folders that contain audio files, or one or more audio files, right-click, and then choose Play. The same rules apply as outlined earlier.

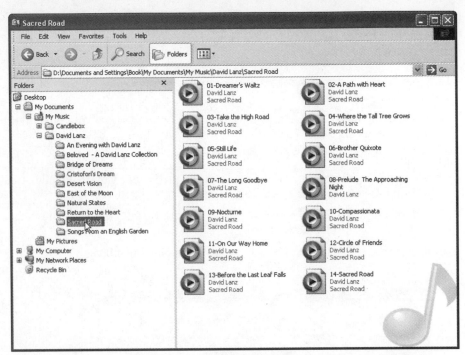

Figure 6-22: You can drill down into the folders list to find the exact location you want.

Shopping for music online

The Shop for Music Online task may seem like an insipid little thing to add to an operating system, but it's actually pretty useful. Here's how it works: Open an artist or album folder that was created when you ripped an audio CD with Windows Media Player, and then click the Shop for Music Online task. This launches IE 6 and brings you to the WindowsMedia.com Buy Now Web site, with a list of choices that correspond to the artist you selected, as shown in Figure 6-23. This site lets you choose a particular CD and then buy it at an MSN partner site such as CDNOW, A&B Music Online, or some other vendor.

Why would you want to do this? Well, you may enjoy a certain CD and want to purchase other music by that same artist. Or maybe you want to buy music that's like the CD you enjoy; this feature is built into this site as well.

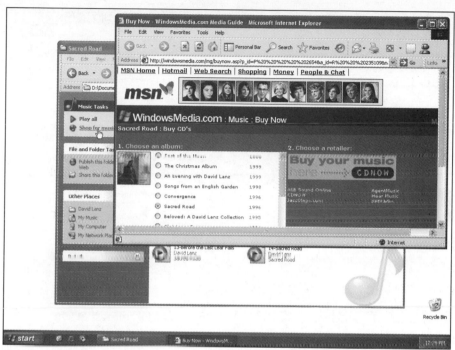

Figure 6-23: The Shop for music online option launches IE 6 and brings you to the WindowsMedia.com Web site.

I have a couple of caveats about this feature. First of all, it obviously requires an Internet connection. But it also requires that you have ripped music with Windows Media Player: If you've got a folder full of MP3 files you ripped with Real Jukebox or whatever, the *Shop for Music Online* task is present, but it brings you to the blank page shown in Figure 6-24. And if you've renamed a music folder (say you prefer *Jackson, Michael* to default, which would be *Michael Jackson*), the *Shop for Music Online* task is present, but it only beeps when you click it. Otherwise, nothing. Microsoft has good reasons for this limitation, but it's something you should be aware of.

And if I can get off my Microsoft marketing bandwagon for a minute, better ways to buy music online probably exist—though you can't beat the spur-of-the-moment convenience of it all. I recommend looking around for the best prices before using this service. And here's one el-cheapo (what we may call *Yankee* frugality in Boston) recommendation for buying music online. If you're only buying CDs so you can rip them to the hard drive and then never use the CD again, you may want to consider used CDs. Amazon.com's zShops (www.amazon.com) is a great place to find them.

Figure 6-24: The Shop for Music Online task only works for music that you ripped with MPXP.

Copying music to an audio CD

When you select an audio file (WMA or MP3) or folder containing audio files in the shell, one other option appears in the Music Tasks list in the Web view; it's labeled *Copy to audio CD* (assuming you have a CD-R or CD-RW drive, of course, otherwise this option won't show up). This option is essentially a front-end to the audio CD-creation capabilities in Media Player for Windows XP (discussed in more detail in Chapter 5). When you click this task, MPXP starts, with the Copy to CD or Device function in place.

Sharing Music with Other Users

Unlike pictures you've scanned or imported from a digital camera, or home movies you've created with Windows Movie Maker, sharing audio files presents a bit of a problem. Most audio files you're likely to have are copyrighted — and though it's permissible to create your own copies of CD audio and then play them on your PC, it is *not* legal to then share that music with your friends over the Internet. That said, some acceptable scenarios still exist if you may want to share music.

Sharing My Music

The first scenario concerns music sharing within your family. Earlier in this chapter, we discussed various ways in which you may share audio files on your system with other users on your local network—say, your wife, husband, or child. Previously, we discussed copying the content in My Music to Shared Music in order to let each user of a PC access the same music, and we also looked at wider sharing techniques, such as the home media server concept.

Another simple way to share your My Music folder on a local network is simply to create a share that points to that folder. Here's how:

1. Navigate to the My Music folder.

2. Right-click and choose Sharing and Security. The My Music Properties dialog box appears with the Sharing tab displayed, as shown in Figure 6-25.

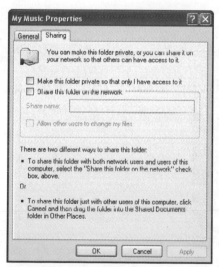

Figure 6-25: The Sharing tab of the My Music Properties dialog box allows you to share this folder with other users if you'd like.

3. Check the option titled *Share this folder on the network*. By default, the share name *My Music* is created, but you can rename this as desired.

4. Check or uncheck the option labeled *Allow other users to change my files* as appropriate. (I don't trust little Jimmy, and neither should you—I recommend that this option be unchecked, but again, that's up to you.)

5. Click OK to close the dialog box. You see a cute little hand appear under the icon for My Music. Now, when other users on the network navigate to your system in My Network Places, they see a share named My Music.

Publishing audio files to the Web

Sharing on the Internet is a bit murkier. One may make the argument that a person should be able to archive even copyrighted audio files to the Internet, so long as they're not publicly accessible. I suppose there is a case for that. Here's how you do it.

1. Select the file, or a folder containing the audio files you'd like to share, and then click the option labeled *Publish this file to the Web* or *Publish this folder to the Web* from the Web view pane. The Web Publishing Wizard appears, as shown in Figure 6-26.

Figure 6-26: Use the Web Publishing Wizard to publish files to support Web sites.

2. Click Next and the Wizard progresses to page two, where you can choose from a variety of Web-hosting solutions, including MSN and Xdrive, which provides online storage space.

3. Choose the appropriate location (we'll use MSN in this example), and log on to the Web-hosting location by using proper authentication (Passport, in MSN's case).

4. Choose the location you'd like to publish to, either a predefined folder or a new folder, as shown in Figure 6-27. At this point, your files are copied, which could be tediously slow, depending on the size of the files to be copied and/or the speed of your Internet connection.

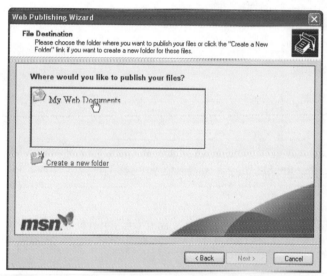

Figure 6-27: When publishing to the Web, you can choose either a preexisting folder location or a new one.

5. Complete the wizard and click *Open this site when I click Finish* to navigate to the Web site where the files were uploaded, as shown in Figure 6-28.

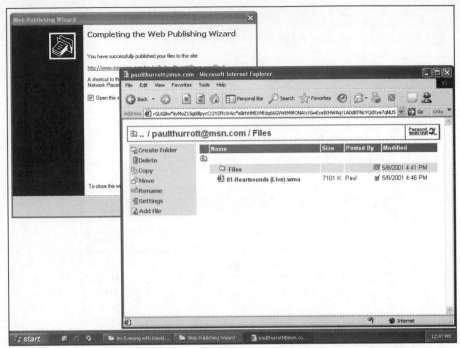

Figure 6-28: After the file copy is complete, you can navigate to your Web folder with IE.

Now that you know how to do this, it's likely that you'll never need to. Audio files tend to be rather large and are therefore not the sort of thing to be moving around the Web.

✦   ✦   ✦

Rip: Copying Audio and Data CDs

Most people these days are probably comfortable with popping an audio CD into a PC's CD drive and playing some favorite tunes while browsing the Web, sending e-mail, or getting other work done. But simply playing audio CDs only hints at the digital-audio possibilities that are now built into most computers — and probably into your computer. In the same way that home CD jukeboxes and car-based CD changers expand your choices, Windows XP expands these choices (almost exponentially) by enabling you to copy music from audio CDs onto your computer. You can use Windows XP to organize your music, copy it to portable audio devices, and even make your own audio "mix" CDs.

The first step, of course, is to get this music onto your computer.

The process of copying songs from an audio CD to the computer is referred to as *ripping* music. You rip music from a CD to the computer with the help of an application such as Windows Media Player for Windows XP; once it's on your computer, you can move it around, organize it, and manage it. And once you get music onto your computer, you might never need those CDs again (though you should keep them around for legal and backup purposes).

This chapter looks at the technology that makes these wonders possible — and provides pointers on how to rip, organize, and manage music from audio CDs as files on your computer — using the tools that are built into Windows XP. Not surprisingly, Windows XP is the *first* operating system to offer such full-featured capabilities right out of the box; you won't need any additional software. Let's give it a test spin (so to speak).

Understanding Digital Audio

As with digital image manipulation, digital audio brings with it a bit of terminology that must be understood before you can dive right in. Although the words are different, the concepts are the same: Using digital music is a compromise between quality and file size. You can record perfect digital copies of CD audio if you want, but the resulting files are too humongous to be workable. So what you need is balance: Typically, you want the music to sound as good as possible while retaining the smallest possible file size. Small files transfer quickly to portable devices, work better over low bandwidth networks, and enable you to store more songs per GB on your hard drive. But larger files tend to sound better.

Historically, companies that have been concerned with providing audio content over the Internet have dealt with these same issues. So in the early days of the Web (way back in 1996), Internet audio was pretty primitive; we were all surfing along at 28.8 or 33.3Kbps. But companies such as Apple (with QuickTime technology), RealNetworks, and Microsoft have been working for years on ways to produce and deliver high-quality music files that don't take up a lot of space.

For digital music, the standard has been a compressed audio format called MPEG Level 3, or MP3. MP3 was first released over a decade ago, but it's only been recently that consumers have come to enjoy it. MP3 format provides impressive-sounding files that can be encoded at a variety of *resolutions*, or quality settings. Audio resolution is measured in *kilobits per second*, or *Kbps*. Reportedly, an MP3 file encoded at 128 Kbps is "CD quality," but this is a bit of a misnomer: As with JPG image files, MP3 files are actually compressed, which makes them *lossy* (it's a trade-off: you lose a bit of quality to gain the advantage of small file size). At 128 Kbps, the lost quality becomes more obvious; it can often be evident that you're not dealing with true CD quality. However, under normal circumstances most people who listen to a 128Kbps encoded MP3 are hard-pressed to hear the difference. A few years back, audiophiles would often encode MP3 files at 160 Kbps or 192 Kbps to offset this problem. The result, of course, is bigger files. It's that age-old compromise again.

At 160 Kbps, the typical 60-minute CD encoded in MP3 format consumes over 60MB of hard drive space. That can add up pretty quickly if you want to copy a number of albums to your PC. And MP3 has other problems that have retarded the acceptance of digital audio formats by the recording industry. Specifically, the format offers no digital rights management features, meaning that anyone can make MP3 versions of songs on their CDs and then hand them out at will. There's no technology to ensure that the listener actually owns that music.

Enter Microsoft

In the mid-1990s, Microsoft Research began working on its own digital audio format, which eventually morphed into Windows Media Audio (WMA). Windows Media Audio was designed to overcome the limitations of MP3 while improving on its strengths. So WMA quickly became available in a version that allowed for MP3-quality audio at lower encoding rates. And Microsoft worked with the recording industry to ensure that its format would work with digital rights management technologies.

In 1999, the company released Windows Media Audio 7, which offered "CD-quality" audio at 64 Kbps, half the encoding rate of a CD-quality MP3 file. Furthermore, the file sizes were smaller, so a song encoded at 64 Kbps in WMA 7 format would take up less than half the space of a 128 Kbps MP3 file. To prove its point, Microsoft launched a media blitz that basically recreated the Pepsi Taste Test: The same music would be recorded in both formats and users could listen to both and try to pick out which sounded better. According to eTesting Labs, an independent information technology testing firm, a consumer test of the two formats revealed that almost 9 out of 10 users could not tell the difference. To the human ear, a 64 Kbps WMA 7 file was (sonically) virtually identical or superior to a 128 Kbps MP3 file.

Windows XP seals the deal

Windows XP and Windows Media Player for Windows XP, however, ship with Windows Media Audio 8; the results are even more incredible. Now, Microsoft has been able to achieve the same "CD quality" audio at only 64 Kbps, but perhaps more importantly, you can get near-CD quality at just 48 Kbps, which really saves on the space.

In my own evaluation of these formats, the quality of WMA 8 has made me a believer. In the past, I did all my CD encoding at 160 Kbps in MP3 format. But since the Beta 2 release of Windows XP and Windows Media Player for Windows XP in March 2001, I've switched to 128 Kbps format. I stuck with the higher encoding rate because I like my "master" copy of audio to be of high quality, and I don't mind using up the disk space. But when I copy music to a portable audio device, I convert it to 64 Kbps to maximize the amount of music I can bring along.

 For more information on portable audio devices, please refer to Chapter 13.

And of course, WMA 8 offers digital rights management features, which enables you to secure any files that you rip with a digital license that prevents them from being distributed illegally. We'll look at this a bit more in the next section.

Making decisions on audio quality

In the end, the audio format and encoding rate you choose is a personal decision; I implore you to experiment a bit with different formats and rates before settling on a standard. Also, you should visit the Microsoft Windows Media Web site (`www.microsoft.com/ windowsmedia/`) and visit their Windows Media Audio and Video 8 section to see how it stacks up. This book focuses on WMA because it's natively supported by Windows XP and Windows Media Player for Windows XP. But I'm convinced it's the way to go, and I'm encoding my own music in WMA format, using this player. (And I make this recommendation after trying just about every other format and player on the market.)

Configuring Windows Media Player to Rip CDs

With terms such as *WMA*, *MP3*, and *encoding* dancing in your head, it's time to configure WMPXP for optimal ripping. All you need do is tweak a few options; some of them have more to do with your hardware than with the actual audio files you'll be creating.

Configuring your CD devices

You should have one or more CD, CD-R, CD-RW, or DVD drives. Each of these types of drives (and any combination drives that provide similar functionality) can be used to rip music from an audio CD. You'll want to ensure that each of them is set up correctly.

There are two basic hardware related options, *copy type* and *error correction*. The copy type can be either *analog* or *digital*; what works best for you depends on your system. A digital copy is generally preferable; it yields the highest-quality output and doesn't require you to shut off other system sounds while you're ripping. If you experience problems with digital copying, however, you can choose analog mode. This works fine, but in that case you should ensure that your system isn't making any *other* sounds during the copy process. Also, analog-mode copying won't let you listen to the CD while you rip it.

The second option, *error correction,* attempts to automatically fix small flaws that can crop up during ripping. If you hear faint scratches or pops while ripping CDs, you should turn on the error-correction feature (even though it slows down the ripping process).

Here's some rule-of-thumb advice: Set your drives to use the digital-copy and error-correction options. I set mine that way to ensure the highest possible quality for my master copies of digital audio. Here's how you set up these options:

1. Open Windows Media Player for Windows XP and choose Tools ⇨ Options.

2. Navigate to the Devices page, as shown in Figure 7-1.

   Note that this page might take a while to render, depending on how many compatible devices (CD drives, portable audio devices, Pocket PC devices, and the like) you have connected to your system.

3. Select a CD device from the list and click the Properties button.

   As shown in Figure 7-2, the Properties dialog box for that device appears; its Copy section is where you decide whether to copy the audio as analog or digital.

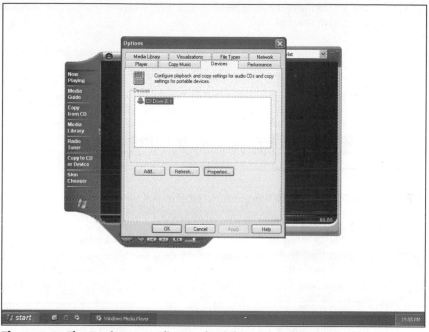

Figure 7-1: The Devices page lists each of the compatible storage devices attached to your system.

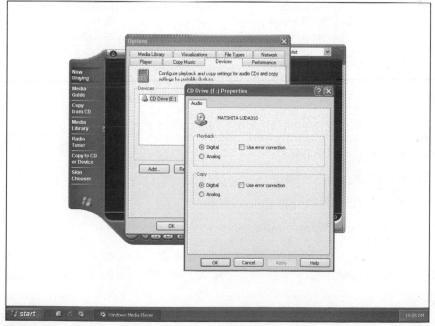

Figure 7-2: Use the CD Drive Properties dialog box to determine how audio is copied to your computer.

4. Ensure that Digital is chosen and that the option labeled *Use error correction* is selected.

Tip If you experience problems later, you can try switching to analog or turning off error correction.

5. Repeat this process for any other CD-type devices that are listed.

Choosing audio format and quality

Next, choose the audio format (MP3 or WMA) and quality (bit rate). The higher the bit-rate number, the better the quality—although this also means a bigger file that takes up more space, which is really important if you're planning to transfer to a portable device. Out of the box, Windows Media Player for Windows XP supports WMA format at resolution levels of 48, 64, 96, 128, 160, and 192 Kbps. If this sounds like Microsoft is loading the deck against MP3, there's a plausible explanation: Windows Media Player 7 didn't offer users *any* way to rip CDs in MP3 format. But Microsoft heard from its PC-maker partners that some users wanted this feature; thus WMPXP has a new plug-in feature that enables these PC makers to add MP3 ripping functionality.

Cross-Reference For more information on portable devices, see Chapter 13.

So if you bought Windows XP in a store such as Best Buy or CompUSA, you won't have any way to rip MP3s out of the box. However if you want to add this feature, click the button "MP3 Information" located in Tools ⇨ Options ⇨ Copy Music. Microsoft has put together a Web site where you can do another taste test or even select a third-party encoder to plug in to WMPXP. But if you got Windows XP from a PC maker who shipped the system with enhanced MP3 technology (what gearheads would call a *codec*) then you might see MP3 copying options on-screen. (Regardless of such variations, what Windows XP offers is—as you might expect—WMA.)

You've got three basic options for audio format and quality:

✦ Format (WMA, MP3)

✦ Digitally protected

✦ Encoding rate (Kbps)

To Set Up Audio Format and Quality:

1. In Windows Media Player for Windows XP, select Options ⇨ Tools, and then navigate to the Copy Music page (shown in Figure 7-3).

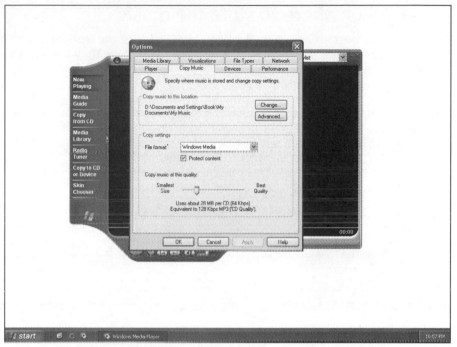

Figure 7-3: The Copy Music page determines how and where CD audio is copied to your system.

2. In the File Format drop-down box, choose Windows Media.

3. Choose an encoding rate on the slidebar labeled *Copy music at this quality.* (I recommend 128 Kbps as a good trade-off between file size and sound quality.)

Before closing the dialog box, you might want to consider the *Protect content* choice as well. When you check this option, all music that you rip is *digital-licensed,* which means that you can play the tracks on your computer, transfer the tracks to a non-SDMI-compliant portable audio device (such as those from Sony), and burn the songs to a mix audio CD. What you can't do is copy them to another PC and listen to them there.

Why would you want to do such a thing? Well, the recording industry would certainly like to see this option become mandatory, since it would aid it in its quest to abolish music piracy. But I find the content-protection features to be difficult to work with, and I recommend against using this feature, well-intentioned though it may be. If you're interested in this technology, please refer to the Windows Media Player for Windows XP help file, which explains (in gruesome detail) what you will go through while working with licensed files.

Deciding where to store the music

Another important option on the Copy Music page of the Options dialog box determines where your digital music files are stored and how they are named. (The next chapter delves into file-management issues, but it's good to think about them a bit before you begin ripping CDs.)

By default, files ripped from audio CDs are stored in your My Music folder, and that's fine for starters. But you can change this location, and how your files are stored, by using the two buttons located in the section of the Copy Music page labeled *Copy music to this location*. Here's how.

To change the location where ripped music is stored, follow these steps:

1. Open the Options dialog box for Windows Media Player and navigate to the Copy Music page.

2. Click the Change button. The Browse for Folder dialog box appears, as shown in Figure 7-4.

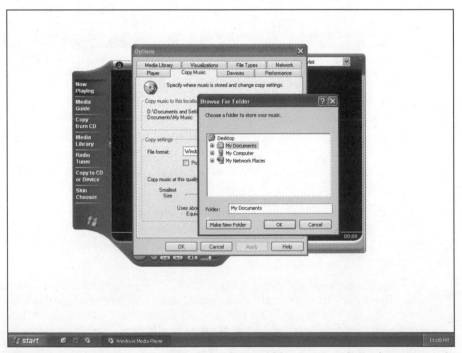

Figure 7-4: The Browse for Folder dialog box enables you to select where to put the CD audio files you copy.

3. Choose a new location.

To change how your digital audio files are created, follow these steps:

1. Click the Advanced button. The Filename Options dialog box appears, as shown in Figure 7-5. This dialog box determines how the filenames generated by Windows Media Player for Windows XP look. (I prefer the *Track number-Song title* format myself, but other folks have reasons for liking other file-naming techniques; feel free to experiment.)

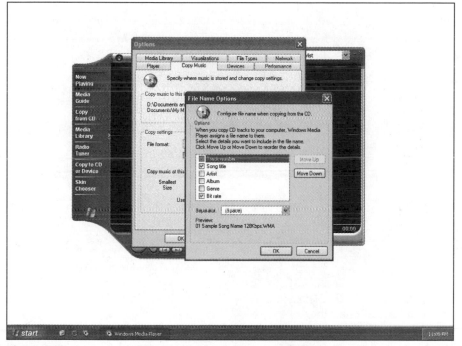

Figure 7-5: A number of file-naming options are available in the Filename Options dialog box.

2. Choose a separator type from the Separator drop-down list box.

3. Click OK when you're finished.

Cross-Reference   File management is a pretty important topic, so Chapter 8 covers it in more detail.

Ripping a CD: Copy Music to Windows XP

Okay, if you've configured Windows Media Player, determined how to copy the music to your computer, and decided where you want to put it when it's copied, then it's time to do the deed. Pick out your favorite audio CD — perhaps a 60-minute gem from some late '80s hair-metal band — and pop it into your PC's CD player.

If your system is configured as it came from the factory, WMPXP launches itself and begins to play the disc (as shown in Figure 7-6), though you might see a dialog box asking you what you'd like to do; if so, choose the Windows Media Player option. As noted previously, if you chose to rip CDs digitally, you can actually allow the CD to continue playing during the rip. If you are recording in analog format, however, you have to stop playback before ripping (I like to stop playback regardless). Also, WMPXP has to be in Full Mode to copy music from the CD: Audio copy features are not available from any of the skins that come with Windows XP.

Figure 7-6: Audio CDs can autoplay when you insert them in a Windows XP machine.

What to do if you're offline

If you are connected to the Internet, you should see the album title and track list appear in the Now Playing view (Figure 7-7). This is crucial for copying music to your system; you need this information for each individual file's *metadata* (the info that identifies what's on a disc so you can organize it), as well as the file and folder names.

If you're not connected to the Internet, you see the CD listed as *Unknown Album (date time)* where *date* contains today's date and *time* provides the total running time of the album, as shown in Figure 7-8. Each track is listed simply as a track number, though the running time for each song is correct.

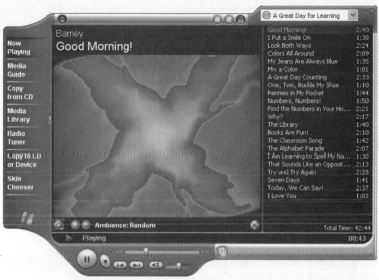

Figure 7-7: When connected to the Internet, WMPXP can automatically supply information about the current CD.

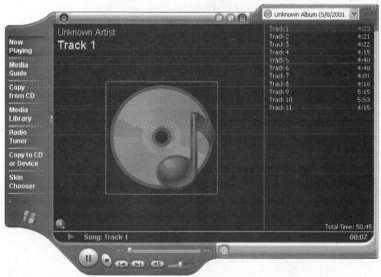

Figure 7-8: Ripping CDs while offline is not a good idea, as each CD would require a lot of information to be manually inputted.

Generally speaking, it's a lot easier to rip CDs when you're connected to the Internet, because WMPXP *autopopulates* (fills in automatically) the album information — or CD metadata — for you. But of course, not everyone has a 24/7 Internet connection yet, so it is possible to manually enter this information if you're offline. I strongly advise against this if it can be helped.

Even if you are connected to the Internet, it's possible that the album you want to rip isn't listed on All Music Guide (AMG), the online database that Microsoft uses to populate the album information. If this happens, you will be forced to input artist, album, and track information.

Copy that CD

In the Windows Media Player for Windows XP taskbar, you see an option called *Copy from CD*. This brings up the interface for copying (ripping) music files from an audio CD, as shown in Figure 7-9.

Figure 7-9: The Copy from CD view lets you determine which songs to copy to your hard drive.

By default, you see a list of each song on the CD, along with a check mark next to the title of each song title to be copied. If you'd like to exclude certain songs, click the checkbox next to their names so the check mark disappears; those files won't be copied. You can alternatively uncheck or check the entire list by clicking the checkbox in the top column header, on the left, as shown in Figure 7-10.

Getting CD names

If WMPXP didn't automatically get the name of the CD, its artist, and the songs on that CD, you can click the Get Names button in the Copy from CD view to try and find the CD online or enter the information manually.

Figure 7-10: Unchecking that top checkbox deselects all songs on the CD.

Viewing CD Album Details

You can also get details about the currently selected CD by clicking the Album Details button, as shown in Figure 7-11. Doing so displays a picture of the album, a way to buy this album online, information about the album, a list to album reviews, and a track listing. There is also a link to an artist profile.

Figure 7-11: The Album Details view offers more information about the current CD.

One thing that's not immediately obvious is that you can display the album information and the normal Copy from CD view at the same time. If you hover your mouse cursor over the top bar in the Album Details view, you can drag down and reveal the Copy from CD view as well, as shown in Figure 7-12.

Figure 7-12: You can drag the Album Details view down to access the normal Copy from CD view.

Click Hide Details to close the Album Details view.

Making sure the information is correct

There's just one last thing to do before you rip your CD: Make sure all the song titles and other information is correct. You can fix this later, as described in Chapter 8, but it's always a good idea to get off on the right foot and fix any obvious problems before you rip. Maybe a song title is incorrect or the genre is different from what you'd expect. (For example, is Sting "rock" or "pop?")

To correct a song title or other bit of information before you copy that music to your hard drive, select the offending text and then click once to display an edit box such as the one in Figure 7-13 (in which you can edit the text). Then repeat the procedure for any other problems you find.

Figure 7-13: You can edit information about each track before you rip them to your hard drive.

Ripping

It's time to rip that CD. Press the Copy Music button. The display changes a bit, as shown in Figure 7-14, to show you the copying operation in progress under the Copy Status heading.

Figure 7-14: While ripping, a copy progress bar is shown in the Copy Status column to show you where you are.

If you want to stop the copy at any time, press Stop Copy.

When the copy is complete, navigate to the My Music folder. You should see a new folder using the name of the artist that recorded the CD you just ripped, as shown in Figure 7-15.

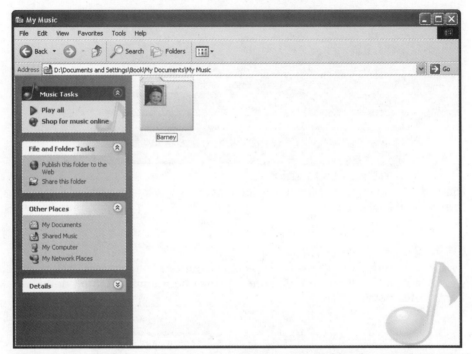

Figure 7-15: When you rip a CD to your system, an artist folder shows up in My Music.

If you open this folder, you see another folder, this one representing the CD you just ripped. This is shown in Figure 7-16. Open that folder and you see a list of files, each corresponding to the individual songs you ripped; this can be seen in Figure 7-17.

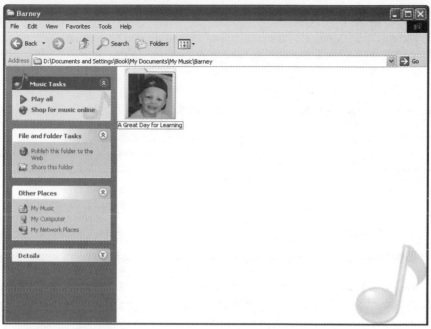

Figure 7-16: Each Artist folder contains at least one Album folder, including one for the CD album you just ripped.

Figure 7-17: And finally, each Album folder contains individual audio files.

When you rip a CD to your hard drive, it is automatically added to your Media Library as well. So you should see new entries under both Artist and Album that correspond to the CD you copied. Easy, eh? Once you see how easy it is to rip CDs, and the high quality of the resulting files, you may never use an audio CD again.

Adding lyrics to the songs you rip

It's not documented very well, but another thing you can do with a ripped CD is add lyrics to each song, and have those lyrics appear in Windows Media Player during playback. Here's how.

1. Select an album you've ripped that contains songs for which you'd like to add lyrics.

2. Navigate to a Web site that contains song lyrics, such as lyrics.com and search for the appropriate artist name. Another option is to break out those liner notes from your CD and see if the lyrics are included.

3. Locate the correct album name and then find a song for which you'd like to add lyrics, as shown in Figure 7-18. Doing so takes you to a Web page that contains the lyrics for that song. You can copy this into the Windows Clipboard by selecting all the song text and then choosing Edit ➪ Copy in IE 6.

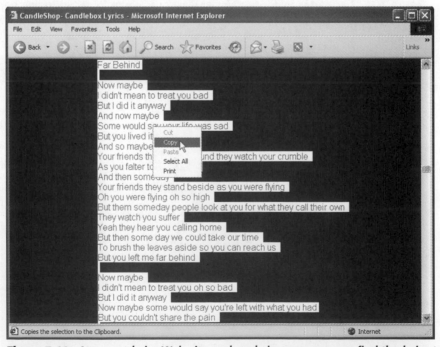

Figure 7-18: At a song lyrics Web site such as lyrics.com, you can find the lyrics to the song and copy them to the Windows Clipboard.

4. Next, launch WMPXP and load up that album, then switch to Now Playing.

5. In the Playlist column, right-click the song and choose Properties. Doing so displays the Properties dialog box for that song (which is curiously different from the one you see when you get properties from the file system).

6. Go to the Lyrics tab.

7. Paste the lyrics into the Lyrics box by selecting the box and pressing Ctrl+V (as shown in Figure 7-19).

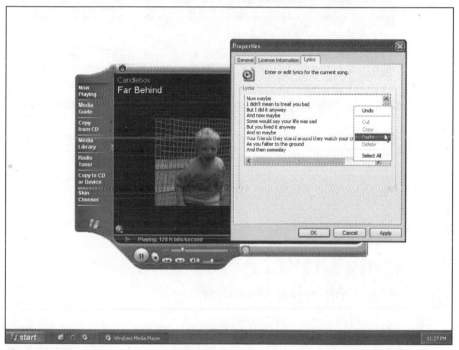

Figure 7-19: In the Properties dialog box for the song in Windows Media Player, paste the lyrics.

8. Click OK to close the dialog box and then play the song in WMPXP.

9. Choose View ➪ Now Playing Tools ➪ Lyrics to see the lyrics while the song plays, as shown in Figure 7-20.

Figure 7-20: Now, you can enable lyric view while that album is playing.

You can regulate the size of the lyric view by dragging the top border up and down. Unfortunately, the lyrics don't scroll to keep pace with the music. To turn off lyric display, you can choose View ➪ Now Playing Tools ➪ Show Equalizer and Settings.

Managing Digital Audio with Windows Media Player

Once you begin ripping CDs to your system, you might not stop until your entire CD collection is copied. (That's what happened to me; I've got hundreds of CDs, so it took a while.) Getting music onto your computer opens up a variety of options, including portable music devices such as the Iomega HipZip and Rio 600 or 800, not to mention *digital audio receivers* such as those offered by Dell Computer, Gateway, and SonicBlue Rio. But all this choice brings a certain amount of complexity with it as well. You want to be sure that your media files are properly set up—associated with the correct genre, recording years, and other metadata so that WMPXP and these other devices can more easily search and sort your music.

Here's an example: Let's say you're having a dinner party and you'd like to get a Jazz mix going, either through your PC directly or through a Digital Audio Receiver. If you didn't correctly label all your Jazz music as the Jazz genre, you might miss out on some great songs. Or what if you'd like to hear a collection of music from a particular year—say, 1985? If the year for each song isn't set up correctly, this can be nearly impossible.

The good thing about this process is that you only have to do it once. And unlike some other tools, Windows Media Player does do a good job of getting that metadata filled in correctly. But there are gaps, mainly due to missing information at All Music Guide, which is used to populate the metadata. If you want to fix them, there are two main ways to do it: Through the shell or from within the media player itself. We discuss shell-based media management in the next chapter, so let's take a look at how you can change audio metadata information directly from within WMPXP.

Back when Windows Me hit the streets, I used Windows Media Player 7 solely for its Media Library. But I burned and ripped audio CDs with other tools because I didn't feel that MP7 was up to snuff. This all changes, of course, with WMPXP, but the Media Library is still a wonderful tool for organizing and managing your digital audio in this release. If anything, it's even better than the version in MP7.

The Media Library provides a number of playlists by default, such as per-artist, per-album and per-genre lists. This makes it easy to play all the songs by one artist, all the songs from one album, or all the music in a certain genre, automatically. Set it to shuffle and you can probably walk away from the player for the rest of the day if you've got enough music.

When you select one of these built-in playlists, you see a list of song titles in the right side of the media player. These are divvied up into columns for song title, artist, album, composer, genre, length, size, type (MP3 or WMA), creation date, bit rate (in Kbps), play count (that is, the number of times you've played each song), filename (with path info), whether the file is protected (yes or no) and copyright (which should be blank unless you're protecting your audio). Some of these items—song title, artist, album, composer, and genre—can be edited directly in the player. And when you do so, the underlying file is changed as well. This is a big difference between Windows Media Player for Windows XP and its predecessor: In MP7, when you edited a song in the player, it only affected the player database, and didn't directly touch the file.

Note The track number and Composer fields are new in WMPXP, and were added based on consumer feedback. Many people don't know the names of the songs they like, but they do know the track numbers they like to listen to on each. Chalk it up to the fact that CD players (and the CDs themselves) don't have the track names on them.

What this means is that it's possible to permanently change some of the metadata for WMA and MP3 files from Windows Media Player. Here's how it works:

1. Start WMPXP and expand the Media Library so that a playlist is visible, as shown in Figure 7-21. This can be an album or a list of songs by a particular artist.

Figure 7-21: Windows Media Player for Windows XP automatically creates playlists such as Album, which displays all the albums you've ripped.

2. Single-click a song title, as shown in Figure 7-22. This highlights the entire line.

Figure 7-22: Clicking a track name once selects that title.

3. Click the song title again. The title appears highlighted, but now in an edit box, indicating that you can rename the title, as shown in Figure 7-23.

Figure 7-23: Click again and you can edit the title or other information about that track.

4. Repeat this process for the artist, album, composer, and genre fields to see how it works.

You can use this technique to find songs that have metadata "holes." Maybe you have an entire album where the genre is missing or incorrect. Or maybe there's a misspelling here or there. These things happen all the time. Fortunately, you can fix them, directly from the media player.

Another time this feature comes in handy is if you'd been using another program — such as Real Jukebox or MediaMatch — to rip CDs before you got Windows Media Player for Windows XP. Those programs work well enough for simple listening, but often they leave out metadata or provide incorrect or proprietary entries — not too useful for organization. (Real Jukebox, for example, uses the current year for the Year field when you rip MP3 files, which is almost never what you want). With WMPXP, you can clean up your digital music collection in no time.

Tip

If you have Windows Media Audio files that you ripped with previous versions of Windows Media Player, you can still add track numbers and composer information automatically to those files from the WMPXP Media Library. Just select an album in the left hierarchy, right-click, and then choose "Update Names". You can even do this for all of your music by selecting "All Audio" and then Update Names.

✦　　　✦　　　✦

Burn: Creating Audio and Data CDs

With Windows Millennium Edition (Windows Me) in 2000, Microsoft issued its first operating system with audio CD-creation capabilities. But these capabilities — offered through the bundled Windows Media Player 7 (MP7) application — came with some serious limitations, and Windows Me offered no way to create (or "burn") *data* CDs. MP7 worked well enough for the time, but it could burn audio CDs only very slowly. And the feature itself was very hard to find within the player; many users never even realized it was an option.

All these issues have been resolved in Windows XP, which is the first operating system from *any* vendor to offer full-speed audio and data CD-burning capabilities. This means that any user with a Compact Disc Recordable (CD-R) or Compact Disc Re-Writable (CD-RW) drive can use Windows XP to create audio *and* data CDs, without having to install any third-party application. And these capabilities are full-featured and complete, able to take advantage of the latest technologies. They're also more *discoverable,* so new users and power users alike can find and use this feature immediately.

In this chapter, we'll take a look at the technologies that make audio and data CD creation not just possible but fairly easy, as well as some of the more typical ways in which you may add a CD-R or CD-RW drive to your system. You'll be burning in no time.

A Quick Look at CD-R and CD-RW Technologies

Long ago, back in the days of Windows 3.1, Compact Disc (CD) technology went mainstream on the PC with the introduction of the first Windows-compatible CD data drives. This first generation of drives became the benchmark against which all future CD devices were measured, so a first-generation CD device is now considered a 1X (or "one-speed") device. So if you're running a 32X or 50X CD drive today, it's transferring data at 32 or 50 times the speed of that first generation of devices, respectively.

Today, of course, CD technology is commonplace on PCs. In fact, most PCs and laptops come with a recordable CD drive (or perhaps a DVD drive) in place of a read-only CD device. Recordable CD devices are available in two major types — CD-R and CD-RW. CD-R devices debuted first, giving users the capability to write data onto a blank, recordable CD for the first time. CD-RWs expand on the CD-R concept by providing an additional benefit: They can also write data onto specially formatted CD-RW discs over and over again, like a hard drive, albeit at much slower speeds.

Today, most recordable CD devices are, in fact, CD-RW devices, though most people continue to use normal CD-R discs in lieu of the more expensive CD-RW substitutes. There are a variety of reasons for this, but for the most part cost is the issue. That, and the fact that audio CD-RWs cannot be read by mainstream CD players, has really slowed the adoption of CD-RW media. And coming down the pike (though it still remains a distant possibility at this point) is DVD+R/W, which will bring recordable capabilities to the much higher-capacity DVD disc. DVD+R/W is natively supported in Windows XP, though only as a removable data disc. Third party products will let you burn true DVD movies, however. For more information see the Web site for this book: www.xpdigitalmedia.com

So what are the differences between CD-R discs and CD-RW discs? Take a look.

Fight of the century of the week: CD-R vs. CD-RW

The CD-R was specified in 1990 and first introduced in product form (by Philips), in 1993. CD-R discs are write-once devices; you can only write once to any given area of the disc, and you cannot erase something once it's been written. But data CD-Rs can be written to multiple times until they are full. Each subsequent write — called a *session* — must, however, take place on a previously unsullied portion of the disc. And once it's full, there's no going back.

So in 1997, Philips and Sony announced the successor to CD-R, called CD-RW. CD-RW works like CD-R, and can use CD-R media. But with special CD-RW media, you can write to the disc a virtually unlimited number of times. So these days, most recordable CD devices are indeed CD-RWs. You may have heard or seen that different CD-Rs are different colors. This is indeed true, and it began a myth that certain colors of CD-Rs are somehow faster or more reliable than others—which is certainly *not* the case. The color of a CD-R is determined by the color of the dye used during the manufacturing process. There are blue CD-Rs, gold CD-Rs, and probably even green CD-Rs, but the color of the disc has no impact on your system's performance or reliability.

But in the early days of the CD-manufacturing process, most CD-Rs were gold, which is the origin of the term *golden master,* used by software developers to describe the final release of a software product. When a product "goes gold" or is issued in golden master form, that simply means that the initial CD-R version has been pressed, and that this CD-R becomes the master for all future product CD duplication.

Choosing a CD-R/CD-RW Drive

So where is CD-R/CD-RW technology today? Well, a variety of vendors offer a variety of products in a variety of form factors at a variety of prices. Put more succinctly, it's a buyer's market. Essentially, you can break down the recordable CD market into two types of products, internal and external. Internal CD-RW devices are cheaper and (generally) faster than the external variety, but they're also much harder to install, and I don't recommend this to typical users unless you're into scraped knuckles and tiny screws. On the other hand, you may be that Mr. Fixit of the PC world and comfortable inside the case of a PC. They're probably not reading this section too closely anyway.

Another problem for internal CD-RW drives: Most PCs are limited to a total of four IDE devices, which are typically hard drives and CD/CD-R/CD-RW/DVD-type devices. So you may have two hard drives, a CD-RW, and a DVD drive in your system, but future disk expansion would require you to remove one of those devices first. This won't be a problem for many people, but it's something to consider. (And combo drives are also appearing that allow you to use DVDs and CD-Rs/CD-RWs in the same drive.)

To combat these problems, a variety of external solutions have appeared over the past few years. The most popular are USB-based CD-RW drives, which plug into the now-ubiquitous USB port. USB is nice, because it's plug-and-play and easy to use. But USB is also slow; the bandwidth for a USB port is generally shared with any other USB devices plugged into the system. This means that using multiple USB devices simultaneously can slow down the entire works—a disaster when you're trying to create a CD. For this reason, many people leave the system alone while it's burning.

External devices also tend to be more expensive than the internal variety because they must include a molded plastic case and a power supply; internal devices need only a faceplate and they derive their power from the system. But a USB device doesn't tax the PCs often-underpowered power supply, either.

To combat the technical problems with USB-based CD-RW devices, a number of manufacturers are starting to ship external devices based on FireWire, also known as IEEE-1394. FireWire devices are 40 times as fast as USB and can often rival the speed of a typical IDE interface, so an external FireWire-based CD-RW may be optimal. Right now, such devices are still fairly rare. This is because most PCs do not include FireWire ports as standard equipment, so the user would have to install an internal FireWire card in the computer, giving in to a hassle that would be avoided by choosing an external device. And FireWire devices are expensive — even more expensive than USB devices.

On the other hand, FireWire is wonderful for Digital Video work, which gets coverage in Part III.

Of course, most people obtain a CD-RW with a new PC anyway, so often this choice is already made ahead of time. But if you're upgrading a decent PC for use with Windows XP and you want to add a CD-RW to the system, these are the issues to consider.

My recommendation is simple. If you're an average PC user and you're not overly concerned with speed, go with an external USB-based device. Although it's more expensive, it's also portable and more easily moved to another PC (which is also a good option for people with two or more PCs). If you're technically competent or can pay someone to install an internal device, then doing so is a good option. The speed benefit is an added bonus — but an internal drive is hard to move to a new PC.

If it means anything, all my current recordable-CD devices are internal. But I'm going external as soon as one of them fails.

About SCSI

You may have heard about SCSI (oddly pronounced "scuzzy") — a type of interface which, like IDE, is used to connect devices like hard drives and CD-RWs to computers. SCSI was seen (earlier on, at least) as superior to IDE — it was once faster and (still is) more expandable — but SCSI is also very hard to configure and use, and most PCs do not use this interface. When CD-writing first became possible on PCs, many of the first such devices were SCSI-based because of the speed improvements there. But modern IDE devices rival the speed of SCSI — as does FireWire — and these interfaces are much cheaper and easier to use. I do not recommend SCSI for anyone using a PC, though certainly it has its place on servers. I certainly don't recommend installing a SCSI card and CD-RW; you don't receive any real performance benefit for your cash outlay. SCSI is just too expensive and hard to use to be a mainstream alternative.

Creating an Audio CD

Before you can make an audio CD, you may find that working with the playlist feature of Windows Media Player for Windows XP (MPXP) is a valuable first step. MPXP includes a number of built-in playlists; you can play all the audio files on your computer, only audio of a certain genre, only audio by particular artists, and so on. But you can also create your own custom playlists. You may want to create a playlist that's appropriate for when you're working ("Work songs"), for example, or a playlist of music for the gym that you expect to use with a portable audio device (called, say, "Workout music" or "Gym songs").

Creating and accessing playlists

A playlist is exactly what it sounds like, a list of songs that's been given a name so you can easily access it later. Generally, you create a new playlist from the Media Library, where the *New playlist* button appears near the top of the MPXP window. Playlists appear under the My Playlists node of the Audio tree in the Media Guide; Microsoft supplies an empty playlist called (imaginatively enough) *Sample Playlist*, but you can safely delete this and make your own (To do so, right-click Sample Playlist and choose Delete). In Figure 8-1, you can see that a custom playlist called "Gym songs" has been created.

Figure 8-1: Playlists can be accessed from the MPXP Media Library.

Adding songs to a playlist is equally easy:

1. Expand various nodes of the Media Guide's Audio tree, such as All Audio, particular artists, genres, or albums, and select the song(s) you'd like to add.

2. Right-click and choose Add to Playlist.

3. This brings up the Playlists dialog box, which you can use to choose from the available list of playlists (or add a new playlist).

Figure 8-2 shows what this procedure looks like.

Figure 8-2: You can add a song to a playlist or create a new playlist.

If you're into drag and drop, you can also drag songs into an existing playlist by scrolling the Audio tree in the Media Library down so the playlist name is viewable. Then, select the file or files you'd like to add and drag them over to the playlist node. This saves the need to open a separate dialog box, but if you've got a lot of music in your Media Library, the right-click method described here is simpler and quicker.

And, of course, there's another way. You can also select a song for inclusion in a playlist and then click the button labeled *Add to playlist*, located at the top of the MPXP window (as seen in Figure 8-3). What's nice about this option is that it doesn't open a dialog box. Instead, it provides a drop-down list of the available playlists, while also providing a way to add a new playlist if desired.

Figure 8-3: Using the Add to Playlist button is probably more convenient than other methods.

If you view the playlist, as in Figure 8-4, it tells you how many songs are in the playlist, the amount of space they occupy on a disc, and the estimated total running time for all the songs. This is exactly the information you need if you intend to later copy that playlist to an audio CD, which can hold 74 minutes of music, or a portable audio device, such as the Iomega HipZIP, which uses 40MB cartridges.

Figure 8-4: When you view a playlist, you can see the songs in the list, and the estimated time and disc space they occupy.

Creating playlists from My Music

Interestingly, you can also create playlists directly from the Windows XP shell, Explorer. To see how, navigate into the My Music folder hierarchy so you can see some audio files, like those in Figure 8-5. If you select one or more audio files and right-click, you see an Add to Playlist option. This actually launches MPXP (if it isn't already available), and then displays the familiar Playlists dialog box so you can choose an existing playlist or create a new one. The capability to add songs to playlists (whether from MPXP or directly from the shell) means you can manage your music exactly as you see fit. Some people feel more comfortable doing so from MPXP; others prefer the Explorer shell. It's nice to have the choice.

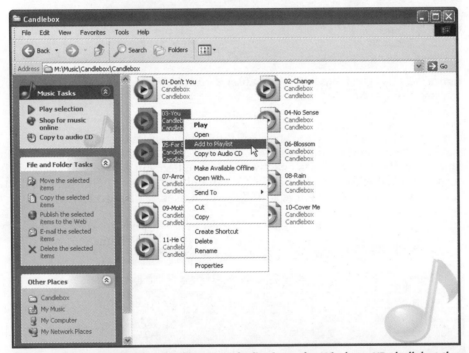

Figure 8-5: You can add audio files to a playlist from the Windows XP shell, but then it ends up launching Windows Media Player for Windows XP.

Managing songs in a playlist

Another nice feature is the capability to change the order of songs in a playlist. Though many people are happy to do no more than shuffle a playlist, some want more control over the songs they listen to. So it's possible to open a playlist in

MPXP and then drag the songs around in the right pane view of the window, in order to change their order of play. You simply use the standard drag and drop skills you developed long ago to change the order of songs in the playlist, as we're doing in Figure 8-6.

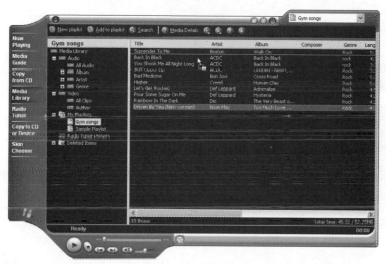

Figure 8-6: To rearrange the order of songs in a playlist, simply drag them with the mouse.

You can also rename a playlist any time you'd like. Simply right-click the playlist node in the Audio tree of the Media Library and choose Rename. Then type the new name into the Rename Playlist dialog box.

Importing and exporting playlists

You can import playlists from other media player applications, such as WinAmp, or export all your Media Player for Windows XP playlists for use in other applications. Playlists created by MPXP typically use the .ASX extension, but MP3-based playlists often use the .m3u file extension. Media Player can work with both types of playlists. This allows you to easily upgrade from your old media player to MPXP.

Exporting a playlist

To export a playlist, choose File ➪ Export Playlists to File (as shown in Figure 8-7).

Figure 8-7: You can easily export all your playlists into a plain text file that other applications can use.

An exported playlist is essentially a plain text file. To see the type of data that's contained, locate an exported playlist, right-click it, and choose Open With and then Notepad. MPXP uses ASX 3.0, which is based on the XML language used on the World Wide Web. ASX files use name/value pairs to provide information about the music files in the playlist. So you see entries for Name, Genre, Artist, and SourceURL, which represents the physical location of the file, among other information. You could hand edit this sort of file, but I don't recommend it for most people. Here's an example of the way in which one song appears in my *Collective Soul CD* playlist:

```
<Entry>
<Title > Heavy</Title>

<Duration value = "00:02:59.766" />

<Param Name = "Name" Value = "Heavy" />

<Param Name = "Genre" Value = "Rock" />

<Param Name = "Artist" Value = "Collective Soul" />

<Author > Collective Soul</Author>
```

```
<Param Name = "Album" Value = "Dosage" />

<Param Name = "MediaType" Value = "audio" />

<Param Name = "MediaAttribute" Value = "0" />

<Param Name = "OriginalIndex" Value = "1" />

<Param Name = "Bitrate" Value = "160000" />

<Param Name = "DigitallySecure" Value = "0" />

<Param Name = "PlayCount" Value - "0" />

<Param Name = "SourceURL" Value - "C:\Documents and Settings\Paul\My
Music\Collective Soul\Dosage\02 - Heavy.mp3" />

<Param Name = "CreationDate" Value - "3/26/2001 1:12:49 PM" />

<Param Name = "Size" Value = "3595328" />

<Ref href = " C:\Documents and Settings\Paul\My Music\Collective Soul\Dosage\02
  Heavy.mp3"/>
</Entry>
```

Importing a playlist

Likewise, you can also import Windows Media and MP3-based playlists into
Windows Media Player for Windows XP. To do so, choose File ⇨ Import Playlists to
Media Library. Then use the standard Windows Open dialog box to navigate to the
location of the playlist you'd like to import.

Setting Audio CD properties

Okay, you've ripped audio CDs into Windows Media (or MP3) format, organized
these media files with Windows Media Player for Windows XP and the My Music
folder, and created custom MPXP playlists. Now you're ready to begin creating your
own custom audio CDs. If you've ever created mix cassettes for the car or home
stereo in the past, you can appreciate how much easier — and faster — it is to create audio CDs with Windows XP. And of course, the resulting audio quality is so
much better.

Before you begin the audio-CD-creation process, you should ensure that Windows
Media Player for Windows XP is properly set up to do so. To begin, launch the
MPXP Options dialog box, which can be displayed by choosing Tools ⇨ Options.
The Devices page of this dialog box (shown in Figure 8-8) contains all the configura-
tion options you need.

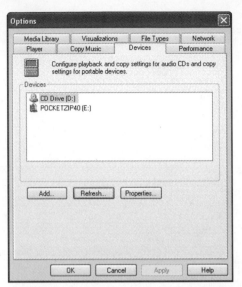

Figure 8-8: The Devices page of the Windows Media Player for Windows XP Options dialog box contains information about all the devices that can interconnect with the player.

Depending on which devices you have connected to your system, the Devices panel on this page should contain at least your CD drive. Select this drive and then click the Properties button to finally display the Properties dialog box for the CD drive. You'll note that there are two main sections, Playback and Copy, as shown in Figure 8-9. We're worried primarily about Copy right now; when you copy music from your computer to a recordable CD, you can do so in either digital or analog mode. *Digital mode* is generally superior to analog for this purpose, assuming you've got a fairly modern system and a supported CD drive. Digital mode ensures that the bits making their way from the computer to the disc don't have to be rerouted through the analog outputs on your sound card (where sound degradation and extraneous background noise can get into the recording). However, if you experience pops or hissing after you use digital mode, and error correction doesn't help (details about that shortly), or you are using a slower PC, you may want to consider *analog mode*. In general, digital *is* the way to go.

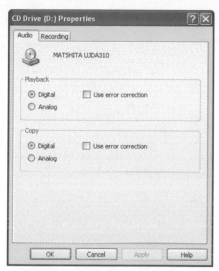

Figure 8-9: The Properties dialog box for the CD drive lets you determine how information is read from, and copied to, the device.

You may notice another option in the Copy section of the CD Drive Properties dialog box, labeled *Use error correction*. This choice can be enabled (it's turned off by default) if you are experiencing problems while creating audio CDs, such as unexpected glitches, skips, pops, and clicks. Error correction attempts to digitally correct errors as they occur during the recording process. So you may wonder why this option isn't on by default. The reason is that error correction dramatically slows down the audio CD creation process. I recommend turning it on only if you hear abnormalities in the audio CDs you create.

On the Recording page of the CD Drive Properties dialog box (Figure 8-10), you can set options for recording speed and so on. (The upcoming section, "Creating Data CDs with Windows XP," goes into more detail about this dialog box). In general, leave this set to the defaults.

Note In Windows Me, Windows Media Player could burn audio CDs only at 2X. In Windows XP, this limitation is completely bypassed for most drives, and you can now create audio (and data) CDs at the full speed of your recordable CD device. This means that Windows XP can write CDs at speeds up to 700 times as fast as Windows Me using modern CD-RW drives.

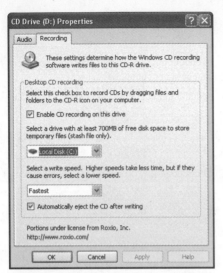

Figure 8-10: The Recording page of the CD Drive Properties dialog box, where you can enable CD recording and set up other recording configuration options.

Creating an Audio CD

Enough of the preliminaries, it's time to burn an audio CD. First, insert a blank CD-R into your recordable CD drive. Note that a CD-RW is generally not acceptable for this, as most consumer grade CD players cannot read CD-RW discs for some reason. Also, Windows XP typically launches a My Computer window when you insert a blank CD; you can close or ignore this window. Now, launch Windows Media Player for Windows XP and click the Copy to CD or Device choice in the Windows Media Player for Windows XP taskbar, or choose Taskbar then Copy to CD or Device from the View menu if you're a menu kind of person. Either way, you'll be shuffled off to the heart of MPXP's audio CD-creation capabilities.

In the left pane of this window, as seen in Figure 8-11, you see the currently selected playlist (remember, you can only copy music from playlists onto a CD). In addition to the list of songs in the playlist, this pane contains the length (in minutes) and size (in MB) of each song, along with the total length of the music, in minutes.

In the right pane, you can see the audio files present on the current device, which should be set to your CD drive (if it isn't, choose your recordable CD drive from the drop-down list box). If a blank disc is inserted, the right pane should simply read, *There are no media items present*, and indicate that you have 74 minutes free.

Figure 8-11: The Copy to CD or Device option lets you burn an audio CD.

Now, you can select the correct playlist for copying. To do so, pull down the drop-down list box in the left pane and navigate to the playlist you'd like. This can be a playlist you've created (which are conveniently displayed right at the top), a music genre, or a CD album. (Interestingly, "artist" is not one of the choices.) When you've chosen the correct playlist, you're ready to start.

Click the Copy Music button, as shown in Figure 8-12, is located near the right top corner of the player window to begin creating your audio CD. This process involves first converting the audio for transfer to CD, and then the actual copying. Depending on the length and number of songs you're copying and the speed of your recordable CD device, it could take several minutes. If you're performing a digital copy, you can listen to the music as you're copying, or listen to other music in your media library if you'd like. What's interesting here is that the player maintains two separate playlists. There's the playlist you're copying, and the Now Playing playlist, which can be accessed from the far top-right corner of the player window. (So you could play some Van Halen through your speakers while copying some serene New Age music if you like.)

When the copy process is complete, the disc is ejected by default and you're done. The resulting disc should work fine in any portable, auto, or component stereo-based CD or DVD player.

Figure 8-12: Once you're ready to burn, simply click the Copy Music button, sit back, and watch it happen. Note that the Copy Music button changes to Cancel when copying begins.

Adding music to an audio CD

Unlike data CDs (described later in this chapter), audio CDs have to be created all at once. You cannot place some files on the CD and then come back later to complete the CD. If you attempt to add files to a previously made audio CD, Media Player for Windows XP warns you that this is impossible as shown in Figure 8-13, and that you must insert a blank CD-R instead.

Figure 8-13: Unfortunately, it is impossible to add music to an audio CD you created previously.

Creating WMA/MP3 Music data CDs

One final bit of miscellany: Audio CD creation is nice, because it allows you to make a CD that can play in any standard audio CD or DVD player, including those in cars and portable CD players. But the growing personal-electronics market has spawned a new type of product that's likely to interest anyone who wants to make music more portable: MP3 CD players—or (better yet) *multiformat* CD players that play both Windows Media (WMA) *and* MP3. Whereas a typical audio CD can hold up to 72 minutes of music, a typical data CD with compressed MP3 files on it can store approximately *10 times that amount* — and with WMA, about 20 times the amount of CD-quality music. And these players are available in portable, auto, and home stereo-component versions, making them accessible to just about anyone. Over 20 hours of music on a single, portable platter: Now, *that's* exciting.

The problem is that Windows Media Player for Windows XP doesn't include native MP3 writing support, though many PC makers are expected to include this capability in their new Windows XP-based PCs; end-users can purchase an MP3 Encoding Pack if desired (see the Web site for this book for details: www.xpdigitalmedia.com). You can also add this functionality yourself by clicking the MP3 Information button located in Tools ⇨ Options ⇨ Copy Music. To make the most of this experience (and get your full 20+ hours' worth), consider getting one of the new multi-format CD players that support WMA as well as MP3. Some examples include Sonicblue's Rio Volt or the Kenwood DPC-MP727. Other portable players, even in-dash players, are expected to support WMA as well and be available shortly. Now because these discs are data CDs and not audio CDs, you can't create them in Windows Media Player for Windows XP. Instead, you have to use the Windows shell. In the next section, we'll discuss the data CD creation features in Windows XP. You can use this capability to make backups of crucial data, and yes, to make WMA/MP3 music data CDs if you so desire.

Creating Data CDs with Windows XP

Data CDs — discs that contain data and document files (which must be played on an appropriate drive) rather than audio files (which you can play in any CD player) — also must be created directly in the Windows XP shell. You can't use use Windows Media Player for Windows XP to create a data CD. To make this process as simple as possible, however, Microsoft integrated CD-burning capabilities directly into the OS, so the system can auto-sense when a CD-R or CD-RW drive is present — and also auto-sense when a blank CD is inserted into such a drive.

In my mind, however, CD-burning in Windows XP is not an obvious procedure. Therefore this section examines the various ways you can get data onto a record-able CD; you can decide which method works best for you. As with other functionality in Windows XP, Microsoft has distinguished between "beginner" and "advanced" methods for performing this task, but this is one area where the line between the two is somewhat blurred: More advanced users may find themselves preferring the so-called beginner method, and vice versa. But first things first: Make sure that your system is properly configured for CD-burning.

Configuring recording capabilities

Assuming you've properly installed a CD-R or CD-RW drive in your system, you should see an icon in My Computer that's labeled *CD drive;* you can find it under the Devices with Removable Storage section (Why this isn't called "Recordable CD drive," as DVD drives are properly labeled, is a mystery.)

To configure the Recordable CD drive for burning, right-click the icon and choose Properties. This displays the CD Drive Properties dialog box. Then navigate to the Recording tab. This page of the dialog box provides configuration options for CD writing, which was shown in Figure 8-10.

The top option, labeled *Enable CD recording on this drive*, toggles the system's data and audio CD-creation capabilities. If the checkbox is unchecked, you can't burn any CDs.

The next option determines which hard drive contains the temporary files—which Microsoft calls the *staging area*—used during the CD burning process. Because of the capacity of a blank CD, this drive must set aside up to 700 MB of space for this task. By default, it uses the System drive (almost always the C: partition, which contains the operating system's boot files). But you can change it to any valid drive by using the provided drop-down list box. I recommend changing this setting to something other than the drive that contains the WINDOWS directory, if possible. Although theoretically you *could* use a mapped network drive for this purpose, Windows XP allows only a local disc to be used for the Recordable CD's temporary files.

The third option lets you choose the burn speed. Typically, leaving this on its default setting, *Fastest,* is a good idea; it lets your device operate at its fastest possible speed. However, if you experience any problems creating CDs, you can use this option to turn the speed down and see whether than corrects the problem. I'm using an internal CD-RW that's capable of writing at 8X currently (and yes, such drives are horribly out of date). Windows XP allows me to choose from among Fastest, 8X, 4X, 2X, and 1X. Your options vary according to the drive type. I don't recommend changing this unless you are experiencing problems.

Tip   You can choose to have Windows XP eject the disc when it's done creating your CD. Note that this option applies *only* to data CDs created from the Windows XP shell: There's no auto-eject option for audio CDs.

For the most part, you may discover that the options here have been set up optimally for you already. In my experience with a several Windows XP systems, I've always been pretty happy with the way Microsoft configures the OS for CD burning. However, you may not want the system to eject the CD after it's done. And of course, this is the place to turn if you're creating "coasters"—recorded CDs that failed to complete for some reason—instead of normal CDs. Reducing the burn speed is usually all that's required.

Getting files and folders into the Recordable CD staging area

The first step in creating a data CD is to insert a blank CD-R or CD-RW disc into the drive. When you do this, Windows XP opens a blank Explorer window that displays the contents of the disc (which should be empty if it's blank); this is shown in

Figure 8-14. This feature departs from previous versions of Windows (which didn't note the insertion of blank CD media at all). As you may expect, the notification is done for a reason: Microsoft wants to make sure you realize that the inserted medium is ready for use. In fact, by presenting the window in such a way, Windows XP is telling you that the drive is ready to accept data.

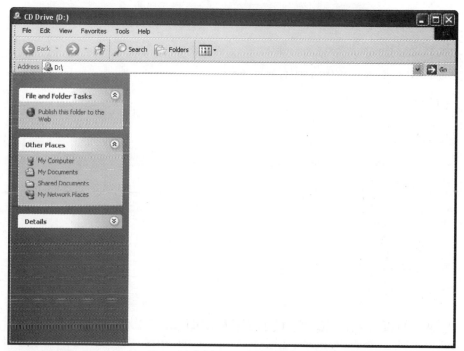

Figure 8-14: Pop in a blank, recordable CD and Windows XP notifies you that it's ready for use by opening a window.

Before you can create a data CD in Windows XP, you have to tell the system which files you'd like to burn. You can do this in a variety of ways, but one of the more obvious is to use the drag-and-drop routine which you've probably been using since Windows 95 — you grab a file, folder, or group of files and folders and drag them to a new target location.

In Windows XP, one possible target location is your recordable CD drive. But thankfully, Windows XP doesn't immediately burn the files and folders onto the disc. Instead, it places them in temporary storage — the staging area discussed in the previous section. It does this for several reasons. You may want to reorganize the layout of files and folders on the recordable CD before you burn it, which (in effect) sets the order in stone. You may want to drag in a large group of files but then hand-pick a few. If you discover you've dragged the wrong files in, it would be a waste of a recordable CD if you didn't have a chance to reorganize them.

Anyway, the drag-and-drop method works two ways; the first is straightforward: You can drag the files and folders into the window that Windows XP opened for you. Of course, that's the reason Windows XP opened that blank window in the first place—it's a drag-and-drop target, as shown in Figure 8-15.

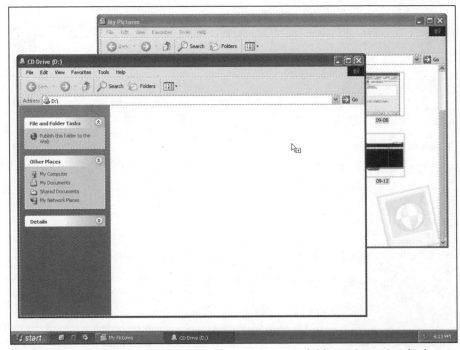

Figure 8-15: One obvious way to get files onto a recordable CD is to simply drag and drop them within the Windows XP shell.

If you're not into that kind of convenience, however, the second method is to drag and drop those files and folders to the CD drive icon in My Computer.

When you do this, the files and folders you dragged and dropped appear *ghosted* (grayed out) in the drive window, under a group heading titled *Files to add to the CD*; this is shown in Figure 8-16. The ghosted icons and the aptly named group help make it obvious that you're not done yet. You can continue dragging and dropping files and folders until you're ready to burn. If you copy enough files, you get the familiar Copying dialog box. But remember that Windows XP is really just copying those files to the recordable CD staging area. They're not burned yet.

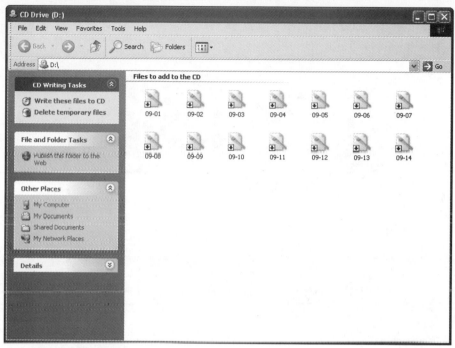

Figure 8-16: Files stored in the staging area are shown as ghosted icons in the recordable CD window.

Tip

It's possible to do other familiar Explorer tasks in the recordable CD window. You can create new folders, for example. This could be useful for organizing files and folders before burning the disc.

Copy data to a recordable CD like a Pro

The drag-and-drop method used above is the "beginner" method for copying data to a recordable CD. You can also use a less discoverable, and arguably more advanced, way to get data onto a recordable CD. This involves the little-used, but useful Send To option that's available from the Windows XP shell. The process is similar to drag and drop but a bit more streamlined: You select the files, folders, or files and folders you'd like to burn, as before. But instead of dragging and dropping them, you right-click and choose Send To ➪ Writable CD from the menu that appears, as shown in Figure 8-17.

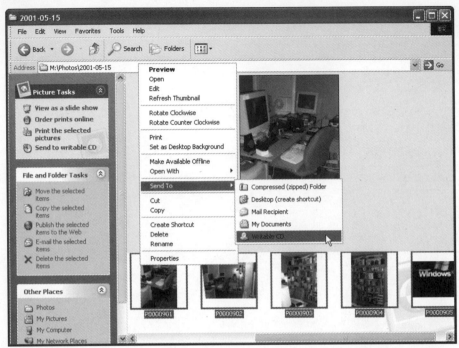

Figure 8-17: Power users may want to use the less-discoverable Send To option to copy files into a CD-R or CD-RW.

The benefit of this approach is that you don't need to have a target window open. This reduces screen clutter. But you can also use drag and drop *without* a target window if you're ingenious enough about it. Simply create a shortcut to your recordable CD drive on your desktop (or Quick Launch taskbar's toolbar) and drag the files there, all without using a target window.

Tip   The method you use, of course, is up to you. I happen to prefer drag and drop. Since I like to organize files before I burn them, I leave a target window open. (I guess that makes me a beginner!)

Burning the CD

Okay, crack those knuckles; we're ready to make a data CD. When you begin copying files and folders to the recordable CD, a new Tasks section appears in the Web view pane in the recordable CD window. The first option under Tasks, unsurprisingly, is labeled Write to CD. Choosing this option launches the CD Burning Wizard, which guides you through the process. Figure 8-18 shows the wizard's opening screen.

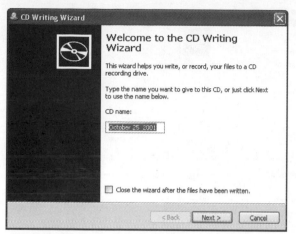

Figure 8-18: The CD Burning Wizard is typically launched from the Web pane view in My Computer.

In the first step of the CD Burning Wizard, you get to choose the name of the CD. On a CD-R disc, you only get to choose the name once, so choose wisely (you can change the name of a CD-RW disc later if you so desire). By default, Windows XP creates a name that combines the current user's logon name with the date. So, for example, I may see a default name such as *Paul 3/21/2001*. Feel free to use any name you like, within reason: You're limited to 16 characters, but you *can* use spaces and many non-alphanumeric characters.

Tip   The first stage of the wizard also offers a choice: whether to close the wizard when the write procedure is complete. You may choose to leave the wizard running if you want to make a second copy of the CD.

When you click Next, the wizard writes the data to the CD, as shown in Figure 8-19.

The length of time this process takes depends on how much data you're writing and on the speed of your recordable CD hardware. It then "closes" the disc. Once the writing is complete, the CD ejects (provided you left that option checked in CD Properties, as mentioned in the previous section). The wizard completes its work but gives you the option of creating a duplicate CD. If you click Finish, the wizard disappears.

Note   The staging area is cleared automatically when you finish the wizard, so you can't recreate that specific CD again without doing a CD copy operation (details coming up).

What happens if you decide that you're not ready to burn a CD and you just want to skip out on the entire process? Well, Windows XP provides a simple option for this as well. Simply open the recordable CD in My Computer and choose *Clear the staging area* from the Web view panel.

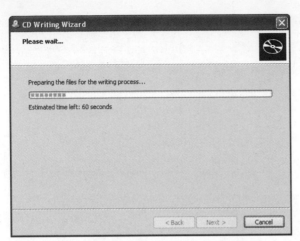

Figure 8-19: The speed of the CD copy process depends on the amount of data you're writing and the speed of your recordable-CD device.

Given the built-in flexibility of Windows XP, you have several ways to abort the CD-creation process. You could eject the blank CD, for example, before the CD burning process begins. This triggers the CD Burning Wizard, which displays an option, *Eject,* and *Delete the files waiting to be written to CD.* Power users can right-click the CD drive icon and choose *Clear staging area* to abort the recording process.

Power users can initiate the CD Burning Wizard without the need to display the Web view. To do so, open My Computer and right-click the CD drive, then choose *Write to CD.*

Haven't had enough? Come back for more

If you're familiar with third-party CD-burning utilities — such as Roxio's excellent EZ CD Creator — you may be wondering how Windows XP handles something called *multisession CD-Rs.* In third-party programs, when you burn a CD-R, you typically have the option to permanently close the CD, meaning that you cannot later add content to that CD. Or, you could leave it open for future writes, which would allow you to add content, at any time, until the CD's capacity was full.

Windows XP doesn't give you that option. In Windows XP, there is *no* way to permanently "close" a CD, preventing you (or anyone else for that matter) from later adding content to it. Instead, CD-Rs are left writable. As you may suspect, this was done for simplicity's sake, so new users wouldn't be confused. If you've got 650 MB of space to write to, you always have 650 MB of space to work with. Once it's full, it's full. But until then, you can always go back and add more information to the disc.

To see how this works, reinsert a CD-R that you've created with Windows XP. The CD drive window appears once again, but now it has a new group called *Files currently on CD*, which contains the data files and folders you've already written. Now, you can drag and drop more files into the recordable CD window (or use the Send To menu). As you do, a *Files to add to the CD* section is automatically created, and the process is identical to what we described above, when you create a new, recordable CD; this is shown in Figure 8-20. And again, you can do this as often as you want, until the disc is full.

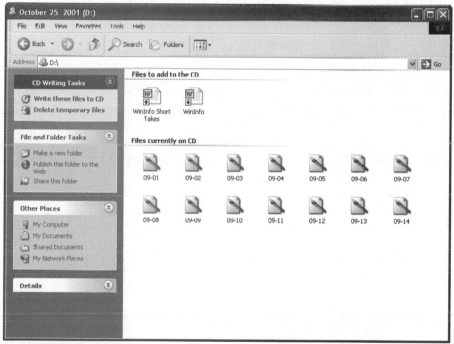

Figure 8-20: You can keep adding files to a CD-R or CD-RW until it is full.

Now, things are slightly different for CD-RW media, which are rewriteable by design. The next section takes a look at the unique options available to you when you use CD-RW media instead of the cheaper (and more easily accessible) CD-R discs.

CD-RW and Windows XP

Why would anyone bother with relatively expensive CD-RW discs when you can buy stacks of CD-Rs for just a few pennies a disc? Well, CD-RW has some pretty obvious advantages over CD-R because it is infinitely rewriteable. But this means that interacting with a CD-RW disc in Windows XP gives you a slightly different experience from what you get with CD-R. When you copy files to a CD-RW, the scenario starts out the same as with a CD-R: You can drag and drop the files to the Recordable CD window as always, and you can fire the CD Burning Wizard by choosing the *Write to CD* option in the Web pane of that window. But here the differences start to crop up: CD-RW rewriting is much slower than CD-R writing—often it happens at about half the speed of a CD-R copy operation.

Speed issues aside, other (more obvious) differences rear their heads. When you reinsert a CD-RW, you can delete all the files and folders previously written to it. Sadly, you can't *selectively* delete files and folders; this option is effectively identical to formatting the disc. And equally problematic. Microsoft doesn't let you use the standard shell methods for deletion. Instead, you have to rerun the CD Burning Wizard using the new *Erase files on CD-RW* option that appears in the Web pane-based Tasks list when you reinsert a CD-RW disc. This is shown in Figure 8-21.

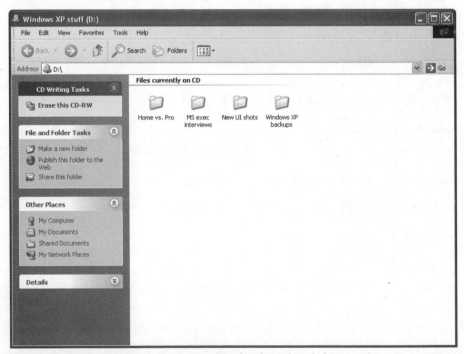

Figure 8-21: If you reinsert a CD-RW disc that has already been written to, you see a new choice in Web view: Erase files on CD-RW.

When you run the CD Burning Wizard this way, you are given the option to delete all the files on your CD-RW disc. When you click Next, the CD-RW is erased. This takes a lot less time than the writing process, however, though the exact time depends on the amount of data that's on there. After a short period of time, the wizard announces that that the CD-RW has been erased.

There's another small difference between CD-RW and CD-R media. If you come back later to a CD-RW that already contains data, and add data to that disc, you can change the name of the disc if you choose. In the first step of the CD Burning Wizard, you see the standard choice to name the CD. With a CD-RW, you can do this as often as you like.

If you're a power user and can't stand the idea of that Web view pane taking up your valuable screen real estate, fear not: An Erase CD-RW option is available, as appropriate, when you right-click the CD drive icon in My Computer.

Harder than it needs to be: Duplicating a CD

Curiously, Windows XP doesn't include a simple way to duplicate a CD. While burning a CD-R or CD-RW with the CD Burning Wizard, however, it is possible to make two copies of the same CD. So it stands to reason that you could "fake out" Windows XP and cause it to duplicate a CD this way. And though this isn't exactly an optimal way to do this, it does indeed work.

The key to faking out Windows XP into making a duplicate of a CD is filling the staging area with the contents of the CD you wish to copy. To do so, just follow a few crucial steps:

1. Make a note of the exact name of the CD you'd like to copy.

2. Navigate to Folder options (My Computer, then Tools, then Folder Options) and open the View page. At least temporarily, choose *Show hidden files and folders*. Then choose OK to close the dialog box.

3. If you only have one CD-style device (CD-R or CD-RW in this case), place the CD you'd like to copy in that device and open CD drive in My Computer. If you have two devices (for example, a recordable CD device and a DVD player), place the CD you'd like to copy in the non-recordable device, and then open CD drive in My Computer.

Many CDs auto-run when you place them in the CD drive or try and open them in My Computer. To avoid this, hold down the SHIFT key while you close the CD door. Then, instead of double-clicking the CD drive icon to open the disc, right-click and choose Open.

4. If you've got one CD-style device, create a new Folder on the desktop, giving it whatever name you choose. Then, copy the contents of the CD to the folder you created on the desktop. Remove the CD, and replace with a blank writable CD, open the folder, select all files, and choose Send To and then Writable CD from the right-click menu. Users with two CD-style devices can simply select all the files on the CD they'd like to copy and choose Send To and then Writable CD from the right-click menu, skipping the time-consuming folder copy step.

5. Now you can write to the CD as normal, but be sure to name the CD identically to the original, since some CDs require a specific name to work properly. If you have only one drive and had to create a temporary folder on the desktop, you can delete this when the CD burning is complete.

6. Return to Folder Options and change the *Show hidden files and folders* option back to the way it was, if you prefer it that way.

Needless to say, this isn't exactly an elegant solution. I expect Microsoft to add a less complicated capability to the shell in a future release of Windows, so you can simply choose a "Copy CD" option, regardless of whether you have one or more CD-style devices. In the meantime, if you find yourself needing to make many backup CDs, you may want to invest in a third-party program such as the excellent EZ CD Creator (www.roxio.com) or Nero (www.ahead.de/).

Failure among us: What to do when CD burning fails

Occasionally, you may encounter problems with writing CDs. This can be caused by many problems, but the most typical is a bad disc. With CD-Rs now sold in bulk, it's not uncommon to see a few bum discs in every pack of 100 CD-Rs. Or maybe the CD-R you're using doesn't really work reliably at its maximum-stated speed. In such cases, you're going to see the Writing to CD Failed dialog box when you encounter a problem, as shown in Figure 8-22. This dialog box gives you three options:

◆ Write the files to another CD.

◆ Exit the wizard and clear the files waiting to be written to CD.

◆ Exit the wizard altogether (the default choice, curiously).

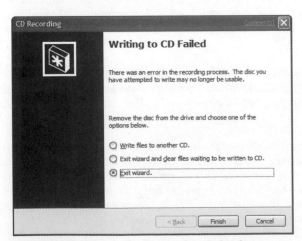

Figure 8-22: Uh-oh. If you see this dialog box, something's not right.

If this is the first time you've seen this dialog box, I recommend the first option. But if your CD burning fails with another CD-R disc, you may choose the third option and then downgrade the speed of your recordable CD device from its Properties dialog box. These two options seem to solve the majority of burn-related problems.

But if you're still experiencing problems, you may consider a different brand of CD-R media. I usually stick with the brand name discs, but each drive seems to have different results with certain kinds of media. If that fails, you may be experiencing a hardware malfunction, so it's probably time to get friendly with your PC maker's support staff.

Note   CD burning in Windows XP is made possible in part through a partnership between Microsoft and Roxio, the makers of EZ CD Creator, and is in part based on that technology. Roxio claims over 700 different CD-R and/or CD-RW drives are supported natively by this technology. In the event that you have a CD-R or CD-RW drive that doesn't have native CD burning driver for Windows XP, Windows XP will fall back to some of Roxio's technology to try to support it. Your burning may be slower—much slower, in the 2X realm—but until an updated driver comes out for your hardware, it's better than nothing!

✦   ✦   ✦

Baby, You're a Movie Star

Digital moviemaking is, perhaps, the most complicated digital-media experience in Windows XP, but may also be the most fulfilling as well. With Windows XP, you can watch digital movies, streaming video, and DVD movies — but you can also record your own home movies and add titles, transitions, and other effects, and then share those movies with friends and family via the Internet. There's a lot to learn, but this part walks you through it step by step.

Playing and Managing Videos

When Windows 95 first came out, one of its most amazing features was a built-in capability to play small videos on-screen. That OS came with a couple of videos on the CD version, including a short, low-quality skiing segment and two music videos in various formats. Back then, it wasn't a given that your computer could even play the things, so they actually formed a good test of your hardware. The 486 on which I originally ran Windows 95 was woefully underpowered for this task.

Today, of course, the computer you're using with Windows XP is more than adequate for playing back very high-quality movies, including video movie files stored on your hard drive, streaming videos that are delivered over the Web, and DVD movies that will make that next business trip a little more bearable. What's interesting is that over the past few years, consumer acceptance of this capability has become almost ubiquitous: It's just a given that you can do this on a PC.

Well, as you might expect, Windows XP has been designed to make your experience with digital movies easier and more exciting that ever before. And that includes movies you've made yourself with a digital camcorder: If you want to play, manage, create, or edit digital movies, Windows XP is the place to be. This chapter explores the video-management, playback, and sharing features built into Windows XP.

Managing Videos with My Videos

You may be aware that Microsoft has elevated the My Music and My Pictures folders in Windows XP to the status of *special shell folder*, which indelibly hard codes their functionality for audio and image management, respectively. Not surprisingly, Windows XP also includes a *My Videos* folder, also found in the My Documents folder, that is designed to hold videos and video-related files. However, Microsoft hasn't deemed to elevate this folder in status as it did for both My Music and My Pictures. Presumably they needed something for the bullet list of features for the follow-up to Windows XP.

In effect, My Videos is just a normal folder found under My Documents — with a few caveats. The folder doesn't even exist on your system until you start Windows Movie Maker for the first time. And it does behave somewhat like the special shell folders (you can't customize it as you can a normal folder).

So before you start working with videos in Windows XP, you might as well create the folder: Launch Windows Movie Maker (Start ➪ All Programs ➪ Accessories) and then close it (more about this application in Chapter 11). When you do so, you see the My Videos folder appear, as shown in Figure 9-1.

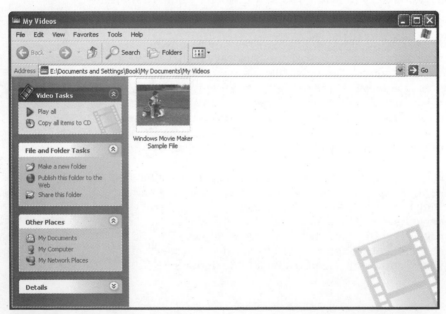

Figure 9-1: The My Videos folder appears after you run Windows Movie Maker the first time.

Inside My Videos is a single digital video file—Windows Movie Maker Sample File—designed to get you started with the program.

At this point, you might want to consider some file-management issues that go hand-in-hand with digital video work. Aside from the considerable space they can take up on your hard drive, digital videos are the most fun and the least hassle if you have efficient ways to create, organize, and download them. The good news is that digital videos aren't yet as common as digital audio files; most people won't need an overly complicated method. But if you do intend to create your own movies, plan ahead and decide on some sort of directory structure that's logical and easy to navigate.

Tip

I suggest separate folders under My Videos for each of your Windows Movie Maker projects—and maybe one folder for downloaded videos.

Power User

As with My Music and My Pictures, the location of the My Videos folder can be moved with a little Registry spelunking. As described in Chapter 6, the Registry Editor (or `regedit.exe` as it's known in code) isn't exactly a friendly little program, but it gets the job done. To change the location of the My Videos folder, for example, you navigate to the following key and change its value to a new location:

```
HKEY_CURRENT_USER\Software\Microsoft\Windows\
CurrentVersion\Explorer\Shell Folders\My Videos
```

You have to reboot before this new setting can take effect.

Watching Movies with WMPXP

To watch a movie in Windows XP, you use Windows Media Player for Windows XP. This player supports a number of video types, including digital movies in a variety of formats, DVD movies, and the streaming movies delivered over the Internet.

Playing digital movies

If you followed the steps in the previous section to display the My Videos folder, you have a sample digital movie called *Windows Movie Maker Sample File* that you can experiment with. To play this movie, simply double-click it. Doing so launches WMPXP, as shown in Figure 9-2, which then begins playing the video. It's a typical (if low-quality) home movie.

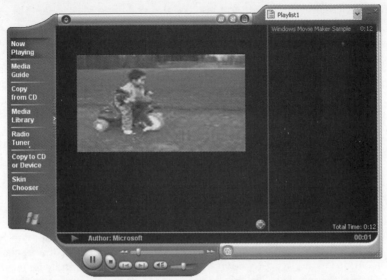

Figure 9-2: Windows XP includes a sample home movie, which you can view in Windows Media Player for Windows XP.

WMPXP can play a number of digital movie types. These include Windows Media video files (file type .WMV), .AVI files (Microsoft refers to these generically as video files), .MPEG- format movie files (.MPEG, .MPG, .MPE, .M1V, .MP2V), and Indeo video files (.IVF).

Power User   What Windows Media Player for Windows XP cannot play, sadly, are movies formatted in RealVideo or Apple QuickTime formats. To play movies of these types— still a requirement for any connected user—you must download and install the RealPlayer and QuickTime player, respectively.

You can configure Windows Media Player for Windows XP to play movies with specific file types by choosing Tools ➪ Options ➪ File Types, as shown in Figure 9-3.

In general, it's a good idea to simply click Select All and let the media player do it all. The Performance tab is also of interest. This tab includes a *Video acceleration* slider and an Advanced button, which launches the Video Acceleration Settings dialog box shown in Figure 9-4.

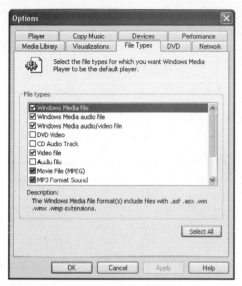

Figure 9-3: Use the File Types tab in the Media Player Options dialog box to specify the media types you want the player to handle.

How you configure this feature depends on your CPU and 3D accelerator video card. If you've got something fairly modern, I recommend enabling all the options on the Video Acceleration Settings dialog box. If you notice any problems with video playback, you might have overestimated the capabilities of your system. In this case, click Restore Defaults or adjust the settings.

Working with DVD movies

Brand new to Windows Media Player for Windows XP is its DVD-playback capability (even though the Windows XP implementation leaves much to be desired). To use it, of course, you need a DVD-ROM (or DVD-RAM) drive. Not so obviously, you need a hardware or software-based *DVD decoder,* a program that decodes the DVD data and converts it into something the computer understands. Oddly, Microsoft doesn't include this crucial bit of software in Windows XP. But depending on how you acquired Windows XP, you may still have DVD-playback capability. At the very least, it's not a difficult feature to add.

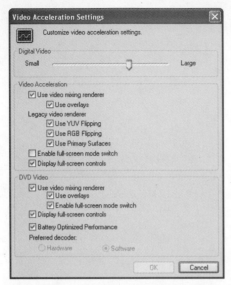

Figure 9-4: You can customize advanced
video options, such as the default size of
the video (and various hardware capabilities),
in Windows Media Player for Windows XP.

Most people obtain Windows with a new PC — and if you got Windows XP with a
new DVD-equipped PC from Dell, IBM, Compaq, or some other major PC maker, then
the required decoder is included right in the box. (It's just one of the many intangi-
ble benefits of going with the big guys.) But maybe you bought Windows XP in a
box at your local Best Buy, CompUSA, or equivalent. In this case, you have to install
your own DVD decoder. This is explained in the next section.

So how do you find out if you need this decoder? Well, if you don't have a DVD
decoder, you won't see any of the DVD options in WMPXP. Of course, even if you do
have the decoder, it's hard to find these options, which are curiously buried in the
UI. The first place to look is the Play menu. If you see a *DVD or CD Audio* entry, then
DVD playback is all set. The other place to look is the Options dialog box (click
Tools ➪ Options), where you should see a DVD tab, as shown in Figure 9-5. If you
don't see this tab, you have to install a DVD decoder on your system.

Installing a compatible DVD decoder

When DVDs first began appearing, PC video cards were fairly underpowered, so a
hardware approach to DVD decoding was used. These days, most people have fairly
powerful video cards, however, and software decoders are far more common
(they're much cheaper than hardware solutions as well.) If you want to add DVD
playback to your Windows XP, you probably need to purchase a commercial DVD
decoder. (If any freeware, shareware or downloadable DVD decoders become available for Windows XP, I will provide information on this book's Web site.)

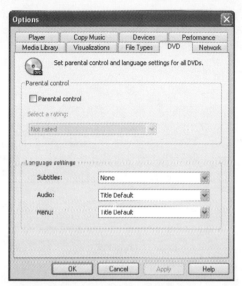

Figure 9-5: DVD options, such as parental control and subtitles, are customized from the DVD tab in the Media Player Options dialog box.

Presently the following DVD decoders are known to be compatible with Windows XP:

✦ National Mediamatics DVD player—www.national.com/appinfo/dvd/

✦ Zoran SoftDVD—www.zoran.com/

✦ MGI SoftDVD Max—www.mgisoft.com/video/dvdmax/

✦ CineMaster 98 and Software CineMaster 98—www.qi.com/

✦ Intervideo WinDVD—www.intervideo.com

✦ Cyberlink DVD—www.cyberlink-usa.com/english/products/powerdvd/powerdvd.asp

These products are available at computer superstores and consumer electronics chains, as well as major online e-tailers. Each of these products is actually a DVD player itself, but the crucial bit you need to play DVD movies in Windows Media Player for Windows XP—the DVD decoder—is installed as part of each application. When you've installed one of these applications, reboot and you can play DVD movies in WMPXP.

There's another option as well. As Windows XP was nearing completion, Microsoft announced that it would offer three *DVD Decoder Packs* for download from its Web site. The DVD Decoder Packs (including DVD technology from CyberLink, InterVideo, and Ravisent) are not free, but they let you add DVD playback to Windows XP without incurring the overhead of a full DVD application install. Check the Web site for this book (www.xpdigitalmedia.com) for more information.

Tip   For the best experience, be sure to open Windows Media Player for Windows XP, choose Tools ➪ Options ➪ File Types, and verify that the DVD option is checked. This causes the media player to auto-play DVD movies when they are inserted in the PC.

Playing DVD movies

If you've configured WMPXP to be the default DVD player, then this application starts automatically when you insert a DVD movie. Otherwise, you can manually start the media player and choose Play ➪ DVD ➪ Audio CD to start the DVD movie. Likewise, you can choose a movie from the *playlist* (a drop-down list in the top right of the player window), as shown in Figure 9-6. However you do it, you should see Hollywood's latest masterpiece begin playing back on the small screen.

Figure 9-6: DVDs should auto-play when inserted, but you can also choose them from the playlist in Windows Media Player for Windows XP.

If you have an Internet connection, WMPXP automatically detects the DVD you're playing and displays information about that movie. (More about this feature in a later section, "Getting DVD Information.")

For simple playback, the main player controls are Play/Pause, Stop, Previous, and Next work. You can use the mouse cursor to select on-screen menu items (Figure 9-7), as you would normally use a DVD remote control if you were playing the movie on your TV set.

Figure 9-7: DVD menus can be controlled with the mouse cursor.

Tip

Watching a DVD movie is one of those rare occasions where you're going to want to sit in front of your computer, doing absolutely nothing, for a few hours, but you don't want power management or a screensaver to kick in. Fortunately, power management is smart enough to stay off while you're watching a movie. But if you are using a screensaver, Windows Media Player for Windows XP gives you the option of disabling it during movie playback. Choose Tools ➪ Options ➪ Player and uncheck the option labeled *Allow screensaver during playback*. (This option is grayed out if you are not using a screensaver, which is a nice touch.)

Using full-screen mode

Of course, if you *really* want to make your cabinmates jealous on that next cross-country flight, then play the movie back *full-screen,* as shown in Figure 9-8 This is accomplished by choosing View ➪ Full Screen (keyboard mavens can press Alt + Enter).

In full-screen mode, a few controls appear briefly on-screen before fading away elegantly (Figure 9-9), along with the mouse cursor. These include a status bar along the top of the screen that includes information about the movie, a Playlist toggle button, and a button that causes the movie to return to normal Full view. On the bottom of the screen, you see the standard WMPXP play controls, with buttons for Play/Pause, Stop, Previous, Next, and Mute/Sound, along with sliders for Volume and Rewind/Fast Forward/Seek.

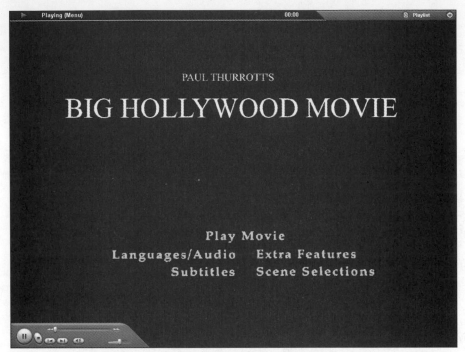

Figure 9-8: DVD playback really shines in full-screen mode, which gives you the biggest possible picture with a minimum of controls.

The on-screen controls disappear if you don't move the mouse or hit a key for a few seconds. They reappear when you do either.

Controlling DVD movie playback

In addition to the basic player controls, which are available in both full screen and Full Mode, Windows Media Player for Windows XP includes some DVD-specific controls. As with many DVD features, these are (unfortunately) hidden pretty well and it's unlikely you'd even run into them during casual use of the player. Even more exasperating, they're not exactly state-of-the-art. Just about every other DVD-player software I've tried offers more elegant controls than those in WMPXP.

To display the DVD controls, choose View ⇨ Now Playing Tools. If Show Equalizer and Settings is not selected, select it now. A new pane appears in Windows Media Player for Windows XP, below the location where movies play, as shown in Figure 9-10.

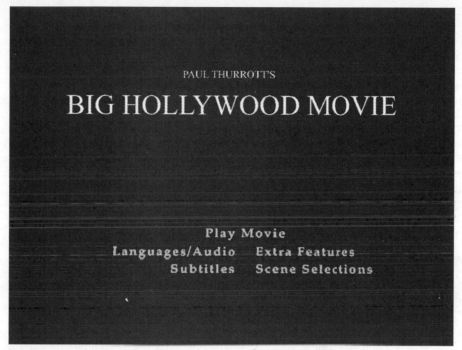

Figure 9-9: In Full mode, the controls and mouse cursor disappear in a few seconds so you can focus on the movie.

Figure 9-10: DVD controls can be displayed to give better control over the movie playback.

Click the Select View button (or choose View ➪ Now Playing Tools) and then select DVD Controls. The DVD controls appear — a *variable play speed* slider and a Next Frame button. The slider lets you play the DVD normally, fast-forward, or rewind in normal increments using the Fast Forward and Rewind buttons. But you can also use the slider to fast-forward or rewind at varying speeds, or play in slow motion or fast motion.

The slider is hard to use, and you have to be very precise to make it work correctly. Here's how it works. The center of the slider is 0 and when the slider is in this position, the movie isn't playing, but is paused. If you move the slider to the right of this mark, it plays in the correct sequence. When the slider is over the Play button, it is playing normally, at position 1. If the slider is between 0 and 1, it is playing forward in slow motion. Drag it so it is over the Fast Forward button, and it is playing at twice the normal speed, or 2. Dragging it further to the right increases the speed.

The reverse is also true: If you drag the slider to the left of 0, it plays the movie in reverse at various speeds. And as you might expect, the farther left you move the slider, the faster it plays in reverse.

If you want to still-frame through a movie, or advance the playback one frame at a time, you can use the Next Frame button. Each time you click this button, the movie advances one frame. Click Play to return to normal play mode.

Changing DVD viewing options

Many DVD movies support a wide range of special viewing options, such as closed captioning, subtitles, various language options, and even camera angles. WMPXP lets you control how you work with thee features. You configure all these options from the DVD tab of the media player's Options dialog box.

To turn on closed captioning, which presents English textual explanations of words spoken by narrators and characters in a movie, choose Closed Captions from the Subtitles drop-down list box in the Language settings section, as shown in Figure 9-11.

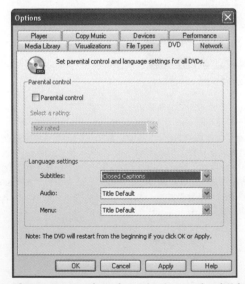

Figure 9-11: Closed captioning and subtitle languages can be chosen in DVD options.

To choose a subtitle, which provides information similar to that in closed captioning, but in a variety of languages. As you can see in Figure 9-12, Windows Media Player for Windows XP supports a wide number of languages. Not all these options are available with every DVD, however. Indeed, many DVD movies do not support subtitles at all.

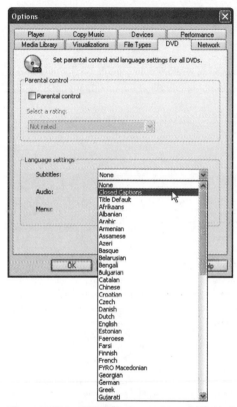

Figure 9-12: WMPXP supports a variety of subtitle languages, but they must be supported by the current DVD as well.

As with subtitles, many DVDs support multiple languages for speech and soundtracks. You can choose a language from the Audio drop-down list box to hear supported DVD movies in that language, as seen in Figure 9-13. And (as with subtitles) this feature isn't supported on all movies. A menu option provides the same functionality for a DVD's on-screen menus.

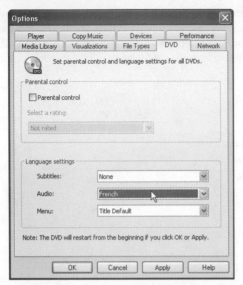

Figure 9-13: Numerous languages are available for the default audio playback as well.

For adults only? Changing the camera angle

A small number of DVD movies — primarily in the "adult entertainment" category — support various camera angles so you can watch the same scene from various angles. Choose View ➪ DVD Features ➪ Camera Angle and specify the camera angle. (The vast majority of DVD movies do *not* support this feature.)

Getting DVD information

When you first insert a DVD, Windows Media Player for Windows XP gathers information about that movie, such as DVD name, director, title names, and chapter names (This requires an Internet connection). Some of this information is auto-populated in the playlist and window title (if present). To view more information about the current movie, choose View ➪ Now Playing Tools then Media Information. As shown in Figure 9-14, information about the current movie now appears in the Now Playing Tools pane, below the movie playback.

Figure 9-14: DVD information can be displayed in the Now Playing Tools area is desired.

If the playlist isn't visible, display the playlist (View ⇨ Now Playing Tools ⇨ Show Playlist) and you see the DVD titles and chapters, as shown in Figure 9-15. You can easily navigate to any portion of the current movie by choosing a title or chapter, rather than having to navigate through the DVD's own menu.

Figure 9-15: When a DVD is played, the Media Player playlist adapts to display DVD titles and chapters.

Curiously, you can rename DVD titles and chapters, though this information is only stored locally and is easily overwritten. To rename a title or chapter name, right-click in the playlist and choose Edit. As shown in Figure 9-16, you can now enter a new name.

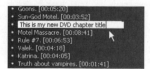

Figure 9-16: You can rename individual DVD chapters if you're so inclined.

You might want to use this feature to create a bookmark so when you have to turn off the DVD for some reason, you can come back to the same point later on. To overwrite the custom title or chapter information you've created, choose View ⇨ DVD Features ⇨ Update DVD Information. This causes WMPXP to go regather the information about the DVD from the Internet.

Capturing a still image from a DVD

If you're interested in capturing a still-frame image from a DVD movie, choose View ➪ DVD Features ➪ Capture Image. This triggers the Save As dialog box (shown in Figure 9-17), which lets you name the image, choose its destination, and specify file type. This option doesn't seem to work on every system — whether the problem stems from particular DVD decoders or specific video hardware is unknown.

Figure 9-17: To save a still frame from the currently playing video, type Ctrl+I.

Configuring DVD options

In addition to all the cool (but well-hidden) playback controls, Windows Media Player for Windows XP also offers a number of other useful options relating to DVD playback. For example, you can set parental controls so certain types of movies cannot be accessed without first entering an administrative account user name and password, which is perfect for that shared family PC. To do so, select Tools ➪ Options ➪ DVD. From the Select a Rating drop-down list box, choose the lowest Motion Picture Association of America (MPAA) rating, such as G, PG, PG-13, R, or NC-17 that triggers the logon requirement. Therefore, if you'd like to restrict PG-13, R, and NC-17 movies, choose PG, as shown in Figure 9-18.

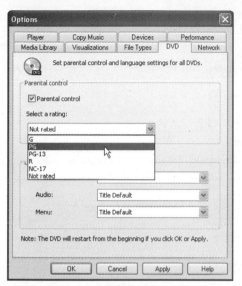

Figure 9-18: If you'd like to prevent your children from viewing inappropriate movies, you can select an MPAA rating.

Unfortunately, some "must-have" DVD options are *not* included in WMPXP. Most glaringly, you *cannot* determine the brightness or contrast of the video being played back, which is crucial, as many DVD decoders appear rather dark by default. Fortunately, you can fix this by going into the DVD decoder-enabled application that was installed to provide DVD playback and adjust these other options there. The results change in Windows Media Player for Windows XP as well. But if you purchased a DVD Decoder Pack, you're basically stuck with the brightness level as is.

Viewing streaming videos

In addition to playing back file-based videos and DVD movies, it's also possible to play streaming videos over the Internet. *Streaming videos* are videos played over a network connection (for example, to the Internet) without ever actually downloading the video to the local PC. And these days, various small video clips are quite common on sites like WindowsMedia.com, MSNBC.com, and others. In fact, many Web sites such as FilmSpeed.com, SightSound.com, and others are now offering full-length feature films for viewing in Windows Media Video format. What a world.

In general, there isn't much to worry about with regards to streaming videos. When you click a hyperlink in Internet Explorer that links to a streaming video, WMPXP starts automatically, caching a certain amount of content to ensure decent playback quality; then the video begins to play. You can play, pause, stop, rewind, and fast forward streaming videos just as you can with file-based video.

To get information about the quality of the connection to the streaming video, choose View ⇨ Statistics, as shown in Figure 9-19.

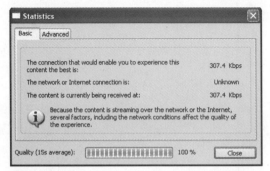

Figure 9-19: During streaming video playback, you can view statistics about the connection you have with the server.

Sharing Videos with Other Users

If you're creating home movies like the ones we discuss in Chapter 11, you're probably going to want to share them with others. This can take various forms: You might set up a home media server, so you can allow others on your home network to view the movies you've created. And though the My Videos folder doesn't have a "Shared Videos" compatriot like My Pictures and My Music, it's possible to create one or share your current My Videos folder on a network if you'd like.

Sharing videos on the Internet is becoming increasingly popular as well. Chapter 11 delves into that topic as it demonstrates the use of Windows Movie Maker to create, edit, and publish home movies.

✦   ✦   ✦

Raw Footage: Taking Home Movies

Before getting into Windows Movie Maker — the Windows XP tool that makes it easy to capture, edit, and share digital movies (as outlined in Chapter 11) — this chapter tackles taking some video footage with a camcorder.

Granted, we can't all expect to be the next George Lucas. But it's reasonable to want to understand the issues that affect the final quality of your home movies. This chapter examines what you can do, ahead of time, to ensure the highest possible quality for your finished movies.

These issues begin at your choice of video camera: These days, digital video cameras are cheap, and if possible, you're going to want to go with one of the newer, smaller units. But many people are going to have to make do with existing (or cheaper) analog units for various reasons, and your; choice of video source will likely involve various tradeoffs.

After you've chosen a camera, the next step is (you guessed it) taking movies. The best idea is simply shoot video, shoot more video, and then shoot even more video. The nice thing about digital video editing, of course, is that you can cut and paste later on as needed. But it's always a good idea to ensure that your original source video is as good as possible; attention to some basic issues when you actually shoot your video can help.

Understanding Home Video

Video shot with a camcorder falls into one of two categories, *analog* or *digital*. Analog video is delivered using a constantly changing electrical signal. The most common example is a standard U.S. TV set. The signal varies constantly and can be adjusted in small increments; when such a signal is lost, you see "snow". Digital signals, however, are encoded in a binary format where each bit of information is represented as a one or a zero. Digital signals aren't as inherently superior to analog signals as you might expect, but we are definitely moving toward an all-digital future as far as video is concerned. In any event, each type of video has its own pluses and minuses.

Most analog video is really *composite* video, which carries the information for video color, image, blanking, and synchronization on a single wire. Typically, composite video is transferred from device to device through a composite video, or RCA-style video connection like the ones you've probably seen on your stereo system. For great distances, coaxial cable—like that found on your cable TV system—is used because it offers little quality degradation over distances. A higher-end form of analog video, called S-video or Y/C signal (so named because the color and brightness information are transmitted on separate wires), generally offers better clarity and resolution. For this reason, high-end TV sets and DVD players often offer S-video inputs.

Analog video, in the United States at least, has a resolution of roughly 525×525. I say roughly, because it's analog, and nothing is ever exact with analog: The perceived resolution varies dramatically according to the reception, the physical connection, and the implementation (VHS video, for example, offers only 250 lines of resolution, while S-video bumps this figure up to about 425).

Digital video, meanwhile, does not offer the variable signal range we experience with analog video. Instead, various bit patterns are encoded in a video stream to represent colors and other information and the resolutions are exact and tend to be higher and more in line with what we're used to on PCs. Nevertheless, digital signals are far more susceptible to electrical interference, and therefore require specially shielded cables. A digital signal is either there or it isn't: It can't come in partially.

What you get with digital video, of course, is clarity. Digital signals tend to be cleaner, and transmit better over long distances. This is because digital data is encoded to know how it should output, resulting in no loss in quality. Analog signals, meanwhile, can only be amplified over distances—a bad signal amplified is still a bad signal.

The primary advantage of a digital video signal is that it doesn't degrade. You can copy digital signals from medium to medium as often as you like—to the limitations of the physical media—and *never* lose any quality. As anyone who's duplicated VHS tapes knows, this is not true of analog video. Each generation of analog video loses quality, often dramatically.

For this reason, I advise sticking with digital video for your home movies, unless you already own an analog camcorder with which you're satisfied. Just remember to archive your analog video digitally as soon as possible to preserve it. The next section looks at some technology choices in the camcorder market.

Choosing a Camcorder

Just as video formats fall into two basic categories, so do camcorders. Today, there is an amazing selection of fairly inexpensive analog and digital video camcorders for the picking. (I do, however, expect the analog market to dry up over the next few years).

Analog camcorders

Analog video is divided into a number of contenders, including VHS, VHS-C, S-VHS, 8mm, and Hi-8. This section takes a quick look at each format.

VHS

VHS is the venerable format we all love to hate, the hardware that plays those hundreds of thousands of video tapes that are clogging Blockbusters from Maine to Los Angeles. VHS camcorders are big and bulky like their living room counterparts, and it's unlikely you've seen one of these dinosaurs since the early 1980's, if only because their humongous size makes them an unwelcome guest on family vacations.

VHS format video offers about 250 lines of resolution, which is pretty low quality by any measure. So I recommend steering clear of this kind of camcorder because of this and because they are just too bulky to be desirable these days. (Despite the fact that you can pop tapes from one into just about any video player in America without the need for an adapter or complicated wire connection).

VHS-C

To solve the size and weight problems of VHS camcorders, the VHS-C ("compact") format was invented. VHS-C cassettes are about half the size of a standard VHS tape, and can be played in a VHS player using a converter cassette. VHS-C isn't as convenient as standard VHS ("where's that converter again?"), and it comes with all the same limits on resolution and quality that you get with VHS.

Like VHS, VHS-C offers only 250 lines of resolution. Ten years ago, VHS-C was a great option. Today, you can do much better.

S-VHS

Super VHS (or S-VHS) was designed to overcome the quality limitations of standard VHS format, but it does so with a cassette that is exactly the same size as VHS. S-VHS camcorders are actually very rare, so it's mentioned here just in case you've had a confirmed sighting of one. (On a technical note, S-VHS offers 400 lines of resolution, which is as high as you can get with semiportable analog video.)

8mm

An eight-millimeter cassette format, adroitly named *8mm format*, appeared in the early 1990s to combat the size issues of VHS camcorders. 8mm cassettes are small, and inexpensive, and camcorders based on this format are widely available at consumer electronics stores. Because 8mm offers 300 lines of resolution, the resulting quality is a bit better than VHS. The problem, of course, is that 8mm cassettes won't play in standard VHS players. So 8mm camcorder owners will need to copy their home videos to VHS or perhaps recordable DVD or hook the camcorder directly to the TV to view their movies on the television.

8mm video quality is roughly identical to that of VHS — it isn't that great. I recommend skipping out on this format.

Hi-8

A higher-quality version of 8mm, called Hi-8 offers compatibility with 8mm tapes, while offering higher-resolution video (about 400 lines) that doesn't degrade across duplications. Hi-8 camcorders can play and utilize 8mm cassettes as well as higher-quality Hi-8 tapes.

Of all the analog video formats, Hi-8 is the best for camcorder use: It's portable and small, and offers S-VHS quality.

Digital camcorders

With the wide variety of analog video camcorders available at bargain basement prices (well, except for S-VHS, which never really hit the mass market), you might wonder why you have to look any farther. When you move up to digital video, however, you open a wide new range of capabilities and features.

Digital video formats tend to be much smaller than most analog cassettes; the camcorders that use these formats are much smaller as well. More importantly, digital video offers higher-resolution video: up to 500 lines of resolution, compared to the 250 to 400 you get with analog.

Digital-video camcorders also offer higher-quality audio capabilities (though it's unlikely that a typical camcorder's built-in microphone can take advantage of it). Of course, many digital camcorders (even low-end consumer units) do support higher-quality external microphones as well.

Digital video has an especially alluring advantage: It won't degrade over time or in later-generation duplications, or cause snowy artifacts when you rerecord over a used cassette, or lose quality when transferred from medium to medium (assuming you're using a digital cable like FireWire—about which more in a minute—to do the job).

And digital camcorders have come down in price. For the foreseeable future, today's generation of digital camcorders is hard to beat.

Consumer-grade digital camcorders ship in two major formats, Digital 8 and Min-DV (Digital Video).

Digital 8 format

To maintain backwards compatibility with the popular 8mm and Hi-8 formats, Sony introduced a digital format called Digital 8, which uses cheap 8mm and Hi-8 cassettes. The nice thing about Digital 8 is that these camcorders can be used to play back analog 8mm and Hi-8 cassettes, crucial if you're upgrading and have a library of tapes. But if you're starting fresh, I recommend staying away from Digital 8. Camcorders based on this format tend to be bigger than comparable Mini-DV units (see below).

Another limitation of Digital 8 is that recording is generally limited to one hour per tape, compared to two hours for 8mm and Hi-8. This is because of the way digital video is encoded on the tape. Digital 8 video offers 500 lines of horizontal resolution.

Miniature digital video format

The preferable mainstream digital video format these days is Miniature Digital Video (Mini-DV). Mini-DV cassettes are the smallest of any camcorder format, analog or digital, and the format offers the highest resolution, about 500 lines.

If you are starting fresh, I strongly recommend going with Mini-DV format.

Buying a camcorder

So you're ready to buy a camcorder. Aside from video format (see the previous section), you have a number of other options to consider; this section looks at each one.

LCD viewfinder

You've seen them at Disney World and the kids' Little League games. Today's camcorders generally offer a flip-out, side-mounted LCD viewfinder (in addition to the standard body-mounted viewfinder that requires you to put the camera up to your eye when you shoot video). Side-mounted LCDs allow you to hold the camera away from your body and observe your surroundings in a manner that may actually prevent you from taking that Chevy Chase-style pratfall into a lake or an unsuspecting bystander.

An LCD is also handy when you want to watch the video you've shot while you're still "in the wild." You can pop open the screen, place the camcorder in player mode, and gather around with your closest friends to relive the day's events on the small screen.

On the downside, LCD viewfinders tend to drain battery life more quickly; they need power to generate the display. It bears repeating: Be sure to pack a few extra batteries, especially if you're going to use this feature.

Battery readouts

Speaking of which: An accurate readout of the remaining battery life is crucial: there's nothing like running out of power during the 8th inning of your son's big game. For this reason, you should hunt down a camcorder that offers an accurate display of this, preferably right on the LCD panel you'll want to be using. Oh, and buy a few extra batteries, regardless of how accurate the display is.

Inputs: FireWire, composite, and S-Video, oh my

Digital camcorders should offer, at minimum, a *FireWire*, or *IEEE-1394* (or, in Sony-speak, *iLink*) connection, which is how you connect the camcorder to your computer. FireWire is a standard, high-speed connection type that first became popular on Macintosh computers but is increasingly common on Windows-based PCs as well. If you don't have a FireWire connection on your PC, you can (and should) buy a FireWire add-on card, which adds this capability to your system; these cards generally cost $30-50 and are fairly easy to install.

It's possible to copy video from a digital camcorder to your PC using other connections, such as an analog USB-based dongle, or a dedicated capture card, both of which typically offer analog, RCA-style connections. But these solutions are limited in various ways: USB can input video at 320×240 resolution maximum, far below even standard VHS quality. And even a dedicated capture card records video in analog format, resulting in some quality loss. To achieve the highest-quality recordings, you really should go with FireWire.

That said, many digital camcorders do offer a variety of analog outputs as well, and if nothing else, this is useful for connecting the camcorder to your TV so you can watch raw footage on the big screen. So look for both composite (RCA-style) and S-video outputs in addition to FireWire.

Image stabilization

Even if your grip is as steady as Gibraltar, it's a good idea to seek out a camcorder with digital image stabilization. This compensates for even small camera shakes by proactively recording an area around the main subject area and filling in the details when needed. The end result is a cleaner, stiller image. In my case—just call me Mr. Shaky Hands—this has been a lifesaver.

Zoom capabilities

As with any consumer electronics product, the typical camcorder maker tries to wow potential customers with a slew of technical-sounding facts and figures. The zoom feature is one such item: *40X! 200X!* the ads scream. But what does it all mean? Well, the figure before the times symbol (the "X") reflects the number of times the camcorder can magnify its display. But you actually have two numbers to worry about here. The smaller figure (40 in my example) refers to the optical zoom, which reflects the physical capabilities of the camera. The higher number (200) refers to the *digital zoom*, which is a software feature that takes the optical zoom, pixelizes it, and enlarges the individual pixels. The end results are actually pretty impressive, given the limitations of what's really happening, but don't base your buying decision on this feature.

In fact, it's a good idea to slowly zoom in on a far away subject with both optical and digital zoom, and then compare the resulting videos. You may end up foregoing digital zoom altogether. Regardless, it is the optical zoom that truly determines the capabilities of the camcorder, not the digital zoom.

Special effects

These days, many digital camcorders offer a slew of special effects so you can add titles, fades, and some fairly bizarre effects like pixelizations and negatives. Why anyone would want this sort of thing is somewhat beyond me, as anyone who would want to add these features should be using a dedicated video-editing software package on a computer (for example, Windows Movie Maker).

You should not purchase a camcorder based on its special effects features. It's better to use the camcorder solely for recording raw video and then add the special effects after you've gotten the video onto your PC. Besides, you're going to want to trim the video down, and you can't do that easily with a single camcorder.

Remote control

Many digital (and analog) camcorders come with a remote control because users want to use the camcorder as a video player when sending output to a TV set. This is actually a handy feature, but you won't need such a thing when interacting with Movie Maker, as this software contains built-in controls for controlling a digital camcorder. But if you plan to watch a lot of camcorder video directly on the TV, a remote is almost necessary.

Still camera capabilities and media

I purchased a Canon XR-25 digital video camera in Spring 2001 and was amused to see that it contained a Secure Digital (SD) memory card, so I could use the camcorder as a still camera, and record still images onto the tiny media card. Some cameras offer this capability without an external media, however, allowing you to capture still images right on the videotape.

The results are mixed: Compared to 2 Mega Pixel (and higher) digital cameras, the quality of image you get from a camcorder is pretty poor. So while it's a nice thought, I can't recommend using a camcorder in this way unless you're unconcerned about the low quality. If a day's experimentation is any indication, I will probably never use this feature in my own camera. But if you think you would want such a thing, several models exist and more are on the way.

Brands

The final choice concerns the brand of camera you buy. As mentioned previously, I'm using a Canon Mini-DV model, and I've been happy with the results. But JVC, Panasonic, Sharp, Sony, and other companies offer a variety of Mini-DV and Digital 8 products that are worth looking at. I recommend investigating the current state of the art in *Consumer Reports* magazine or the ZDNET/CNET Web sites, which are updated more frequently. The Web properties in particular seem to be more taken with fairly useless gee-whiz features, but they are more likely to have had recent experience with modern equipment.

On a related note, I recommend buying a digital camcorder locally, if possible, rather than on the Web. These devices are expensive and delicate, and it's nice to have a local place to turn to for repairs and returns, if necessary.

As always, *caveat emptor*.

Taking Home Movies — Some Basics

Once you get the camcorder home, it's time to get the battery charged and start shooting some video. While you're waiting for the batteries (you did buy extras, right?) to get up to speed, take some time to review the manual that came with your camcorder. Unlike PCs and software these days, most of these devices come with a pretty thick book. Read it. Know it. Do your best to love it.

Now have some fun with it.

Video recording basics

Before committing an important personal event to tape, spend some time getting to know the camera. Take at least an hour's worth of meaningless video, such as a family day at the park or your child riding a bike (in retrospect, you might later find that such video is far more compelling in the future than the family trip to the giant theme park). You're going to eat up an entire tape and make a bunch of mistakes. Go ahead, it's fun. Besides, you can later edit out the mistakes in Movie Maker and turn 60 minutes of amateur video into a 3 minute tour-de-force. It could happen.

Get a feel for how your camera frames the scene: Does the recorded video seem to encompass the entire area seen through the viewfinder during shooting? How does your shaking hand affect the completed video? Do you have image stabilization turned on? Compare video shot with and without this feature.

The idea here is to shoot, shoot, and shoot some more. Move the camera quickly around a scene, then slowly. Learn what looks (and sounds) good and what doesn't.

Avoid using built-in camcorder features

As discussed previously, many camcorders offer a number of extra features, like special effects, that (by and large) you should avoid. Experiment with them to find out why if you must. But remember: All these features can be implemented through software (better, for that matter) when you import the raw video onto the computer. Let the camera do what it's good at — shooting video — and leave the editing feature to Windows Movie Maker (to find out how, see Chapter 11).

Zoom and pan issues

Optical and digital zoom (mentioned earlier in the section on camcorder features) bears a repeat visit here: Experiment with digital zoom to see whether it's something you want or need. If not, don't be afraid to turn it off; sometimes a feature is added simply because it's possible, and not necessarily because it's useful (think of "Clippy," the animated Microsoft Office Assistant, if you're unclear on this point).

Likewise, you may find that certain camera movements cause the camera to lose focus, blurring the image: Moving the camera quickly from side to side (or *panning* in AV speak) is such a movement. Play around with the camera to see how fast you can move it without blurring the image; then work to ensure that you never exceed this speed when you shoot video.

Go Forth and Shoot Video

Granted, an in-depth explanation of all the issues you're likely to face while making home movies could easily fill (and has filled) entire books. And of course, I'm still learning myself: Unlike point-and-click digital cameras and audio CDs, digital video is still a process that many people have not yet mastered. But it's a learning process and fun; when all else fails, just enjoy it.

But be mindful of the technology and spend time with your computer and camera. For many people, the computer offers a chance at digitally and permanently archiving their memories, a powerful and responsible goal. At the very least, ensure that you are doing so at the highest possible quality, with the best current tools, using the most stable medium presently available. The next chapter looks at one of those tools, a freebie that comes in Windows XP — Windows Movie Maker. It's not the end-all-be-all video-editing suite (you may not be looking for that anyway). But experience with Windows Movie Maker teaches you whether you want to take this hobby to the next level and work with digital video in a more "professional" manner. Who could ask more of an integrated OS technology?

✦   ✦   ✦

Creating Digital Videos with Windows Movie Maker

CHAPTER

11

◆ ◆ ◆ ◆

In This Chapter

Assessing your system needs for digital video

Getting around the Windows XP Movie Maker interface

Comparing digital and analog video

Creating and editing your first digital movie

◆ ◆ ◆ ◆

Every digital media task you attempt with Windows XP comes up against some barrier to entry. The stumbling block can take many forms — difficult technology with obscure purposes, dense technical lingo, myriad of hardware requirements, or other big helpings of information to digest before you can make the most of the features.

For video work, this rule of thumb is doubly true. Creating and editing digital video raises familiar issues — for instance, the tradeoff between file size and image quality. But creating good digital video is far more difficult than ripping a CD or acquiring images from a digital camera; there's just more to learn and master. Digital video work is often more expensive than any other digital-media technology. In addition to an analog or digital video camera (as discussed in Chapter 10), or some other video source, you need some sort of hardware interface to give you control of that video source — and copious amounts of hard drive space, RAM, and CPU power — if you intend to work effectively with video.

The good news is that the software side of digital video is handled with a feature called Windows Movie Maker, which is included in Windows XP. Windows Movie Maker is a fairly simplistic program, but don't look at that as a limitation. Instead, think of Movie Maker as the perfect way to get started with digital videos. If you find yourself wanting more, there are plenty of options out there. But for now, let's focus on the basics and see what you can do in Windows XP, right out of the box.

Introducing Windows Movie Maker

Despite its name, Windows Movie Maker is an application that can record audio and/or video data from a hardware source such as a camcorder, Digital Video (DV) Camera, VCR, or even an audio CD player, and store that data in digital form on your computer. (Microsoft should have called it Windows Media Maker instead, since few people are aware of this program's audio capabilities.)

When you've got those digital audio and video files on your computer, you can edit them into a finished movie using Windows Movie Maker. You can then share the finished product with others via the Web and e-mail.

The original version of Windows Movie Maker debuted in Windows Millennium Edition (Me) in late 2000. The version in Windows XP includes everything from the version in Windows Me and adds new features, such as better recording quality, support for higher, DVD-quality video resolutions, a more refined user interface, and more. Because Windows Movie Maker is now running on the stable and powerful Windows XP platform, it's a much better solution for video work. Frankly, Windows Me had enough problems on many systems without trying to manipulate large videos too.

Here's an interesting problem that you probably never experienced before you began working with digital videos. The file system of the disk to which you record your videos is suddenly very important because the old FAT32 file system — from Windows 9x/Me — is limited to files no bigger than 4GB. If you want to work with large videos, you have to ensure that you're using NTFS, the native file system of Windows XP. Fortunately, it's easy to convert a FAT32 drive to NTFS, although doing so makes that drive inaccessible to Windows 9x if you're dual-booting. Open a command-line window and type **convert /?** to learn more about converting your drive to NTFS. But remember that this is a one-way conversion to NTFS — once you do the conversion, you can't go back to FAT32.

Windows Movie Maker concepts

Before getting into the specifics of Movie Maker, a review of the lingo is probably a good idea. To Movie Maker, the video and audio you record from your video source is called the *source material* — which can be a home movie stored on a digital or analog camcorder, a VHS tape, a live TV show, an audio tape, a DVD, or any other audio or video source that can be connected to the computer. (For more about these connections, see Chapter 10.)

Movie Maker records a *source file* from the video source using audio/video capture hardware, as described in the previous chapter. This file, which is stored locally on your hard drive, should be considered "raw" data because it is essentially unchanged from the original and should certainly be edited before you can be declared the next Steven Spielberg. Movie Maker lets you edit this raw source file and combine it with other source files, such as still images, music, and voice-overs, to create a finished movie. This is what you'll want to show your friends and relatives.

A Windows Movie Maker *movie* can consist of any combination of still images, audio, and video, and is stored in a Windows Media format (WMA audio or WMV video) only. Movie Maker is further limited when it comes to valid source materials that it can import. For example, Movie Maker can import MP3 audio and MPG video, in addition to its native Windows Media formats. But it cannot import QuickTime or Real Audio movies.

And when it comes to output, Movie Maker is likewise limited: It can only create movie files in Windows Media Video format. If you want to work with other video formats, such as MPEG or Quicktime, you'll need to look elsewhere. And if you want to output to video tape, you're likewise out of luck.

While using Movie Maker, you work with a variety of file types. Each movie you create is organized in the application as a Movie Maker *project* (⋋.mswmm). A Movie Maker project describes the interaction between the various source files used to create a movie. When you have completed editing your project, you save it as a stand-alone movie file (*.wmv) or audio file (*.wma) that can be viewed or heard by others with Windows Media Player. There is also a *collections* file that contains information about the clip collections you work with in WMM. Each time you import or record a video source with WMM, the resulting source file is broken down into smaller clips by default (you can turn this off if desired) and stored in named collections within your project. We'll look at this more closely later in the chapter.

But first, let's take a quick look at the Movie Maker interface and see how it all fits together.

A tour of the Windows Movie Maker interface

Windows Movie Maker is available from the Accessories portion of the Start Menu, though you might see it directly in the recently used programs list in the left half of the Start Menu when you first install Windows XP). As shown in Figure 11-1, Windows Movie Maker consists of a multi-pane window, where each section plays a crucial role in the development of your digital movies.

In this section, we'll take a quick look at each major section of the Movie Maker user interface.

Toolbars

Like most Windows applications, Windows Movie Maker includes a set of toolbars at the top of its application window which include toolbar buttons for the most often needed functions. By default, all four of the toolbars—Standard, Project, Collections, and Location—are displayed, as shown in Figure 11-2, and I recommend leaving this as-is. Unlike more complex applications such as Word or Excel, you're going to be using virtually all of Movie Maker's features.

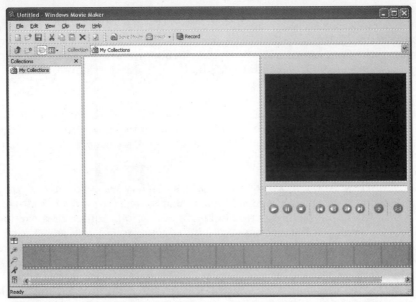

Figure 11-1: Windows Movie Maker is a one-stop shop for all your digital movie creation needs.

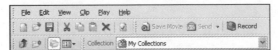

Figure 11-2: By default, all Movie Maker toolbars are displayed; you should probably leave it that way.

Collections

When you record a raw video from a video source, a new *collection* is created. This represents a data file on your hard drive in which the video (or audio) is stored. By default, each collection is broken down into *clips* during the recording process. A *clip* is a logical section of video or audio. For example, in a video, clips are created for each scene change: The number of clips you have depends on the number of scene changes in the video source, as shown in Figure 11-3.

Monitor

On the right side of the Movie Maker window is the monitor (Figure 11-4). This is used to play back video clips or an in-progress video production. The monitor area sports the standard playback controls; synchronizing its timeline with the timeline in the workspace. You can also use the monitor to play a movie full-screen or split a clip; both are described in detail later in this chapter.

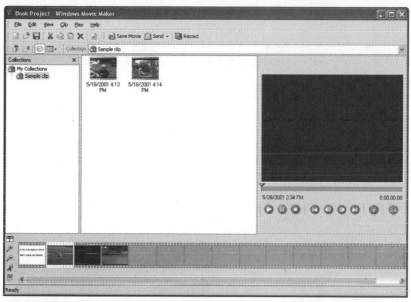

Figure 11-3: The collections area contains the collections you've created, all of which are divided into clips.

Figure 11-4: The monitor allows you to view clips, raw video footage, and your target movie, in progress.

Using the workspace

The *workspace* is where the magic happens (so to speak). You drag clips from the collections area into the workspace to visually construct a finished movie. The workspace can be viewed in *Storyboard* view (Figure 11-5), which displays each clip in the same size, or in *Timeline* view, which accurately displays the relative length of each clip, as shown in Figure 11-6. The workspace represents the *final* version of the movie you are creating.

Figure 11-5: In Storyboard view, the workspace displays each video clip in the same size.

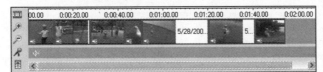

Figure 11-6: In Timeline view, each clip is shown in its relative length.

Setting default options

Before doing anything else, you may want to set up a few default options. This is done from the Movie Maker Options dialog box which, (as you may expect) is accessible by choosing Tools ⇨ Options. As shown in Figure 11-7, this simple dialog box controls a number of important settings, such as the default author name (this would be you, but it automatically uses your logon name, which is generally not what you want), whether Movie Maker automatically creates clips as raw source material, as imported (a recommended option), and so on.

For the most part, you can leave these options unchanged, though you'll want to make sure the default author is correct. The E-mail Options button determines what e-mail application is used to send e-mail movies you create in Movie Maker. The default is to use whatever e-mail application you have set to be the default for all of Windows—the one that shows up at top left in the Start Menu—but you can change it as needed.

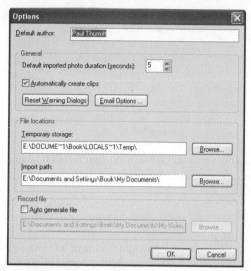

Figure 11-7: The Options dialog box allows you to determine where files are stored and search and the default name for the author of movies.

Overview of the movie making process

Okay, you've dealt with lot of jargon and have been described an application before you actually did anything with it. It's time to get down to business and make a movie, but let's take a quick look at overall steps of what we're about to do, an executive overview, if you will.

In the coming sections, you will

✦ Connect a video source of some sort to the computer.

✦ Create a new Movie Maker project.

✦ Record video footage from that video source with Movie Maker.

✦ Save the resulting file (the so-called raw footage) to a location on your hard drive. Movie Maker automatically creates a new collection that represents this footage, and it is broken down into bite-sized chunks called clips.

✦ Drag one or more clips to the workspace.

✦ Trim content from at least the beginning and end of the video contained in the workspace.

✦ Add a title graphic to the video.

✦ Add one or more transitions.

✦ Optionally add a voice-over to the video.

✦ Save the video in various formats and share the resulting files with others.

Hopefully it doesn't seem so complicated when it's described like this. But then again, you can see that creating even a simple video requires a number of steps. They become second nature after you've done them a few times. But as we discussed previously, there's just more to learn in the realm of video.

Acquiring Video Footage

The way you copy footage from your video source — called *video acquisition* — can vary somewhat depending on the type of video source you're using, analog or video. We discussed some of the differences between these formats as well as limitations and capabilities of various hardware devices that allow you to acquire video in the previous chapter. So now, we'll look at the ways in which you can acquire analog and digital video. If you're using an analog video source, the next section can get you started. Otherwise, FireWire users can skip ahead to "Acquiring Digital Video and Controlling a Digital Camera."

Using an analog video source

You can use analog video sources such as VCRs and 8mm or VHS-C camcorders with Windows Movie Maker through a video-capture device like the Belkin VideoBus II. But some digital video sources are usable in analog mode as well; they offer analog outputs like S-Video ports and RCA-style audio plugs. So depending on the video source you want to work with, an analog capture device could be crucial. And some of these devices, like the previously mentioned Belkin device, are quite cheap, letting you get started with digital video on a budget.

 Tip   The differences between analog and video sources are covered in Chapter 10.

Whatever device you choose, the basics are the same: Some video source is connected to your computer through a video capture device, which is installed and working on Windows (see the previous chapter for details). Click the Record button to bring up the Record dialog box, as shown in Figure 11-8. This dialog box controls which hardware device(s) captures video and audio together, just video, or just audio, the quality of the recording, and other options.

When recording off an analog video source, you're typically going to want to ensure that the source video and audio devices are the same; in our example, we're using *USB Video Bus II, Video* as the video source and *USB Video Bus II, Audio* as the audio source. Click the Change Device button to change a video or audio source to the correct device and, in the case of the video source, to configure certain settings as shown in Figure 11-9.

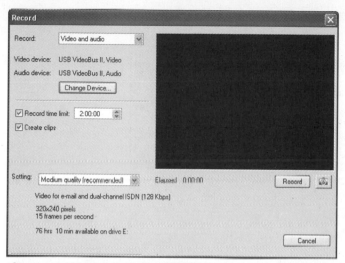

Figure 11-8: When recording video from an analog source, you are limited by the capabilities of the underlying hardware.

Figure 11-9: Available audio and video devices appear as options in the Change Device dialog box.

Once the source hardware is correctly set up to work with Movie Maker, you need to think about the quality setting you're going to use when recording the raw, unedited source material. Movie Maker supplies three preset settings, Low Quality (56 Kbps), Medium Quality (128 Kbps, Microsoft's recommended recording quality), and High Quality (256 Kbps); you can choose Other to make a second drop-down appear, as shown in Figure 11-10. This list includes a range of choices that may be somewhat limited by the source hardware. If you're using a USB-based capture device, for example, you are limited to quality settings that max out at 320x240 due to that hardware's bandwidth limitations. (IEEE 1394, also called "FireWire" and "iLink," digital camcorders, which are discussed in the next section, can record at "near-DVD-quality" at 720 × 480 resolution).

Other options in this dialog box include one that limits the recording time to a pre-set time limit, which can be useful for hands-off recording, and one that controls whether clips are created as the source media is recorded. For more home movies, clip development is desired, so you should leave this option checked.

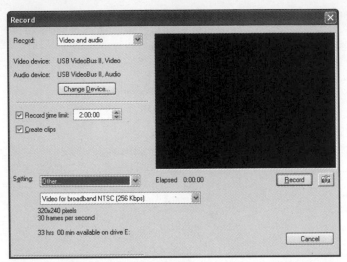

Figure 11-10: If you choose a quality setting of Other, a wider range of quality templates appear.

When you're ready to record, begin playback on the video source and click the Record button in the Record dialog box. The button changes to Stop (as shown in Figure 11-11); click it again when you're done.

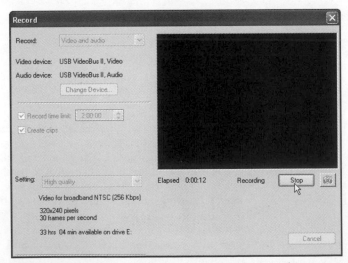

Figure 11-11: When recording, the Record button changes to Stop and a flashing Recording indicator appears.

When you're done recording, Movie Maker prompts you to save the raw footage using the Save As dialog box. Once you've given this movie a name, it creates a collection in Movie Maker with that name and generates clips, as shown in Figure 11-12.

Figure 11-12: Recorded movie is imported as a collection and divided into clips.

At this point, you're ready to begin editing. Save the Project and skip over the next section unless you're interested in the advantages of a full digital environment.

Note

The way in which Windows Movie Maker determines how to make clips depends on the video source. For analog video, scene changes and individual sessions — where the person taking the video pressed the record or stop button on the camera — are used. Microsoft calls this "automatic scene detection;" the technology was developed by the company's Research division. For digital video, only individual sessions are used because this data is more intelligently transmitted to the PC with timestamps and other information.

Acquiring digital video and controlling a digital camera

If you're fortunate to have a digital camcorder (DV or Digital8 format) and a 1394 (FireWire) connection, acquiring video in Windows Movie Maker is an even better experience. Digital camcorders are designed to be controlled by external devices and video software, and Movie Maker offers this capability.

As with an analog video capture, the first step is to turn on the camera and ensure that it is in *play (VCR)*, rather than *camera*, mode. Then, click the Record button to display the Record dialog box, which is (ideally) set to record video and audio, using your DV camera. If this isn't the case, select the camera using the Change Device button. Then, the dialog box should resemble Figure 11-13.

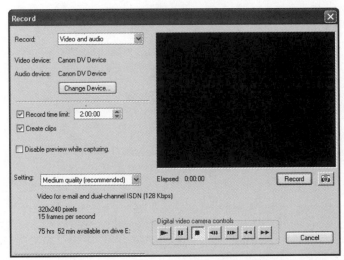

Figure 11-13: Digital video acquisition is much nicer in Movie Maker, with controls for controlling the DV camera automatically through software.

What's new here is the Digital video camera controls, which appear in blue near the bottom of the dialog box. These controls allow you to play, pause, stop, rewind, fast forward and navigate a frame at a time forward and backward without needing to use the camera's controls. And the video output is shown on the Record dialog box's preview window.

To test this, first choose a quality setting. Digital video recording allows you to get the maximum quality and resolution possible by choosing Other ⇨ DV-AVI (25 Mbps). This format is uncompressed, so it makes for massive file sizes, but if you are looking for the nicest possible video, this is the way to go.

Note   AVI files are also more compatible with third-party video applications, such as MGI VideoWave and Adobe Premiere. If this compatibility is important to you, you might consider acquiring your source video in AVI format (assuming you have the hard drive space to do so).

Once you've settled on a quality setting, you can use the digital video camera controls to control the camera. Cue up the video, as shown in Figure 11-14, until you're ready to begin recording.

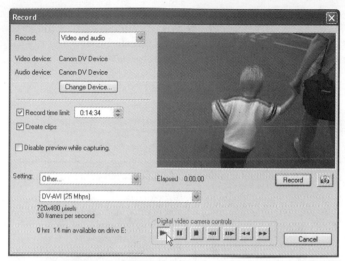

Figure 11-14: The DV camera controls work just as they do on a VCR or other video device.

When you find the spot where you'd like to begin, simply click the Record button. As shown in Figure 11-15, a small "Recording" text message blinks next to the Record button (now renamed Stop) and an elapsed-time text field appears. The digital video camera controls are grayed out and unavailable during this sequence.

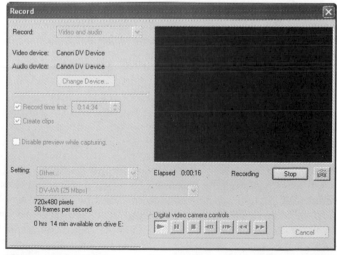

Figure 11-15: While recording, the process is similar to analog video: The DV camera controls are grayed out and you can click Stop when you're done recording.

When you're done recording, click Stop. Movie Maker will prompt you to save the raw video footage on your hard drive. Generally, you should store this file in the folder that contains the current Movie Maker project, but that's up to you. Movie Maker will generate clips as the file is saved, as shown in Figure 11-16.

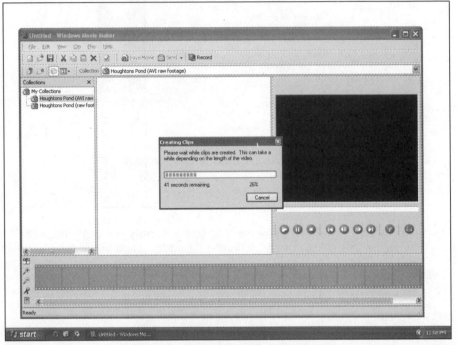

Figure 11-16: After the recording process is complete, Movie Maker will automatically generate clips of the video.

Depending on how many scene changes there are, you will see a number of clips appear in the collection section of the window, and a collection will appear under My Collections with the same name as the file you just saved (Figure 11-17). Now it's time to edit.

Note   I like to save my raw video footage with an annotation in the file name such as "raw footage" so I can more easily tell the difference between the finished videos and the raw, unedited stuff. Therefore, a file I want to call *Mark playing in the yard* may be named *Mark playing in the yard (raw footage)*. How you organize your videos is, of course, up to you, but it's a good idea to do something to differentiate the unedited video from the finished product.

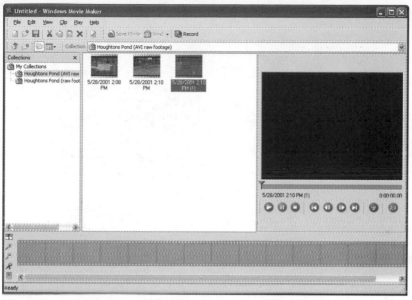

Figure 11-17: Clips are displayed in the center of the window; a new collection is added to the Collections list.

Composing a Video Production

Regardless of the method—digital or analog—you used to acquire the video, you should now have a Movie Maker project with one collection. This collection will have one or more clips, generated by Movie Maker, which you can now manipulate to your heart's content. Clips generated from an analog source are named Clip 1, Clip 2, and so on, whereas digitally acquired clips are named for the date and time the video was actually taken, which is another nice reason to use this format. So you may see clips with names like *5/28/01 2:08 PM, 5/28/01 2:11 PM.*

You can select any clip and play back that clip in the monitor window, as shown in Figure 11-18. The standard playback controls are available, along with an option to display the clip full screen. This makes it easy to preview video clips to determine whether they are part of your final movie.

To include clips in your final movie, you drag them down to the workspace section, as shown in Figure 11-19. By default, this area uses Storyboard view, which graphically shows you the order of the clips in your final movie. You can drag down clips one at a time, or in groups, to determine their position in the final movie. The Storyboard clip represents, visually, the order in which these clips are played.

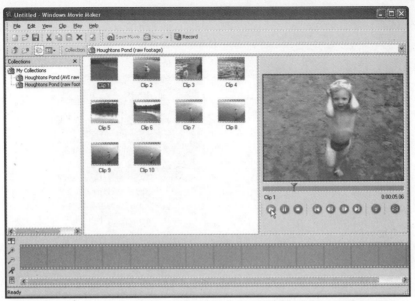

Figure 11-18: Individual clips can be played back in the monitor window.

Figure 11-19: Simply drag clips into the workspace area to create a final movie.

When you've got a rough idea of the clips that will make up your final movie and their positions in that movie, you can play back the entire sequence of clips in order to see how it looks. Oddly, there's no toolbar button or keyboard shortcut to do this. Instead, you have to choose Play ➪ Play Entire Storyboard/Timeline. The video will then play in the Monitor section of the window.

Okay, there are other (equally unobvious) ways to do this: Click a blank area of the workspace and then click Play under the Monitor preview window to play back the entire movie. Alternatively, you can hit Stop twice to reset the monitor to display the entire video, instead of just the current clip.

Storyboard view is nice for dragging and dropping and ordering clips, but it doesn't accurately reflect the length of each clip, which you will need for editing purposes. To work with video clips in a more time-centric way, you can switch the workspace to Timeline view by clicking the Timeline button as shown in Figure 11-20. Alternatively, you could choose View ➪ Timeline.

The Timeline view, shown in Figure 11-21, displays the relative length of each clip, using, well, a timeline. This view is used to trim clips — make them shorter in some way, adjust audio levels, add transitions, and perform other editing tasks. In general, you will perform simple positioning tasks with the Storyboard view, but then switch to Timeline for most of your editing work.

Figure 11-20: Switch to Timeline view by clicking the Timeline button.

Figure 11-21: Timeline view is useful for editing clips and adding transitions and titles.

One other interesting feature of the Timeline view is that you can zoom in and out to reduce or increase the displayed time increments. This can be useful when you're editing and want to ensure that a video trim or title transition occurs at a specific point. To zoom in, click the Zoom In button, as shown in Figure 11-22. The Zoom Out button can be found directly below it.

Saving your first movie

Now, you have to edit the raw footage in various ways, but before we get into that, let's see how you go about saving a final movie. Once you've dragged one or more clips into the workspace, you can save them as a movie that can be played in Windows Media Player or streamed over the Web. Movies can be saved at various quality levels and resolutions, so you can target an appropriate media, such as the Web or e-mail. And you can add information about the movie that appears as it is played back.

To save a movie, first drag one or more clips from the Collections area into the workspace. Normally, you'd want to edit these clips (by trimming them, creating transitions, or adding titles) before saving a movie. But we'll get into that later. Click the Save Movie button on the toolbar to display the Save Movie as shown in Figure 11-23.

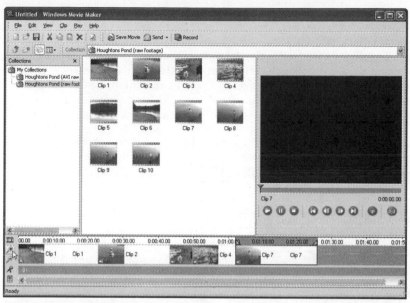

Figure 11-22: Click the Zoom In button to expand your view of individual clips in Timeline view.

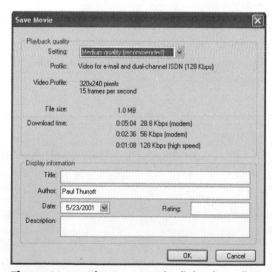

Figure 11-23: The Save Movie dialog box allows you to create a finished movie you can share with friends and family.

This dialog box lets you choose the quality of the finished movie, primarily through the Setting drop-down list box. This provides a few preset quality levels, such as Low Quality (176 × 144 pixel resolution, 15 frames per second, or FPS), Medium Quality (320 × 240, 15 FPS; this is the default), High Quality (320 × 240, 30 FPS) and Other, which displays the Profile drop-down list, shown in Figure 11-24. If one of the three preset quality levels isn't appropriate, check out the options in Profile. Note that USB-based video capture is limited to 320 × 240, so it won't make sense to create a final movie that exceeds the resolution with which you captured the raw footage.

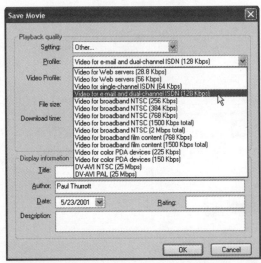

Figure 11-24: If you choose a quality setting of Other, a variety of new quality profiles become available.

In the Profile drop-down list, you will see a larger variety of quality levels, as shown in Table 11-1.

Table 11-1 Quality Levels			
Profile name	Resolution	FPS	Compressed?
Video for Web servers (28.8 Kbps)	160 × 120	15	Yes
Video for Web servers (56 Kbps)	176 × 144	15	Yes
Video for single-channel ISDN (64 Kbps)	240 × 176	15	Yes

Profile name	Resolution	FPS	Compressed?
Video for e-mail and dual-channel ISDN (128 Kbps)	320 × 240	15	Yes
Video for broadband NTSC (256 Kbps)	320 × 240	30	Yes
Video for broadband NTSC (384 Kbps)	320 × 240	30	Yes
Video for broadband NTSC (768 Kbps)	320 × 240	30	Yes
Video for broadband NTSC (1500 Kbps total)	640 × 480	30	Yes
Video for broadband NTSC (2 MB total)	640 × 480	30	Yes
Video for broadband film content (768 Kbps)	640 × 480	24	Yes
Video for broadband film content (1500 Kbps total)	640 × 480	24	Yes
Video for color PDA devices (225 Kbps)	208 × 160	20	Yes
Video for color PDA devices (150 Kbps)	208 × 160	8	Yes
DV-AVI NTSC (25 Mbps)	720 × 480	30	No
DV-AVI PAL (25 Mbps)	720 × 525	25	No

The option you choose depends on your goals for the movie and where you want to use it. For now, use the High Quality option in the Setting drop-down list to get the best possible quality from your 320 × 240 output.

The Save Movie dialog box changes dynamically as you choose Settings and Profiles options, showing the file size and download time of your final movie, based on the options you choose.

In the bottom of the dialog box, you can add display information about the video, as shown in Figure 11-25. The title should be something short and descriptive (*My first movie* is a good choice). Type in your name as author, and if you set up Movie Maker properly, it is auto-filled with your name (otherwise, you'll see your logon name). The Date option is auto-filled with today's date, but you can edit this as appropriate. You can add a rating (G, PG, whatever) and description if you like.

When you're ready to save the movie, click OK and the Save As dialog box appears, giving you the option to choose the location to which you want to save the video. Unless you chose one of the DV-AVI options in the Profile drop-down list, your movie is saved in Windows Media Video (WMV) format; the DV-AVI options allow you to save in uncompressed AVI format, which produces great quality but does result in massive file sizes. (More about AVI later in the chapter.)

Once you've chosen a target location, give your video masterpiece a logical name and click Save. The Creating Movie dialog box appears and provides a progress bar while the movie is created, as shown in Figure 11-26.

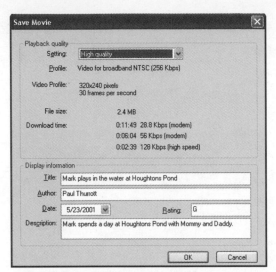

Figure 11-25: Before saving your movie, be sure to fill in the display information, which shows up in Windows Media Player during playback.

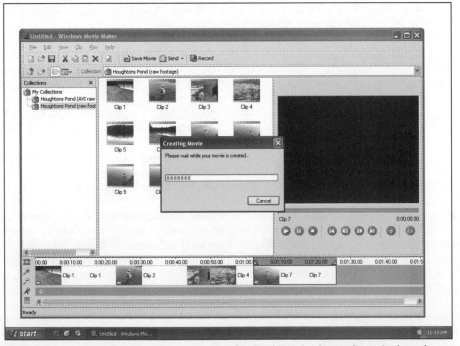

Figure 11-26: How long it takes to create the final movie depends on its length and the quality setting you've chosen.

When your movie is done, Windows Movie Maker asks whether you'd like to see the movie in Windows Movie Maker. Click Yes to see your first movie in all its digital glory, as shown in Figure 11-27.

Figure 11-27: Now you can enjoy the fruits of your hard work. Hi, Mark!

Okay, this isn't too shabby, but unedited video is unedited video. In the following sections, we'll see how easy it is to add trim video, transitions, titles, and other professional effects. Remember that you can save your movie at any time, in any format you like, as you go along.

Trimming video content

Because it's highly unlikely that you will want to use every second of every clip you've imported into the workspace, Windows Movie Maker allows you to trim video clips in a variety of ways. You can trim off a portion of the beginning of a video clip, trim off a portion of the end of a clip, or trim an arbitrary area out of the middle of a clip. Also, you can split clips into two or more separate clips, and combine contiguous clips into a single clip if desired. We'll look at each of these cases here.

Trimming from the beginning of a clip

To trim the beginning off of a video clip, first drag that clip to the workspace (if it's not there already). Then, click the Zoom In button once or more as appropriate so you can see what you're doing. The workspace should resemble Figure 11-28.

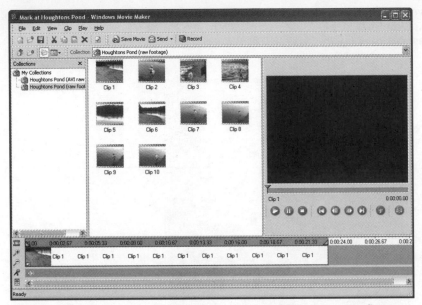

Figure 11-28: By continually clicking the Zoom In button, you can fine tune your video editing.

Now, click the clip and ensure that the small triangular Start Trim handle is available in the upper left corner of the workspace, as shown in Figure 11-29.

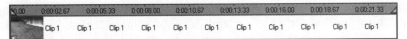

Figure 11-29: The Start Trim and End Trim handles allow you to trim video from the beginning and end of the clip.

Drag the Start Trim handle to the right, as shown in Figure 11-30, noting the video display in the Monitor section. When you've reached the point where you'd like the clip to begin, release the Start Trim handle and the beginning of the clip is trimmed off.

Note that this edit only affects the version of the clip that will appear in the final movie. The original clip, which is still up in the Collections area, is unaffected.

If dragging the Start Trim handle isn't your style, there's another way to trim video from the beginning of the clip. Select the clip you'd like to trim and then click inside the blue timeline area, as shown in Figure 11-31. The mouse cursor changes into an up arrow cursor and a thin black line, indicating the current position within the clip, appears. As you click inside the blue timeline, the position of the black line changes.

Figure 11-30: By dragging the Start Trim handle to the right, you can trim video from the beginning of the clip.

Figure 11-31: Alternatively, you can use this method to set a trim point.

You can use this up arrow cursor to precisely position the point at which the video is trimmed. When you've found the right place, simply choose Clip ➪ Set Start Trim Point. Voilà! The beginning of the video is trimmed.

Trimming from the end of a clip

Trimming the end of a clip involves similar skills, except that you'll be working with the End Trim handle, as shown in Figure 11-32.

Figure 11-32: To trim video from the end of a clip, move the End Trim handle to the left.

This handle is the counterpart to the Start Trim handle, and it's used to set the end trim point, which is handy when you want to trim video off the end of a clip. To do so, drag the End Trim handle to the left until you reach the point where you'd like that clip to end. Again, be sure to zoom in enough beforehand so you can make an accurate edit. As before, the video appears in the Monitor section to give you a visual guide.

There is also an alternative way to trim video from the end of the clip. As with the start trim, you can use the up arrow cursor to position a thin black line, which indicates the current position within the clip. As you click inside the blue timeline, the position of the black line changes.

Use the up arrow cursor to precisely position the point at which the video is trimmed. When you've found the right place, simply choose Clip ➪ Set End Trim Point to trim the end of the video.

Trimming an area from the middle of a clip

Once you see how trimming the beginning and end of a clip works, it probably makes a lot of sense. But how do you trim a segment from the middle of a clip? Well, you don't. Instead, you split the clip where you want the trim to begin and then trim the beginning of the next clip, which is created by the split. And if you want, you can then recombine the two clips back into a single clip. Here's how.

Splitting video clips

Using the up arrow cursor and that thin black positioning line, find the position in the timeline where you'd like to split the clip. Then, choose Clip ⇨ Split. As shown in Figure 11-33, the clip in the workspace is split into two clips (again, this doesn't affect the original clip found up in the Collections area). Now, you can trim the beginning off the second of the two clips as described above.

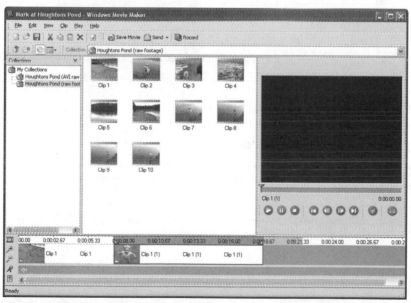

Figure 11-33: It's possible to split a clip so you can trim video from its middle.

Combining video clips

Sometimes you may want to combine two clips into a single unit, which may make them easier to work with. This is particularly useful for contiguous clips, where the action continues seamlessly from one to the other, and you never have any intention of creating a transition between them or editing them further. Or perhaps you split a clip so as to edit out a sequence in the middle, but now you want to recombine them back into a cohesive whole.

Combining video clips is as easy as splitting them. Simple select two or more contiguous video clips in the workspace area and then choose Clip ➪ Combine. As shown in Figure 11-34, the clips are then combined and treated as a single clip. Also, note that this doesn't affect the original clips found in the Collections area, just the clips you're working with in the workspace.

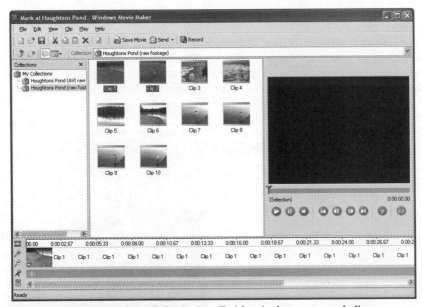

Figure 11-34: A combined clip is visually identical to a normal clip.

However, you *can* combine clips in the Collections area too! As before, select two or more clips, this time in the Collections area, and then choose Clip ➪ Combine.

Adding transitions

Depending on the quality of the scene changes, the transition from one clip to another may be somewhat visually jarring. To counter this effect, Windows Movie Maker allows you to add *transitions* to your videos, which eases changeover from one clip to another. Movie Maker is pretty basic in this regard, as it offers only one such transition, the *cross-fade* transition, where one clip fades out as the next begins, creating a fairly seamless experience. The good news is that the cross-fade transition is the most common type of transition and a good introduction to this editing feature. And the cross-fade transition in Windows Movie Maker works quite well, to boot.

To transition from one clip to the next, make sure that at least two video clips are present in the workspace and zoom in (as required) to fine tune your work. Then, select the second of the two clips and, as shown in Figure 11-35, drag that clip to the left. While you're dragging the clip, you'll see a weird black and white "staircase" graphic that denotes the area in which the two clips will overlap. The further you drag the clip to the left, the more time is used by the transition. Refer to the blue timeline to precisely time the transition.

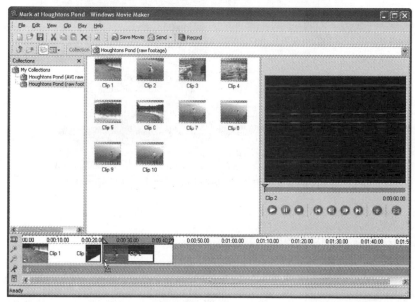

Figure 11-35: To create a transition between two clips, simply drag the second clip to the left.

When you let go of the leftmost clip, it is positioned over the end of the first clip, as shown in Figure 11-36.

Now, play the entire workspace to preview the transition in the Monitor area.

It's unlikely that you're going to get a transition right the first time, but you can go back and drag the second clip around to your heart's content, in order to make the transition longer or shorter as you wish. You can even remove the transition all together by carefully dragging the second clip to the right. This can often be a bit more delicate than it should be, but if you're careful as you move the mouse cursor, you can remove the transition.

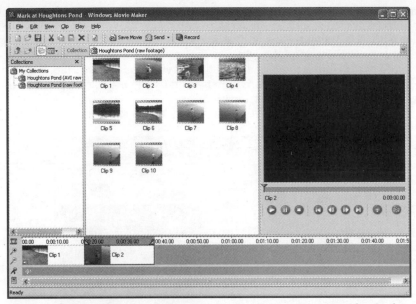

Figure 11-36: Clips that transition into each other appear to overlap in the Timeline view.

Transitioning with still images

In addition to transitioning between video clips, you can transition from a video clip to a static bitmapped image, or vice versa. One interesting effect that's possible in Movie Maker is to create still images completely in black or white and then transition from a video clip to one of these images. This allows you to "fade to black" or "fade to white".

There's one little caveat for this technique: The still images you create must be the same resolution or, at the least, must have the same aspect ratio of the final movie you're going to create. We'll discuss this later in the chapter, but when you're done editing, you have to save the finished movie in one of several formats. And any still images you insert into the movie need to have the same dimensions as the final product, or you'll see weird black bands on the top and bottom or left and right of the video when it's complete.

If you're making a movie for the Web, the most common format is 320 pixels wide by 240 pixels in height, which is generally expressed as 320 × 240. But other formats, such as 176 × 144, 208 × 160, 640 × 480, 720 × 480 and 720 × 525 may be possible as well, depending on how you depend to output the final video. For now, we'll assume that the output is 320 × 240, which is the maximum you can achieve for video that was acquired with a USB device such as the Belkin VideoBus II. But in the future, you can experiment with higher resolutions as well if your hardware permits it. Just remember that all your still images will need to be in the same resolution as the target video if you want to avoid banding.

To create a black still image:

1. Open Microsoft Paint, which can be found by navigating to Start; then choose All ⇨ Programs ⇨ Accessories ⇨ Paint.

2. Choose Image ⇨ Attributes. The Attributes dialog box opens, as shown in Figure 11-37.

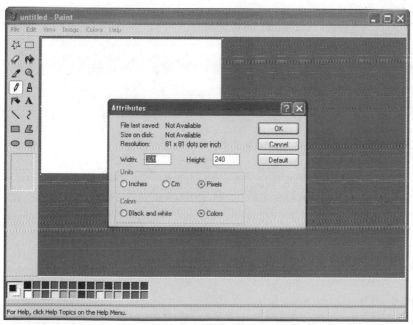

Figure 11-37: To create a still image transition, make sure that the image is the same resolution as your target movie.

3. Enter **320** for the width and **240** for the height; then click OK to close the dialog box. The image resizes to those dimensions.

4. Using the Fill With Color tool, fill the entire image with the color black as shown in Figure 11-38.

5. Save the file in your video project folder with a logical name such as *black* or *black still frame*.

6. Exit Paint.

You can repeat these steps to make a white still image, or an image of any other color.

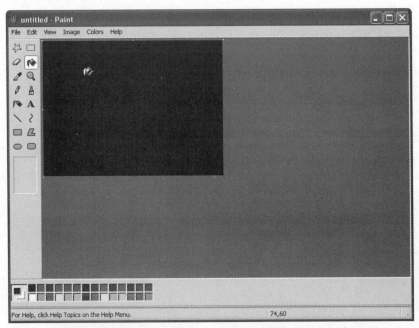

Figure 11-38: Fill the image with the color you'd like to transition to.

Now, you need to import at least one of these images into Windows Movie Maker. In Movie Maker, choose File ➪ Import to display the Select the File to Import dialog box shown in Figure 11-39 (Alternatively, press CTRL+I). Navigate to the folder where the black still frame was stored and import that image.

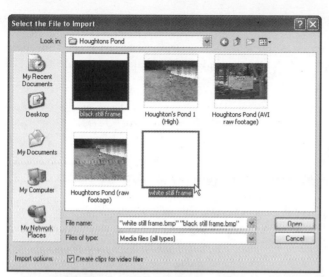

Figure 11-39: Once you've saved your still image transitions, you can import them into Movie Maker.

The image is imported into the current collection and stored as a clip, as shown in Figure 11-40.

Figure 11-40: Imported still images appear as clips inside the current collection.

Now you can drag it into the workspace area to add the image to your movie. You can drag a still frame to the beginning of the movie, to the end of the movie, or between any two clips which do not have a transition between them. One typical use for this type of image is to create a fade to black from one clip and then fade from black into the next. We'll add that type of effect now as an example.

To begin, make sure that you've got two contiguous clips in the workspace area and that there is no transition between them, as shown in Figure 11-41. The workspace should be in Timeline view.

Figure 11-41: To add a still image transition, ensure that you've got two contiguous clips in the workspace...

Now, drag *black* (the black bitmap image) down into the workspace and drop it between the two clips as shown in Figure 11-42.

By default, a still image is given five seconds of air time. You may want to zoom into the Timeline view a bit to get a better view. It's possible to lengthen or shorten the amount of time the still image displays, but only if there is no clip directly after the image. This may seem like a problem, but there's a workaround: If you want to change the length that the still image appears to something other than the default, simply drag it to the end of the workspace first, and then use its End Trim handle to resize it. Then, drag it back to its intended location between two clips. In Figure 11-43, we can see the still image being lengthened at the end of the Timeline.

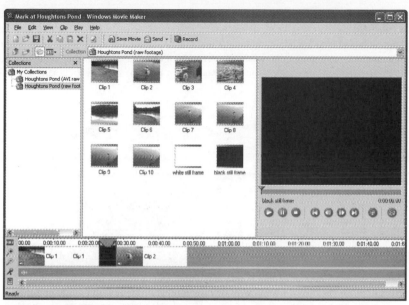

Figure 11-42: ...then drag a still image clip between them.

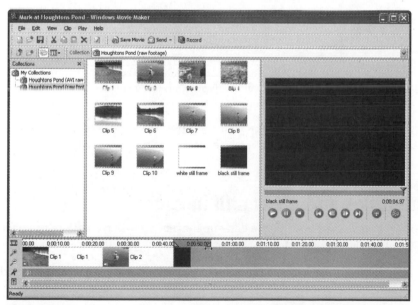

Figure 11-43: If you want to expand the length of time a still image appears, drag it to the end of the timeline first.

Once the still image is the correct length and has been positioned between two clips, you can use your transition skills to create a cross-fade transition between the first clip and the black still image and another cross-fade transition between the black image and the second clip. It's the same process, but this time you're dragging a still image instead of a video clip. When you're done, the workspace may resemble Figure 11-44.

Figure 11-44: Still image transitions will overlap with nearby video clips.

You're probably going to want to experiment with this a bit to find an effect that you like. Also, be sure to try it with a white bitmap as well; you may like that look better.

Adding titles and other still images

Once you've determined how all the clips in your movie will transition into each other, you may want to add a title to the movie for that final professional touch. For example, you could place a still image at the beginning of the movie that displays a title with a date or explanation of the video. You can also create end credits and other transitionary titles this way if you'd like.

To create a title for your finished movie:

1. Open Paint and resize the image as described in the previous section.

2. Using the Text tool, create a textual title image for your video, as shown in Figure 11-45.

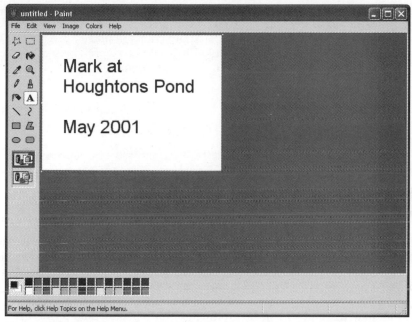

Figure 11-45: You can also use Paint to create simple textual titles for your movies.

3. Save the image when you're happy with it and import it into Movie Maker.

4. Drag the title to the beginning of your movie in the workspace.

5. Making sure that the workspace is in Timeline view, create a transition between the title image and the first video clip.

6. Preview your movie in the monitor and edit the transition until you're happy with it. You may want to experiment with titles that have white and black backgrounds.

Also, be sure to experiment with end titles. You can create simple credits lists in Paint and use images, perhaps even still frames from your movie, as titles and transitions if you'd like.

Adding voice-overs and background music

Given how easy it is to work with video clips and still images in Movie Maker, you may not be surprised to discover that it's equally easy to manipulate the audio soundtrack in your movie extravaganza. And Movie Maker makes it possible to add voice-over narration as well as background music to your movies.

When working with audio in Movie Maker, you deal with *audio clips*, which is logical enough. Audio clips get imported, recorded, and inserted into the workspace just like video clips, with a few differences. Audio clips are placed in a special area of the workspace, in Timeline view, just below the area where video clips are dragged. (You can see it in Figure 11-46 next to the microphone icon.)

 Figure 11-46: Audio clips have a special area in the workspace.

Importing an audio soundtrack

If you'd like to import an existing audio file (such as a Windows Media Audio or MP3-formatted file) to use as audio soundtrack, the process is very similar to when you import video. Simply choose File ⇨ Import and then navigate to the file you'd like to import. When you select an audio file and import it into Movie Maker, you will see it appear in the Collections area, as shown in Figure 11-47.

You can play the audio file through the monitor as you would a video—select it in the Collections area and then click the Play button under the video monitor. You won't see a video play, but the audio will play back normally.

Figure 11-47: Audio clips are placed in the current collection alongside video and still image clips.

You can also drag the imported audio file into the workspace area, just as you would with a video file. You have to be in Timeline view for this to work, however; if you attempt to drag the file down while the workspace is in Storyboard view, you will receive a warning and the view will change automatically. Audio files dragged into the storyboard are automatically placed in the audio area below the video area, as shown in Figure 11-48.

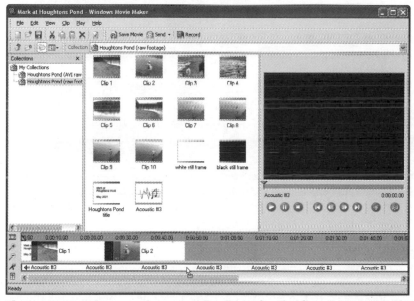

Figure 11-48: When you drag an audio clip to the Timeline, it is automatically placed below the video area in the audio area.

Now, the biggest problem with this scenario is going to be timing: It's unlikely that your audio file is the exact length of the video, so you're going to have to deal with audio that's either too short or too long for the otherwise-finished video. You can trim overly-lengthy audio with the Start Trim and End Trim handles, just as you do with video, though this is less of an exact science since you can't hear the audio as you do so. In Figure 11-49, you can see the end of a long audio clip being trimmed back to match the length of the video.

More importantly, there's no way to fade audio in or out elegantly, as you can with video. So if you trim the end of an audio clip, the sound is simply going to end abruptly.

There are ways around this problem, but they involve using tools other than Windows Movie Maker. For more sophisticated audio editing, check out the Windows Media Web site (www.microsoft.com/windowsmedia) for downloads and additional information. The Web site for this book also has information about more sophisticated audio tools (www.xpdigitalmedia.com).

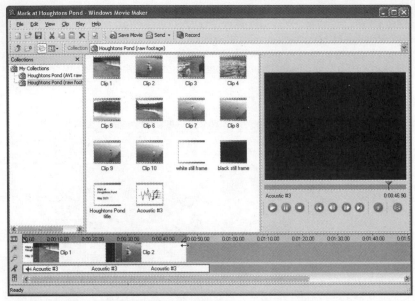

Figure 11-49: An audio clip can be trimmed in the same way that a video clip is trimmed, using the Start Trim and End Trim handles.

Adding narration

In addition to audio soundtracks, you can also add narration to your otherwise finished movie. To do so, click the Record Narration icon (the one that looks like a small microphone next to the audio area in the Timeline). This displays the Record Narration Track dialog box, shown in Figure 11-50, which allows you to choose an audio capture device and line (typically your PC microphone), determine the recording level, and record your narration.

Figure 11-50: When you click the Record Narration button, you are presented with this dialog box.

When you click the Record button, the video begins playing and you can start the narration, matching it to the video. When you're done, click Stop and you are prompted to save the narration as an uncompressed WAV file. When the file is saved, it will automatically be imported into your current project. You can then drag the narration into the workspace as desired.

Working with audio levels

Movie Maker doesn't offer many sophisticated tools for editing audio, but one thing you can do is adjust the audio level so as to favor the audio that's built into the video track of the workspace or the separate audio track. By default, Movie Maker gives equal precedence to each type of audio, so the audio level is split 50/50 between the two. But you can click the button labeled *Set the audio levels* (found just below the Record Narration button in the workspace) to adjust the audio level to give precedence to one or the other.

When you click the *Set the audio levels* button (or select Edit ➪ Audio Levels), you see the Audio Levels dialog box shown in Figure 11-51. This dialog box features a slider that lets you select whether the audio or video track outputs more volume. As you move the slider toward the Video track side, the volume of the audio found in the video track is increased and the audio in the audio track is decreased. The reverse is also true.

Figure 11-51: If you've added an audio clip or narration to a video, you can choose to favor the addition or the underlying video.

If it's not obvious, this feature has one limitation: You can *only* apply it to your entire finished movie, and not to individual parts of it. It would have been nice to selectively adjust the audio levels at discrete points of the movie—perhaps in a future release.

✦   ✦   ✦

Working with the Outside World

In today's connected world, no PC is an island, so this part examines the ways you can use your Windows XP-based digital media in that wider world beyond your PC. This section looks at the Internet-integration features of Internet Explorer and MSN Explorer, which allow you to take advantage of rich media experiences on the Internet. It outlines ways to connect a Pocket PC or portable digital-audio device to your Windows XP PC — and copy music, images, or even videos for use on the road. This part also shows how Windows XP can connect you to the instant-messaging phenomenon started by ICQ in the late 1990s — so you can stay in touch as never before.

Internet Explorer Digital-Media Features

◆ ◆ ◆ ◆

In This Chapter

Web Integration and Windows

Internet Explorer 6

MSN Explorer

◆ ◆ ◆ ◆

Throughout the history of Windows, feature integration has been an important part of every major OS release. Today, Internet integration is a familiar feature of Windows; with Windows XP, Microsoft has improved the usefulness of these features, especially with digital media.

So, to address the various audiences that find Windows XP compelling, the company has included two major Web browsers in this product — Internet Explorer (IE) *and* MSN Explorer. IE is geared more to business and power users; MSN Explorer addresses the more casual user. But both offer an interesting amount of integration with digital media, such as pictures, sound, and video. This chapter addresses those features.

A Look Back at Internet Integration in Windows

During the development of Windows 95, Microsoft made the crucial decision to integrate Internet functionality into Windows. At the time, Windows 95 was far enough along in its development that the original shipping version of the OS had room to include only some of the "plumbing" for this functionality (such as an integrated TCP/IP stack for internetworking and a simple FTP client for remote file access). But the company also made a Plus! Pack available when Windows 95 first shipped in August 1995; it included the first version of Internet Explorer (IE), Microsoft's Web browser. IE was available for free download from the Web as well, mimicking the delivery mechanism that made rival Netscape Navigator so successful.

Over the next few years, Microsoft improved its Web browser and worked on integration technologies that would make it work more seamlessly with Windows. In July 1996, the company shipped Windows NT 4.0 with IE 2.0. Microsoft shipped IE 3.0 a month later—the first version truly integrated deeply into the OS. As the first version overwhelmingly preferred by consumers *and* technical reviewers, IE 3.0 began eating away at Netscape's market share.

But IE really rose to prominence with the next release, IE 4.0, which arrived in late September 1997. IE 4.0 actually replaced the shell navigation functionality in Windows with a Web-like interface that gave users consistent-looking access to both the Internet and their local files. IE 4.0 was integrated into the retail version of Windows 98, which shipped in May 1998. As you might have heard, this action got Microsoft into a little bit of legal trouble with the federal government, which charged Microsoft with illegally tying one product (IE) to a monopoly product (Windows). For its part, Microsoft says it was simply providing functionality that clearly benefited users; the subsequent death of Netscape was a result of strategic blunders by that company and not because of the Windows/IE tie-in. I'll leave it to greater minds than mine to debate this, but a number of consequences of Microsoft's ongoing legal problems have affected Windows. In Windows XP, for example, PC makers and consumers are now able to remove the IE user interface (the browser icons, for example, if desired).

Anyway, the integration of IE and Windows continued in subsequent OS releases, such as Windows 98 Second Edition (SE, 1999), Windows 2000 (2000), and Windows Millennium Edition (Me, 2000), each of which offered the then-latest version of the browser as a standard part of the OS. So it's only natural that Windows XP would continue this trend (which it does) with IE 6 and a relatively new product called MSN Explorer.

Web Integration in Windows XP

Windows XP was designed with the notion that users are increasingly connected to the Internet and look to this vast resource as an important part of their everyday lives. In addition to the obvious inclusion of Internet Explorer (more about this in the next section), Windows XP adds a number of Internet-related features.

In Windows XP, the concept of the Active Desktop is gone. Instead, functionality that used to require the Active Desktop just works when you need it (what a concept) including such capabilities as displaying Web pages (along with GIF and JPEG images) right on the desktop. The Web view folders from previous versions of Windows carry on in Windows XP, of course, but they are far more powerful in this release, with task lists appropriate to the content you're currently viewing.

Windows XP also comes with Windows Messenger, Microsoft's Instant Messaging (IM) and Real-time communication client. Windows Messenger, shown in Figure 12-1, allows you to communicate with buddies using text, audio, and video chat, and the version that comes in Windows XP offers a number of other features related to Microsoft's .NET strategy. I take a closer look at this exciting product in Chapter 14.

Figure 12-1: Windows Messenger is an instant messaging client that's also key to .NET integration in Windows XP.

A number of Internet-enabled games come with Windows XP, including Internet Backgammon, Internet Checkers, Internet Hearts, Internet Reversi, and Internet Spades. These games link to the MSN Gaming Zone (shown in Figure 12-2), where you can connect with players from around the globe.

And .NET Passport integration is included in Windows XP so you can optionally link your Windows logon to a .NET Passport account (which logs you on to .NET Passport automatically when you browse Passport-compatible Web sites). The .NET Passport allows you to control personal information, as well as store credit card information, so you don't have to manually enter that data every time you visit an eCommerce site. You can integrate .NET Passport through the .NET Passport Wizard (shown in Figure 12-3), available from the User Accounts applet in the Control Panel.

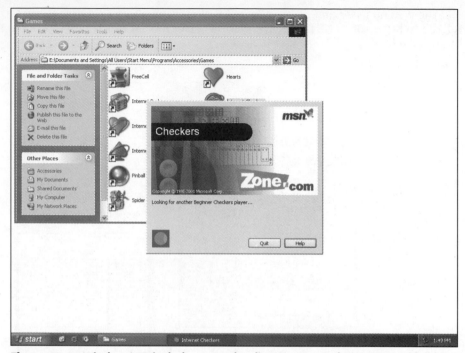

Figure 12-2: Windows XP includes several online games, such as Internet Checkers, which can be played against other people through MSN Gaming Zone.

Finally, Microsoft knows that access to the Internet is of vital importance to its customers, so it has included links to a Web browser (IE by default) and e-mail client (Outlook Express by default) right at the top of the Start menu, as shown in Figure 12-4.

These links cannot be removed, but they are modifiable through the Properties window for the Start menu (shown in Figure 12-5). You can choose Internet Explorer or MSN Explorer as your default Web browser, and designate Hotmail, Outlook Express, or MSN Explorer as your e-mail client. Other applications can add themselves to this list as well: Any application that can configure itself as the default Web browser, for example, will automatically appear as such in the Start Menu. And when you install Microsoft Outlook, it assigns that e-mail program as your default, so that is what shows up in the Start menu.

The remainder of this chapter examines the digital-media features of the two Web solutions provided right out of the box, Internet Explorer 6 and MSN Explorer.

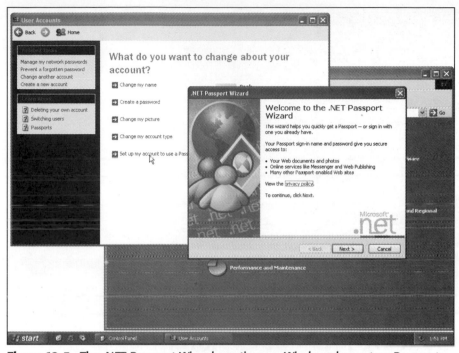

Figure 12-3: The .NET Passport Wizard can tie your Windows logon to a Passport account.

Figure 12-4: Your default Web browser and e-mail client show up in the top left of the Start menu.

Figure 12-5: You can easily change the default Web browser and e-mail client through Start menu Properties.

Introducing Internet Explorer 6

Internet Explorer 6 is an evolution, rather than a revolution, when compared to its IE 5.*x* predecessors. In Windows XP, IE has been modified to take on the pleasant Windows XP look and feel, as shown in Figure 12-6. And of course, some new features have been added as well.

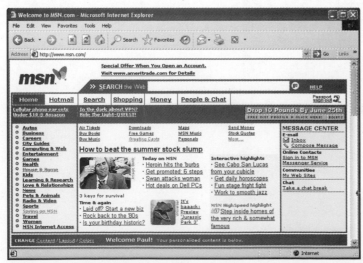

Figure 12-6: Internet Explorer 6 is an evolutionary improvement over previous versions.

Some of the new stuff is hidden from the user. IE 6 browses faster and is more compliant with ever-important Web standards such as HTML and Cascading Style Sheets (CSS); this guarantees that your Web experience is as fast and easy as it can be.

Microsoft introduced a number of Explorer Bars back in 1997 with IE 4.0, and IE 6 improves on this concept with new bars and new features. An Explorer Bar, like the one shown in Figure 12-7, exposes functionality without requiring the user to open a dialog box (which would effectively block access to the browser window).

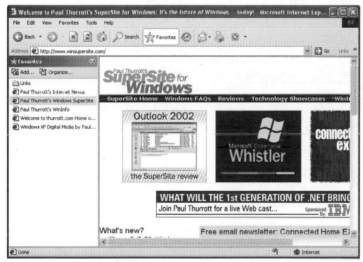

Figure 12-7: The Favorites Explorer Bar is a typical example, offering the capability to access commonly used features without opening menus or dialog boxes.

Trying out the new Explorer Bars in IE 6

In IE 4.0, Microsoft introduced the Folders, History, Search, and Favorites Explorer Bars. IE 6 has changed a few of these (in subtle but important ways) and added some new ones:

Search the Web

Providing a front-end for the MSN Search functionality (search.msn.com), this Explorer Bar lets you type in search topics and then view the results in the main Web window, as shown in Figure 12-8. If you're wondering what the difference is between "Search" and "Search the Web," just remember that "Search the Web" searches *only* the Web (not the entire Internet). Search provides for finding people, addresses, businesses, maps, and other items of interest, as shown in Figure 12-9.

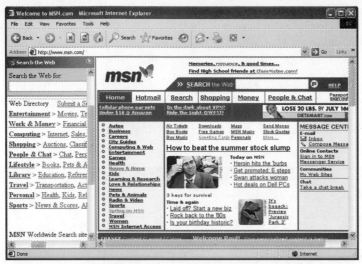

Figure 12-8: The Search the Web Explorer Bar provides instant access to MSN Search.

Figure 12-9: The more general Search Bar is reminiscent of the Windows Search functionality, and it offers a wider range of online search types.

MSN Calendar

Everyone with a .NET Passport account can use MSN's Calendar service (calendar. msn.com), and with IE 6, you can do so without needing to load a full browser window, as shown in Figure 12-10.

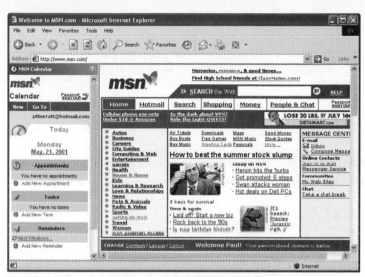

Figure 12-10: MSN Calendar is probably more useful in an Explorer Bar than it is as a dedicated Web site.

Expedia

The Expedia Web site (www.expedia.com) is a site for booking travel arrangements, including flights, car rentals, and hotels. As with other Explorer Bars, you can use this Bar without having to navigate to the Expedia Web site (as shown in Figure 12-11).

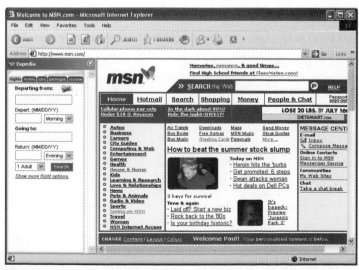

Figure 12-11: With the Expedia Bar, you can check prices for flights, hotels, and cars.

MSNBC News

The News Explorer Bar aggregates the same sort of MSNBC-based local weather, stock quotes, and stock news information you can get from the MSN home page (www.msn.com). As shown in Figure 12-12, the News Bar can also be personalized with news, health, business, technology, sports, opinion, and living/travel headlines from MSNBC. And each section can be collapsed and expanded, like the task areas of the Windows XP Web view.

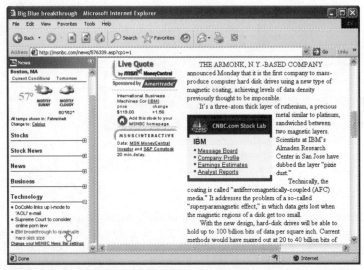

Figure 12-12: Personalized news and weather, all in a convenient Explorer Bar you can leave running as you browse the Web

Slate

Sometimes derided as a "great failed experiment" in online paid subscription content, this Microsoft online magazine is *still* some of the best reading on the Internet. With the Slate Explorer Bar (Figure 12-13), you can navigate the latest article headlines and search Slate without manually visiting the site.

Media Player Bar

Back when Windows XP was in development, Microsoft tested a feature called the Personal Bar — basically an enhanced Explorer Bar. It bristled with ambitious options such as *Search the Web*, *MSNBC News*, and another section called *Media*, all in one Bar. In response to tester feedback, the company scrapped plans for this Bar and moved its components into separate Bars. Of these, the Media Player Bar is important enough to us that it gets its own (upcoming) section of the chapter.

Figure 12-13: Slate is MSN's opinion and commentary Web site; this Explorer Bar provides quick access to the latest articles.

Using the IE Media Bar

Shown in Figure 12-14, the IE Media Bar basically places a small, Web-based front-end to Windows Media Player in the corner of the IE window. The first time you attempt to access any digital audio or video on the Web, IE asks you whether you'd like to use the built-in player or the full Windows Media Player. The choice is yours.

The goal of this player is to provide seamless integration with Web-based media. Many users get confused if a separate application launches whenever they click a hyperlink. Thus the embedded Media Bar can be undocked so it becomes a floating window, as shown in Figure 12-15 (handy if you want to stretch out the display to show a video).

The IE Media Bar can also be used to play Internet-based radio stations, using the same interface that Windows Media Player uses, as shown in Figure 12-16. This feature is described in detail in Chapter 5; the only difference here is that the radio can be controlled through the browser window.

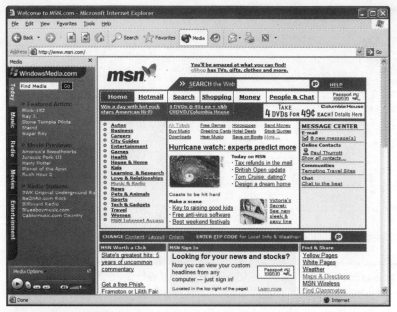

Figure 12-14: The Internet Explorer Media Bar provides an in-browser player for Web-based media.

Figure 12-15: An undocked media player can be stretched to show videos in a larger size than is possible when the player is attached to the IE window.

You can also access the Windows Media Player Media Guide from this interface (Figure 12-17), which gives you a lot of media-player functionality without making you open that application.

You should experiment with the embedded Media Bar to determine whether it fits your needs. (Personally, I prefer the full Windows Media Player. Your mileage may vary.)

Figure 12-16: The embedded media player allows you to access Internet radio stations from a Web site.

Figure 12-17: The same Media Guide you get in Windows Media Player for Windows XP is available on the Web.

Imaging Features in IE 6

In addition to integrating digital audio and video into Internet Explorer, Microsoft added a couple of interesting image-related features to the new browser as well. These include an image toolbar that makes it easier to work with Web-based pictures and an automatic image-resizing feature that autofit large images into the current browser window.

Using the Image Toolbar

If you open Internet Explorer and hover the mouse cursor over any image, you see a small floating toolbar appear, as shown in Figure 12-18.

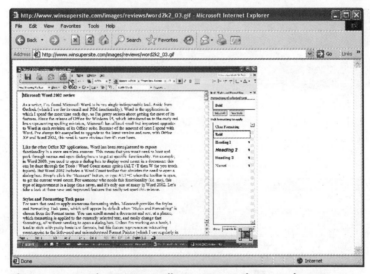

Figure 12-18: The Image toolbar appears when you hover over any image on a Web page.

The toolbar has four icons designed to give you quick access to the most common tasks you encounter when you work with Web-based images. You can save the image, which defaults to the My Pictures directory; print the image without first saving it to the hard drive; e-mail the image, again without first saving it; or open the My Pictures folder.

When you choose the send the image via e-mail, you get the same *Send Pictures via E-mail* dialog box discussed in Chapter 1. You can use it to automatically resize images that are larger than certain sizes, which keeps the size of the resulting e-mail to a minimum, as shown in Figure 12-19.

The e-mail option uses the default e-mail client, as determined by the Start menu.

Figure 12-19: You can keep images small when sending via e-mail.

Using automatic image resizing

A less welcome addition is the automatic image resizing feature, which autofits large images to the browser window. Consider Figure 12-20, which depicts an image in normal size, and compare it to how it looks when shrunk to fit a small browser window.

Figure 12-20: The same image, shown in its native size and automatically resized by IE

Fortunately, you can manually toggle between the shrunken version and the normal view of an image. If you move the mouse cursor over the lower left of the image, a small button appears, as shown in Figure 12-21. Click this button and the image is displayed normally. Click it again and the image once again shrinks to fit the window.

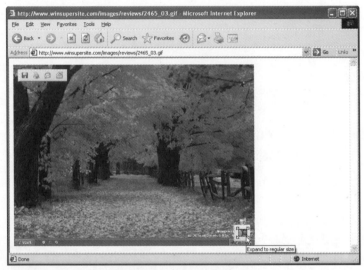

Figure 12-21: The Image Resize button toggles a Web-based image between resized and normal displays.

The theory is good, but the reality is less appealing: Unlike the excellent Image Preview applet, IE seems incapable of generating decently resized images, though it does pretty well with photographic JPEGs for some reason. Unless you have a compelling need for this feature, I recommend turning it off. Here's how.

Turning off IE imaging features

Both the Image Toolbar and the automatic image resizing feature can be turned off if you find them annoying.

1. Open Internet Explorer and choose Tools ⇨ Internet Options to view the Internet Options dialog box.

2. Switch to the Advanced tab and scroll down to the Multimedia section, as shown in Figure 12-22.

3. Uncheck *Enable Automatic Image Resizing* and/or *Image Toolbar (requires restart)* as you see fit. Note that toggling the Image toolbar does not actually require a restart.

4. Click OK to finish.

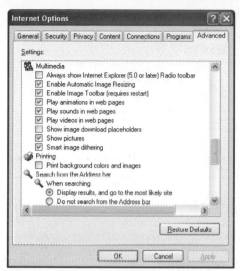

Figure 12-22: The Advanced tab of Internet Options can be used to set a number of features, including some image-related ones.

Using MSN Explorer

One interesting application that has been somewhat overshadowed by Windows XP is MSN Explorer, a consumer-oriented Web browser that integrates Microsoft's MSN Web properties into an America Online-style shell. MSN Explorer is designed to be simple, fun, and friendly, and I guess it's all that, assuming you're into that kind of thing. Of course, this application shares most of its best features with IE 6, but many home users may want to use MSN Explorer for Web browsing and e-mail, despite its limitations.

Those limitations are deadly to the power-user. If you choose MSN Explorer, you can't change the default home page, for example, or use an external e-mail program.

Shown in Figure 12-23, MSN Explorer is an attractive and surprisingly integrated package. I'll leave it to you to explore its many features; it does include a nice tour for that purpose. But back to business: the next section examines the MSN Explorer digital-media features.

Note When you launch MSN Explorer for the first time, it asks whether you'd like to make it your default application for Web and e-mail access. You can change your choice later if you like, but I recommend choosing No until you're sure that you want to stick with this application for both of these critical services. Also, you will need to configure MSN Explorer for your .NET Passport account the first time it's run, so you'll have to be online and be prepared to answer a couple of questions.

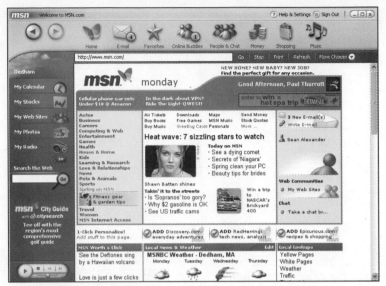

Figure 12-23: MSN Explorer offers a bright, friendly interface to Microsoft's Web properties.

The MSN Explorer Media Player

Like IE 6, MSN Explorer includes an integrated Media Player (to be fair, this feature debuted in MSN Explorer). You can expand the player into a floating window, as shown in Figure 12-24, and access the MSN Music Web site to find Internet radio stations and other digital audio. This site is also accessible by clicking the Music icon in the MSN Explorer toolbar.

Figure 12-24: Like the Media Player in IE, the MSN Explorer version can be expanded into a floating, resizable window if need be.

The Media Player in MSN Explorer offers no choice about playing media. While browsing the Web with MSN Explorer, you have to use the internal player to play any digital audio or video; using the full Windows Media Player is not an option. For people that prefer to use Media Player for Windows XP (MPXP), this might be a problem.

Using My Radio

You can add a My Radio item to the My Stuff bar in MSN Explorer that provides you with one-click access to the My Radio section of MSN Music, as shown in Figure 12-25.

Figure 12-25: You can use the My Radio item in the My Stuff bar to access MSN Music and online radio stations.

Using My Photos

MSN Explorer also offers a My Photos item in the My Stuff bar, which integrates with the MSN Picture It! Web site (communities.msn.com/PictureIt). Every .NET Passport user (that is, anyone with a Hotmail or MSN account, or any MSN Explorer user) can create online photo albums on this Web site and share the contents with others. As shown in Figure 12-26, MSN Picture It! provides links for uploading photos, creating albums, inviting others to view your albums, and other related tasks.

Figure 12-26: The MSN Picture It! Web community is available to all Passport users.

For the seasoned Windows user, MSN Explorer may be a nice application to visit — but you may want to move beyond it before too long.

✦   ✦   ✦

Working with Portable Devices

Technology is improving so rapidly these days that it's almost impossible to keep up. One good example of this is the portable device market, which encompasses such things as handheld and palm-sized computers, portable gaming devices like Nintendo's GameBoy, portable audio devices that play back MP3 and WMA files, portable CD players that are compatible with MP3-formatted data CDs, and much more. Some of these devices are clearly entertainment-oriented; others have a foot planted firmly in the business-productivity camp. But certain portable devices allow you to take digital music and, believe it or not, digital video on the road in a format that is small, light, and extremely portable. The two that get most of this chapter's attention are palm-sized Pocket PC devices and handheld portable audio devices from a variety of manufacturers.

The Pocket PC is Microsoft's most successful iteration of Windows CE-based devices, designed to bring Windows compatibility to a format that is small and portable. Pocket PC devices are currently offered by such companies as Compaq, Hewlett-Packard, and Casio. A Pocket PC is useful as an instant-on tool for personal information management (PIM), desktop synchronization of portable data, and even eBook reading on those long, boring flights. But the Pocket PC platform distinguishes itself from the Palm OS-based competition by integrating multimedia features that push the limits of what people expect of these useful devices. That is, you can play digital audio and videos on a Pocket PC, with stunning clarity and quality.

For the more traditional consumer-electronics market, a vast number of companies offer portable digital audio players that use embedded RAM or some type of medium to store audio (from 32 MB to over a gigabyte of audio, though these RAM figures will probably seem quaint in an embarrassingly short time). As with a Sony Walkman, portable digital audio players allow you to bring your music on the road—but you can bring much more without having to lug cassettes or CDs around. And because most of these devices have no moving parts, battery life is exceptional.

Many people express surprise when they see what's possible these days with portable devices. You will soon be amazing friends and family alike with this technology. The next section outlines how it all comes together.

Working with Portable Devices

If you think about it, what's the point of creating a digital library of music and video if you can't take it with you? In today's, ahem, *digital lifestyle*, you can use a PC as the focal point (or *hub*) of a connected home—and connect that PC with a variety of devices. Bill Gates once talked about *information at your fingertips*, but let's face it, most of us just want to be entertained. With portable digital devices, you really *can* take it with you.

Some people, of course, simply choose to use a laptop. And this makes things easy. If your digital-media files are already on a hard drive that you carry around the country, you can watch DVDs on a plane or in a hotel room, listen to your music collection with Media Player for Windows XP (MPXP), or watch home movies you've created in Windows Movie Maker (WMM). But laptops aren't always appropriate. For example, often there isn't enough room to open one on a plane. And why pop a laptop open during the morning commute via train or bus? Sometimes something a little more portable is called for.

Many solutions to this problem are possible. Through integration with portable devices, Windows XP is designed to become the hub of your digital lifestyle, making digital audio and video easy to use, even while you're on the go.

Regardless of the type of device you use, eventually you have to connect it to your computer—typically through a ubiquitous USB port (though serial devices are still around, and newer 1394 ("FireWire") and USB 2.0 devices are waiting in the wings). Depending on the type of device you connect to the system, Windows XP responds accordingly. It interprets a portable audio device as an external disk drive to the OS; if the device contains audio files, Windows XP pops up a dialog box asking what you'd like to do when the device is connected. (Figure 13-1 shows this kind of arrangement.) Choices include playing the music, opening a My Computer window so you can manually manage the files it contains, or simply doing nothing and clicking Cancel. (In fact, you can turn off the dialog box; see the last section in this chapter for details.) Pocket PC devices, meanwhile, are typically handled with an application called ActiveSync (which comes with the device) so the OS knows to do nothing and let ActiveSync do the work.

Figure 13-1: When you connect a portable digital audio device to the PC, you see this dialog box by default.

Most users, however, are likely to prefer Media Player for Windows XP as the front-end for their portable devices — mostly because the number-one use for these devices is to copy digital audio back and forth — and MPWXP includes functionality designed specifically to work with these devices.

Integrating Media Player for Windows XP with devices

As Chapter 8 relates, creating audio CDs can be pretty straightforward if you use Copy to CD or Device, a component of Media Player for Windows XP. As its name suggests, this component (shown in Figure 13-2) can also copy digital audio to a portable audio device or Pocket PC; the interface is basically identical, regardless of the type of device you're using. The only difference is the storage space on the respective device.

As with audio CD creation, you want to have a playlist ready before you copy audio over to the device. This can be a prefab playlist such as All Audio or one that you've made beforehand (for more about playlist creation, see Chapter 8). Synchronizing playlists with portable devices is somewhat tricky, however; each device has specific storage capabilities. For example, I use an Iomega HipZIP for my portable audio needs (such as they are), and this device uses 40MB cartridges. The Hewlett-Packard Pocket PC I use, however, has only 32 MB of RAM, which cannot be removed. But the HP supports Compact Flash expansion, so I could theoretically add media with 16, 32, 48, 64, 128, or 256 MB — or even gigabytes more with miniature hard-drives such as the IBM Microdrives.

Figure 13-2: A Pocket PC or portable digital audio device appears in Media Player for Windows XP in basically the same form.

In effect, you have to tailor your playlists to your specific device—a playlist's total length *must* not exceed the capabilities of your portable device. But you can also create multiple playlists and just drag over the songs you want, selecting a few from each playlist. Since Media Player for Windows XP tells you how long each song (and each playlist) is, it's easy to see right away how much capacity you've got left and plan accordingly.

Changing media-quality level before copying

As always, there's a catch. Media Player for Windows XP includes a wonderful bit of functionality designed specifically for portable devices (even though it makes the amount of available space left on your device harder to gauge). Through a feature called *transcoding*, you can "downgrade" music as you copy it to a device. For example, you store your WMA files at 128 Kbps on your computer, because you want a high-quality master copy of the data from your media, but you don't want the file to take up too much hard-drive space. For this purpose, 128 Kbps is the right compromise. But for a portable device with limited storage, 128 Kbps files put a severe limit on how much music you can carry around with you. The Iomega device I mentioned previously can only store 6-8 songs at this quality level.

Avoiding the pitfalls of transcoding

A couple of caveats here. The transcoding feature works with MP3 files as well as WMA format, but in my experience, WMA downgrades much more cleanly than does MP3. Also, transcoding is only as good as the source: Downgrading from 64 Kbps to 48 Kbps might not make much sense. You should experiment with varying quality levels before you hit the road and discover you've just recorded 45 minutes of scrambled mush.

Also, transcoding is slow. When you choose to transcode media on the fly, copying music becomes a bit excruciating. Each song must first be converted to the new quality level before it is copied to the device.

But there is an even bigger problem with transcoding — maybe the deal breaker if you're the impatient type: Once you've decided to transcode music before copying, the file size estimates in the media player are almost completely useless. So even though you might be converting from 128 Kbps to 64 Kbps as you copy, the size estimates for the songs you want to copy are still made at the higher rate. And music that you want to copy to the device is labeled *Might not fit* (more about this problem coming up shortly). Phooey!

Given these limitations, I still recommend using this feature *unless* you have a humongous storage capacity. Otherwise, experiment with transcoding and see the kinds of results you can get. Just don't wait until the last minute before a flight to do the conversion; do all your transcoding ahead of time.

Thankfully, you can get the media player to convert your audio while it copies songs to the device. For example, you could tell the media player to downgrade, or *transcode*, audio to 64 Kbps when using the Iomega. This gets a more acceptable amount of music on the HipZIP's removable storage (17-18 songs); the technology built into the media player gives you reasonable audio quality, especially when you consider the background noise and aural distractions in the places where you're likely to play it back.

One nice thing about this feature is that it's device-specific. For example, you could set up a Pocket PC to transcode audio down to 48 Kbps and a HipZIP to 64 Kbps. Each device can have different settings. (More about this technique later in the chapter.)

Here's how you can use transcoding to maximize the storage capacity of your portable device.

1. Plug the device into the PC and open Media Player for Windows XP.

2. Navigate to the *Copy to CD or Device* component of the player and, if necessary, choose your device from the drop down list on the right side of the player, as shown in Figure 13-3.

Figure 13-3: You can select a device from the drop-down list in the right side of the media player.

3. Select Tools ⇨ Options and then navigate to the Devices page.

4. Select your device from the list and click Properties. As shown in Figure 13-4, the Properties sheet for that device appears.

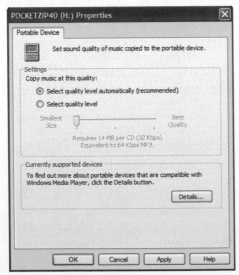

Figure 13-4: By default, Windows XP uses the native quality level when copying digital audio.

5. If you'd like Media Player for Windows XP to automatically select the quality level of audio that is copied to the device — that is, you'd like it to do no transcoding and simply copy music at its native resolution — opt for the default choice, labeled *Select quality level automatically (Recommended)*.

6. If you'd like to transcode audio while it's being copied to the device, click *Select quality level* (as shown in Figure 13-5) and choose a quality level on the slider. Generally acceptable choices include 32 Kbps, 64 Kbps, and 128 Kbps.

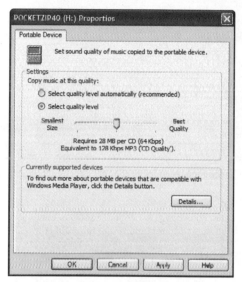

Figure 13-5: To manually enable transcoding, simply select a quality level and pick a transcoding rate.

7. Click OK to exit the dialog box.

Okay, when you've set up your transcoding rate, you can begin to copy music to the device. Simply select the playlist or individual songs you'd like to copy and click *Copy Music* when you're ready.

But here's where transcoding hits some turbulence, at least from the "user experience" perspective. In the left pane of the Copy to CD or Device component of Media Player for Windows XP, the Status field indicates whether songs you want to copy can actually fit. But when you use transcoding, many of these songs are listed as *May not fit* (Figure 13-6) because the player can't accurately know the final size of the files until after they're transcoded. In fact, many of these songs *will* fit, but you have to try copying them before you know.

When you copy music with transcoding on, each song is converted before it's copied, as shown in Figure 13-7. This is the time-consuming part of the process, which is otherwise identical to the process of writing music digitally to a device without transcoding.

Figure 13-6: When transcoding, size estimates are incorrect.

Figure 13-7: When transcoding is enabled, WMP must convert each audio file to the target quality rate before copying.

If you attempt to copy more music than you have storage available, you have to sit through an annoying conversion phase before Media Player throws up the error message shown in Figure 13-8 (telling you, in effect, that you're out of luck).

Figure 13-8: An unexpected error indeed. When there's not enough room on the target device, you see this error message.

 Portable devices are treated like a hard drive (not a CD-R/CD-RW) by Windows XP. That is, you don't need to worry about "sessions." You can simply keep adding music and other data to the device until it is full.

Pocket PCs for the Digital-Media Jet Set

Back in 1996, Microsoft introduced Windows CE, its operating system for handheld PCs. The handhelds of the era were designed to offer much of the functionality in a true PC, but with a smaller form and price. Windows CE was designed to look and feel like Windows, so users and programmers alike could bring their Windows skills along for the ride when they ran out and adopted CE devices for their own.

The anticipation seemed to make sense at the time—but most of the first-generation devices that ran Windows CE offered tiny keyboards, hazy monochrome screens, and a clamshell design that was too small to type on but too big to fit in a pocket. They failed miserably in the market. Meanwhile, a company called Palm introduced a much smaller, much simpler, and less-expensive product called the Palm Pilot. These devices delivered only basic functionality, and were nothing like PCs, but they offered synchronization capabilities so people could transfer PIM information back and forth between the device and the PC. It was an instant success, and today, Palm and compatible products *still* dominate the market.

Microsoft bounced back with a revision that included color; some manufacturers began building devices to run the new Windows CE (most were just a hair smaller than a laptop). These failed in the market as well. One small glimmer of hope came from the first generation of palm-sized PCs (originally called Palm PCs, though Palm Inc. soon put a stop to that). The palm-sized PCs still used the basic Windows desktop; they, too, failed to ignite dramatic sales. Perhaps mighty Microsoft was going to fail with its mini-OS. Indeed, by March 2000 the next version of Windows CE (version 3.0) was considered a make-or-break release for the company. If that failed in the market (as it seemed sure to do), Microsoft was going to pull the plug on its handheld products.

Then, in April 2000, Microsoft announced the Pocket PC — palm-sized devices from a variety of manufacturers running Windows CE. And something unexpected happened: They started selling- and selling very well. Throughout all of 2000 and most of 2001, market-leader Compaq couldn't even keep its best-selling iPaq Pocket PC in stock. By early 2001, the Pocket PC was eating into Palm's market share in a way that was previously unimaginable. Companies that had abandoned Windows CE were back with new devices, and new companies came on board with their own Pocket PC devices. A year after the release of the Pocket PC, Microsoft had established itself as a true competitor in the handheld market and simultaneously resurrected the notion that everything the company makes only succeeds after three revisions. (From the perspective of someone who has been observing the PC industry for over a decade, I can honestly say that only the financial turnaround at Steve Jobs' Apple Computer rivals the sudden turnaround experienced by Windows CE.)

The secret to the success of the Pocket PC is simple: Microsoft finally listened to its users and made the machine they were asking for. Bringing the desktop Windows user interface to a handheld device might have seemed like a good idea at the time, but the market has proven that users want a *simpler* interface on a handheld. So the Pocket PC user interface revolves around a PIM-based Today screen, shown in Figure 13-9, and a Start menu that's found in the upper left of the screen, as shown in Figure 13-10. This is because most people are right-handed; it's easier to use a menu that cascades down from the top left.

The Pocket PC comes with "Pocket" versions of Microsoft Outlook, Word, Excel, and PowerPoint. What makes the Pocket PC truly interesting is that most of the devices come with color screens and all of them are compatible with Windows-based digital media, so you can play digital audio and video when desired.

Microsoft facilitates these features through a version of Windows Media Player designed specifically for the Pocket PC. Like its XP-based cousin, this version of the player (shown in Figure 13-11) works with playlists and utilizes the same audio and video formats. Of course, trying to shoehorn most audio and video directly into a device with so little storage makes little sense — so you can convert these formats and produce smaller files that work better with a typical Pocket PC's small screen and limited storage space.

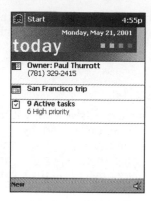

Figure 13-9: Rather than use a desktop metaphor like Windows, the Pocket PC is based on PIM functionality.

Figure 13-10: The Start menu cascades from the top left (a response to user feedback).

Figure 13-11: Windows Media Player 7.1 for the Pocket PC is compatible with WMA and WMV 8 for the PC.

Tip   If you own a Pocket PC and haven't yet updated your media player, you can do as a free download from www.microsoft.com/windowsmedia. Just select downloads from the site and you'll easily find the version that's right for your device.

Copying digital audio to the Pocket PC

The previous section discussed ways to transcode digital audio as you copy it to a portable device such as a Pocket PC. Doing so gives you more for the money, storage-wise, without dramatically reducing the quality of the music — provided you stick with Windows Media Audio (WMA) format. What's nice about using this format with a Pocket PC is that you don't have to take as many devices on the road. If you have a Pocket PC, it probably makes more sense to buy a few extra memory modules instead of a dedicated portable audio device. These days, most Pocket PCs are compatible with Compact Flash storage, which is fairly cheap and very small. Future devices will (no doubt) work with other types of storage, such as Secure Digital (SD) media cards.

When you use Media Player for Windows XP to copy music to a Pocket PC, you don't have to worry about *where* the music is copied. Media Player knows to copy these files to the My Documents folder on the device. But if you have external storage, such as the aforementioned CompactFlash card, you might want to use that for media storage instead. In this case, you can choose to manually copy music files to the device, and choose the exact location where the music goes. You lose the capability to transcode, unfortunately, but this might not be an issue if you are already encoding audio at a lower rate or aren't concerned about converting audio as it's copied to the device.

Here's how you can manually copy digital audio directly to a Pocket PC.

1. If ActiveSync isn't already running, start ActiveSync. (For information about installing and configuring ActiveSync, please see the Web site for this book, www.xpdigitalmedia.com.)

2. Attach your Pocket PC device to the PC and turn it on to enable the connection. This causes ActiveSync to synchronize with the Pocket PC, as shown in Figure 13-12.

3. Click the Explore button in the ActiveSync toolbar to bring up the Mobile Device Explorer window, where you can navigate around your Pocket PC as you would folders on your hard drive, as shown in Figure 13-13.

4. Navigate to the location where you'd like to store your audio files. For example, this might be the My Documents folder on your Storage Card.

5. Open the My Music folder on your PC's hard drive and navigate to the song files you'd like to copy to the Pocket PC.

Figure 13-12: Microsoft ActiveSync is the front-end to your PocketPC.

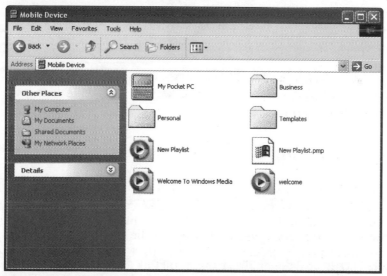

Figure 13-13: You can browse around your Pocket PC as if it were just another drive on your system.

6. Drag and drop the files normally, as shown in Figure 13-14. The Copy and Conversion dialog box appears as the files are copied (no conversion takes place for this file type).

7. When file copying is complete, detach your Pocket PC from the PC; you can then play the audio in Windows Media Player 7.1 for the Pocket PC.

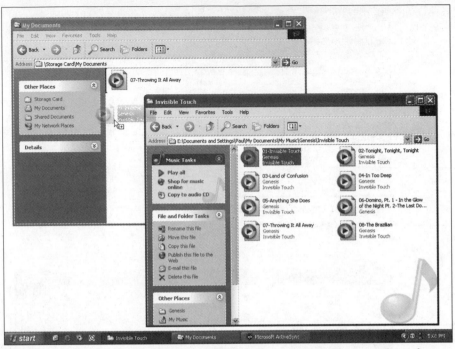

Figure 13-14: Like any other drive, a Pocket PC is an acceptable target for a drag and drop operation.

Using pocket digital video

Pocket PCs are also compatible with MPWXP digital-video formats; you can copy videos directly to a Pocket PC if you've got the storage space. But a more elegant solution is to first use Windows Movie Maker to convert existing videos to a format that matches the capabilities of your Pocket PC. This results in smaller, lower-resolution videos that are more appropriate for the format.

Microsoft CEO Steve Ballmer likes to show off this feature during speeches about digital media because it *really* shows off what Windows XP and the Pocket PC can do — in a way that most people wouldn't normally expect. So Ballmer explains how he can be on a flight and bore people with his home movies instead of having to take out his wallet and bore them with wallet-sized photos. (Admit it: Part of you is gleefully anticipating that look of amazement from fellow passengers. Not to mention the props from family members you might be visiting. It's a win-win for the geek at heart.)

To make this happen, you just fire up Windows Movie Maker and convert an existing movie to a format that shows up properly on the Pocket PC. (For a closer look at Windows Movie Maker and its video-creation capabilities, see Chapter 11.)

To convert a movie for use on the Pocket PC, follow these steps:

1. Open Windows Movie Maker and choose File ⇨ Import to find a movie you'd like to convert, as shown in Figure 13-15. Alternatively, you can open an existing WMM project and choose a raw or final movie you've been editing.

Figure 13-15: Windows Movie Maker now supports the Pocket PC natively.

2. If you've chosen to import a raw movie or a WMM project, you can edit the movie with titles and transitions. Note that the Pocket PC screen is 240 × 480, so you should make sure that the title screens you create are in that resolution (again, see Chapter 11 for more information).

3. Once your storyboard is complete, you can save the final movie. Click the Save Movie toolbar button to display the Save Movie dialog box shown in Figure 13-16.

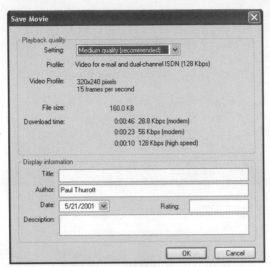

Figure 13-16: The Save Movie dialog box comes with preset quality templates.

4. In the Setting drop-down list, choose Other. The Profile drop-down list — normally hidden — appears (see Figure 13-17).

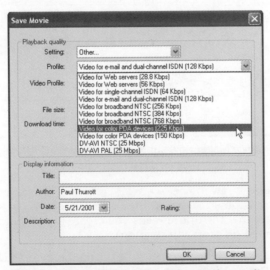

Figure 13-17: If you choose Other as the quality setting, a plethora of new options opens for you.

5. In the Profile drop-down list box, choose *Video for color PDA devices (225 Kbps)* or *Video for color PDA devices (100 Kbps)*. The Video profile then changes to reflect the format's capabilities (both offer 208 × 160 resolution, but the 225 Kbps version offers 20 frames per second while 100 Kbps is only 8 FPS). You can also adjust the file size and download times accordingly, as shown in Figures 13-18 and 13-19.

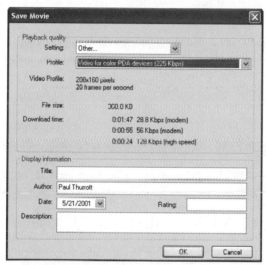

Figure 13-18: The Video for color PDA devices (225 Kbps) setting offers 20 FPS.

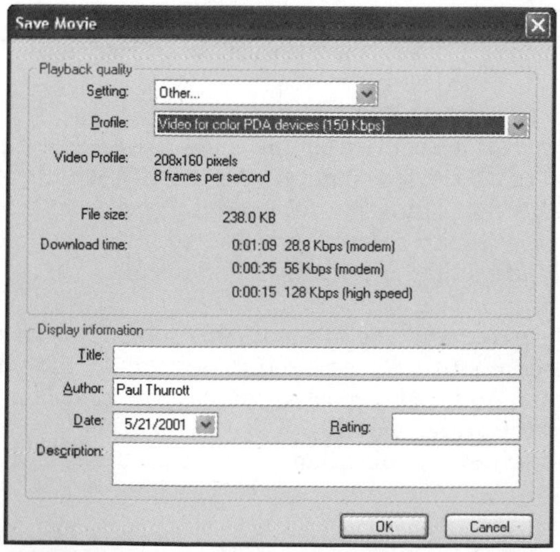

Figure 13-19: *Video for color PDA devices (150 Kbps)* results in smaller files sizes but runs at only 8 FPS.

6. Fill in the appropriate display information (explained in Chapter 11) and then click OK to save the movie. You are prompted to choose a destination and then the movie is created. Windows Movie Maker prompts you to view the movie in Media Player for Windows XP; this isn't a bad idea since you can preview the quality and see how it came out.

The standard caveats for quality-versus-size apply here, of course: A 225-Kbps movie has a higher image quality but it also requires bigger file sizes. Experiment a bit and see what works best for you.

Once you've created your mini-masterpiece, you're going to want to copy it to your Pocket PC. Use the instructions in the previous section about copying digital audio to accomplish this; the steps are the same. When you're done, you can watch short home movies on your Pocket PC.

Using Portable Digital Audio Devices

If you're not in the market for a Pocket PC but want to take digital audio on the road in a format that is portable and fairly inexpensive, a portable digital audio player may fill the bill. These devices all offer similar capabilities, including a certain amount of storage, connection to the PC via an USB port, and headphones. Some come with internal memory and some sort of external expansion, usually through a CompactFlash slot or similar technology. Whatever the specifics, most of these devices are quite small and offer wonderful digital quality music.

However, if you want to use such a device Media Player for Windows XP, be sure to get one that's compatible. Of course, Microsoft is careful to make sure that all the most popular devices work with its software, but a few glaring omissions still exist. For the most up-to-date list, be sure to visit the Microsoft Web site before you drop $300 on a player and discover that it doesn't work with MPXP. Here's the URL: www.windowsmedia.com/mg/portabledevices.asp.

The market for portable audio devices is divided into a few obvious segments. For example, a growing collection of CD devices can play MP3 and WMA files in addition to standard audio CDs. But today, most portable digital audio devices fall into the handheld, ROM-based-memory-card category pioneered by Sonic Blue (then under the aegis of Diamond Multimedia) and its Rio 300 device.

Since then, Sonic Blue has improved and expanded its Rio line and other companies have jumped in with suitable competition. Some market leaders include the Sonic Blue Rio, Compaq iPaq Personal Audio Player, Nike psaPlay, Creative Nomad II, Iomega HipZIP, RCA Lyra, and the Sony Vaio MusicClip. The market is vigorously competitive—and growing—so new and formidable devices are sure to keep coming.

Using a portable digital audio device is generally identical to using a Pocket PC (as described earlier) to play digital music: Compatible devices integrate directly into Media Player for Windows XP, making it easy to copy songs from your playlists onto the device. But portable audio devices interact with the OS in a slightly different way than Pocket PCs. Also mentioned previously, you're generally greeted with a dialog box when you connect a portable audio device to your Windows XP-based PC. But XP also lets you configure how the system interacts with the device in a more elegant fashion.

Configuring a portable audio device

If your portable audio device is connected and turned on, you can navigate to My Computer, where you see a new entry under the grouping *Devices with Removable Storage*. In the case of the Iomega HipZIP, this new entry is called *PocketZip40* and it provides a way to navigate the device as if it were a small hard drive—thus you can configure the device so Windows behaves accordingly when you attach the device.

To configure the portable audio device, follow these steps:

1. Right-click its icon in My Computer and choose Properties. The Properties sheet for the device appears, as shown in Figure 13-20.

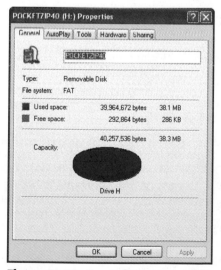

Figure 13-20: To configure a portable audio device, just display its Properties sheet from My Computer.

2. On the AutoPlay tab, you can configure what happens when the device is connected, as shown in Figure 13-21. Select Music Files from the section of content types at the top and then an appropriate action. (Note that you can choose *Take no action* if you'd prefer for nothing to happen. What a concept.)

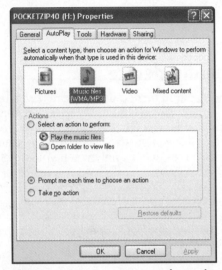

Figure 13-21: Here you can determine what happens when the device is connected.

3. Click OK to finish. You can come back later and choose the option labeled *Restore defaults* if you are unhappy with your selection.

Navigating your device as a drive

The other interesting thing you can do is treat the portable audio device as a hard drive and manually copy audio files to it from My Music. This is similar to the steps earlier in the chapter for the Pocket PC, except an external application (ActiveSync) is not required. To navigate around the storage on your portable audio device, simply open it in My Computer as you would any other drive. You can play music from the device directly, delete audio files, copy new audio files to the device, and perform any other kind of file-related task that's possible on a hard drive.

✦   ✦   ✦

Communicating with Windows Messenger

One of the more awesome capabilities made possible by the Internet is peer-to-peer communication; Microsoft takes advantage of this reality in Windows XP with its new Windows Messenger application. Windows Messenger extends the Instant Messaging (IM) technology of the past with new features — including audio and voice chat and application sharing, and other features. This chapter takes a look at instant messaging in general, as well as the specific Windows Messenger features available to you in Windows XP.

Instant Messaging

About five years ago, a friend and co-author calling me, convinced that his wife had just installed a virus on his computer. He asked if I had ever heard of something called "ICQ" (as in "I seek you"), an application that placed a cute little flower icon in his Windows 95 tray. After looking over the company's Web site, he was convinced that there was something wrong with this picture.

I had never heard of ICQ, but I visited the Web site. ICQ was a new product by an Israeli company called Mirabilis, which had created a new way to communicate over the Internet, using text chat boxes — similar to what you'd get on an online service such as America Online (AOL), but free and open to anyone with an Internet connection. I installed ICQ on my system to check it out, but I was never that interested in online chatting and quickly dismissed the tool as a plaything for teenagers and college students. I assured my friend that it was nothing to worry about (unless his wife became addicted to online chats and never left the computer).

It turns out my friend's wife was actually on the leading edge (embarrassing both my friend and I, as purported PC experts); ICQ took the Web by storm, establishing a new application category in which it quickly became the *de facto* standard. Within a year, over 100,000 people were logged onto ICQ simultaneously; the figure quickly grew to 500,000 simultaneous users by the end of 1997. Proprietary online services such as AOL began opening their chat clients to the Internet; companies such as Yahoo! and Microsoft quickly jumped on board. Today, instant messaging lags behind only e-mail and Web browsing for usage on the Internet.

From ICQ to AOL

In June 1998, AOL bought Mirabilis for its ICQ technology — which it then integrated into AOL Instant Messenger. ICQ itself still exists today as a free download (from the ICQ Web site (www.icq.com), and still one of the more bizarre locations on the Internet). But the tiny company from Israel started an industry all by itself, and today the major players battle for market share in the crowded but increasingly important instant-message market.

Microsoft enters the fray with MSN Messenger

Microsoft's entry, MSN Messenger, arrived in 1999 as a free download for Windows users. The service quickly established itself as a popular alternative; over 700,000 subscribers signed on in its first six days of availability. MSN Messenger didn't begin life as a feature-rich tool (as did AOL's products) but it was quickly enhanced with stock quotes, mobile-device compatibility, Hotmail integration, and other attractive capabilities. MSN Messenger is also a key component of MSN Explorer, the Web tool detailed in Chapter 12. The company introduced a Macintosh version of MSN Messenger as well, which is now up to par with Windows version.

Throughout 1999 and 2000, Microsoft attempted to make it possible for MSN Messenger users to communicate with AOL and ICQ users, but AOL kept changing its proprietary communications software to block Microsoft. This lead to a nasty public spat between the two companies, with the short-term result that MSN Messenger users can only communicate with other MSN Messenger users. Although AOL agreed to open up its Instant Message software to competitors (as a compromise during its successful bid to merge with Time Warner) the agreement has yet to be implemented.

Today, MSN Messenger (Figure 14-1) is a powerful communications tool that offers a deep level of integration with Microsoft's MSN Web properties — and with millions of users, it's easy to find people to chat with.

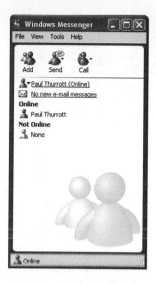

Figure 14-1: MSN Messenger brings instant messaging to the Windows OS.

Introducing Windows Messenger

In Windows XP, Microsoft includes a new version of its instant messaging program, which it calls Windows Messenger to denote its integrated status: Windows Messenger will not be made available for free download on the Internet. Windows Messenger differs from MSN Messenger in several key ways; it extends the feature-set of MSN Messenger by incorporating features that were previously available only in NetMeeting, the company's legacy tool for real-time collaboration and video conferencing.

Tip NetMeeting fans will be happy to hear that their favorite tool is still available in Windows XP for backwards compatibility purposes, though it won't be upgraded in the future and isn't found anywhere in the Start Menu. To find NetMeeting, navigate to C:\Program Files\NetMeeting (assuming you installed Windows XP on the C: drive). The executable is named conf.exe.

So Windows Messenger, shown in Figure 14-2, now incorporates the text chatting and file sharing features found in MSN Messenger, but it also adds the audio and video chat capabilities, whiteboarding, and application-sharing features that were previously found in NetMeeting. Windows Messenger can also integrate with various .NET services, such as MSN Alerts, so you'll be able to participate in Microsoft's upcoming Web jihad. And most interestingly, Windows Messenger integrates your Windows logon with .NET Passport, so you are signed on to Passport — and to any Passport-enabled Web sites — automatically when you log on to Windows. This optional (but powerful) feature is likely to change the way you use the Internet in the near future; upcoming sections provide details.

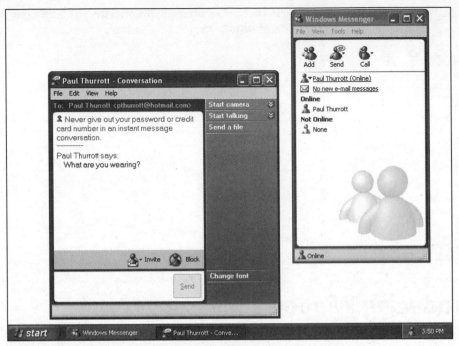

Figure 14-2: What you see when you open Windows Messenger

Configuring Windows Messenger

Windows XP installs Windows Messenger automatically and then offers you a chance to create a new account (or load an existing one) the first time you boot XP. But you can configure Windows Messenger at any time. Previous versions of Windows accomplished this feat solely through the MSN Messenger application. But in Windows XP, you can integrate your Windows logon with the Microsoft .NET Passport service, so we'll start there.

.NET Passport logon integration

A few years back, Microsoft started the Passport service, which was designed to offer an online wallet (or "e-wallet") that could hold personal information about a user, such as name, address, and credit card information. The idea was that Web sites could utilize the Passport service to obtain this information when a user wanted to make a purchase online; that way people wouldn't have to laboriously type in this information every time they made a purchase online.

For a variety of reasons, this vision was more promise than reality. Few Web sites took advantage of the feature; many people felt uncomfortable about storing such information online.

In Windows XP, Microsoft is taking another stab at this initiative. This time, they've integrated the functionality into a secure version of Windows (Windows XP) so users are more apt to trust the service's security and functionality. And because Passport—now renamed to .NET Passport—is integrated into Windows, more and more Web sites are signing on board.

Here's how .NET Passport is integrated with Windows XP: When you log on to Windows XP using a logon and password, you can optionally allow your .NET Passport to be activated as well, an action that was previously manually initiated at each Passport-equipped Web site. .NET Passport accounts are tied to Hotmail and MSN e-mail addresses, so you have to get one of those first. (Because Hotmail is free, it's an option worth looking at here. If you already have a Hotmail or MSN account, you can skip ahead to the section titled "Adding a .NET Passport account to your Windows logon.")

Obtaining a .NET Passport account

The easiest way to get a free .NET Passport account is to sign up for Hotmail. Here's how:

1. Open Internet Explorer and navigate to `hotmail.com`.

2. Click the option labeled *Sign up now* (near the top of the page).

3. Fill in the registration information as required.

   You get an e-mail address (which takes the form *[username]*@`hotmail.com`) and a prompt to pick a password that is at least 8 characters long.

 Tip

On the Hotmail registration page, I strongly recommend unchecking the options titled *Hotmail Member Directory* and *Internet White Pages* for security reasons—and to help you avoid getting a ton of spam e-mail.

4. When sign-up is complete, log on to Hotmail via the Web-based interface at `www.hotmail.com` and enjoy your new e-mail account. (When you create a Hotmail account, this account is automatically configured for .NET Passport.)

Adding a .NET Passport account to your Windows logon

Now that you have a .NET Passport account, you can choose to have this account log on, through Windows Messenger, when you log on to the PC. To do so, follow these steps:

1. Open Control Panel ➪ User Accounts.

   The User Accounts application opens, as shown in Figure 14-3.

2. Select your user account under the section labeled *Pick an account to change*. This displays the page labeled *What do you want to change about your account?* (This page is shown in Figure 14-4.)

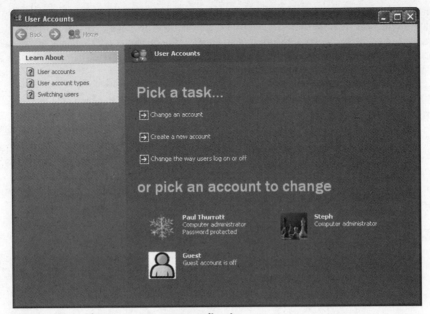

Figure 14-3: The User Accounts application

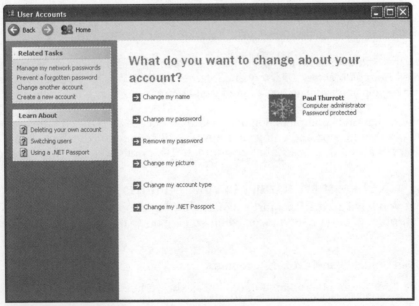

Figure 14-4: How to change your account

Note You *must* be logged on to an account to set up a .NET Passport for that account. You cannot tie a .NET Passport account to a user account other than the one you are currently using. Also, you will have to be connected to the Internet for this work.

3. Click *Set up my account to use a .NET Passport*. This displays the .NET Passport Wizard, as shown in Figure 14-5.

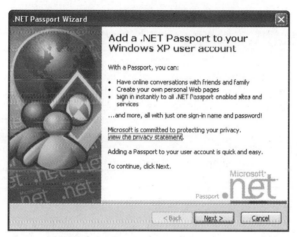

Figure 14-5: The .NET Passport Wizard opens.

4. In the first part of the wizard, you can choose to use an existing e-mail account, or create a new one. Choose the option labeled *Yes, use an existing email account*.

5. Now, enter your Hotmail (or MSN) account and password when asked. You can optionally decide here whether you want to be logged on automatically when you log on to Windows.

6. After the Wizard verifies your username and password, you're done. Click Finish to close the Wizard.

If you set it up that way, Windows XP logs you on to your .NET Passport account whenever you log on to Windows. The big question, of course, is whether doing so is a good idea. I think so: Passport-enabled Web sites are becoming more common all the time; it's handy to not have to worry about authentication every time you enter a new site. And Microsoft will be adding tons of .NET related functionality to this program after Windows XP ships. If you're not logging onto your .NET Passport account when you logon, you'll never even hear about it. See the Web site for this book about exciting updates to Windows Messenger: www.xpdigitalmedia.com.

Either way, when you set up a .NET Passport account through User Accounts, Windows Messenger is set up to work with that account. It alerts you when you have new e-mail, and gives you access to chat with other users. Windows Messenger appears as a small green man in your system tray as shown in Figure 14-6. Let's take a look at how you configure this application.

 Figure 14-6: Little green man from Microsoft (Windows Messenger)

Setting Windows Messenger options

To configure Windows Messenger, right-click the Windows Messenger icon in the tray and choose Open. This displays the Windows Messenger window, shown in Figure 14-7. The window displays contacts who are online and offline; you can add contacts, send invitations, and call contacts.

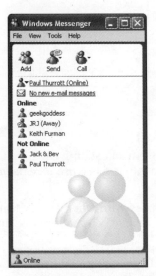

Figure 14-7: The Windows Messenger window shows you who's online and who's offline.

You can also configure Windows Messenger by choosing Tools ➪ Options, which display the Options dialog box shown in Figure 14-8. This dialog box allows you to determine how Windows Messenger behaves, with options for such things as display name (how others see you), password, and other preferences.

Using the Audio and Video Tuning Wizard

In addition to the Options dialog box, Windows Messenger also offers an Audio and Video Tuning Wizard, which allows you to configure how the application interacts with microphones, speakers, and video cameras. You can access this wizard by choosing Tools ➪ Audio and Video Tuning Wizard.

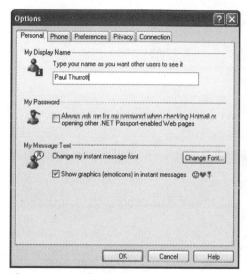

Figure 14-8: The Options dialog box in Windows Messenger

Using Text Chat

Text chat is the "bread-and-butter" IM application; Windows Messenger offers a full-featured client application for this purpose. You can send instant messages — in text format — to any user in your contacts list by double-clicking that person's icon in the main Windows Messenger window or by choosing Tools ➪ Send an Instant Message. Either way, the Conversation window appears, as shown in Figure 14-9.

You can only send instant messages to contacts who are online. If the contact you wish to message is offline, Windows Messenger offers to let you send that person an e-mail message via your Hotmail or MSN e-mail account, as shown in Figure 14-10.

When someone sends you a text chat message, you see the small alert window shown in Figure 14-11. A Windows Messenger Conversation window opens as well. You can click the alert window to open the Instant Message window, or simply right-click it to dismiss the alert window. If you take no action, the alert window disappears on its own in a few seconds; the minimized Conversation window stays on your taskbar. This must be closed manually.

Figure 14-9: The Conversation window for Windows Messenger

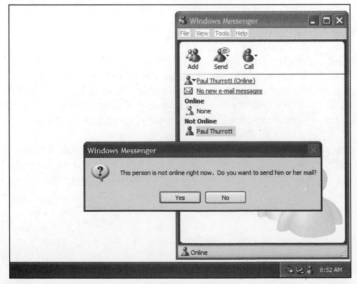

Figure 14-10: Sending an e-mail message to an offline contact

Figure 14-11: The alert window that signals the arrival of a text-chat message

Note The alert window shown here will be extended with other functionality after Windows XP ships. For example, you will be able to sign up for MSN Calendar (www.calendar.msn.com) Alerts, which will provide alert windows that correspond to appointments and to-do items in your schedule. I have more information about this and other exciting Windows Messenger developments on the Web site for this book, at www.xpdigitalmedia.com.

When two or more people are chatting, Windows Messenger provides the name of each person next to each message so you can see who is typing what. When someone is typing a response, the window's status bar notes that, as shown in Figure 14-12; you won't see the message until that user hits Enter or the Send button.

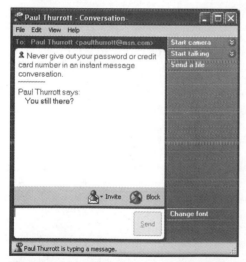

Figure 14-12: The status bar signals that someone is typing a response.

While in a text chat session, you can invite other users to join in too. Simply choose Invite ➪ To Join This Conversation; then choose the name of the contact to invite another contact to take part in the chat (Figure 14-13).

You can close the Instant Message window at any time to close the session, but other contacts can still send you instant messages: That small alert window appears if the Instant Message window is closed and someone sends you a message.

Figure 14-13: Inviting another person to join a chat

Text chat is fun, I suppose, but I don't want to spend too much time here on a feature that's been around for years. What's far more interesting in Windows XP is the ability to use digital media features such as audio and video to chat. The following sections delve into these exciting new features.

Goodbye Phone, Hello Audio Chat

Windows Messenger supports audio-chat capabilities that mimic the style of voice communication everyone's familiar with from the telephone. Audio chat is two-way, which means that both users can speak and be heard at the same time. However, audio chat is limited to two users only, a limitation that does not apply to text chatting.

Of course, the audio chat functionality in Windows Messenger requires that the person speaking has a microphone connected to the computer, and that the person listening on the other end has speakers installed. To communicate together most effectively, of course, both users need microphones and speakers. In the past, typically you would have to plug a microphone into the microphone port on your sound card, and then use your standard PC speakers for output. However, to get the best performance out of this feature, it's better to purchase a dedicated USB-based headset that sports one or two headphones and a microphone. Then, you can configure Windows XP to use that unit for voice chats (that is, for both voice playback and recording), and use your standard speakers for other sound output.

Configuring your PC for audio chat

To configure your system for a USB-based headset:

1. Install the headset hardware and any associated drivers, if required, using the instructions provided with the headset. Typically, Windows changes your default audio output to go through the headset, which is probably not what you want.

2. Open the Control Panel and select Sounds, Speech, and Audio Devices. Then, click Sounds and Audio Devices to display the Sounds and Audio Devices Properties dialog box, as shown in Figure 14-14. (If you're displaying the Control Panel in Classic View, simply choose Sounds and Audio Devices instead).

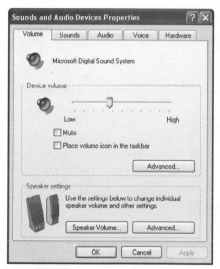

Figure 14-14: The Sounds and Audio Devices Properties dialog box

3. Navigate to the Audio tab, which is shown in Figure 14-15. Ensure that the default device for sound playback is your usual speaker set, not the headset. The sound recording device should be set to the headset, however. Click Apply when it's set up how you want it.

4. Navigate to the Voice tab, shown in Figure 14-16. Here, you probably want to ensure that the default device for voice playback is the headset, not your normal speakers. And the voice recording device should be set to the headset as well, of course. This gives you a telephone-like capability when using the headset for audio chat.

Figure 14-15: The Audio Tab for the Properties dialog box under Sounds and Audio Devices

Figure 14-16: The Voice tab of the Properties dialog box

5. Click the Test hardware button to launch the Sound Hardware Test Wizard. This wizard, shown in Figure 14-17, helps you test and configure your headset.

It's really designed for a variety of other applications, such as online games and voice control of the OS, but it's a good idea to make a quick run-through of the Wizard to make sure your headset is working properly.

6. In the first stage of the wizard, your hardware is tested and you don't have to do anything. In the Microphone Test phase, shown in Figure 14-18, you can speak into the headset microphone to make sure it's configured for your voice level.

Figure 14-17: The Sound Hardware Test Wizard

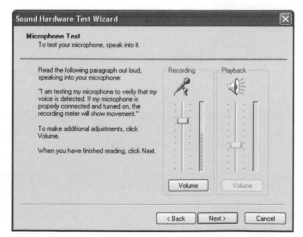

Figure 14-18: The Microphone Test of the Sound Hardware Test Wizard

7. In the Speaker Test phase, you also speak into the headset microphone, but this time, the audio is replayed through the headset headphone so you can adjust the playback volume. This is shown in Figure 14-19.

8. After that, you can complete the wizard. If all went well, your hardware is working and you're ready to begin.

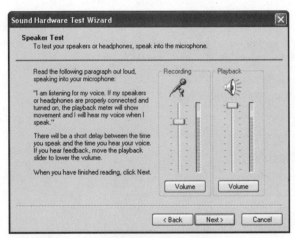

Figure 14-19: Adjusting playback volume

Using Windows Messenger's audio-chat feature

To initiate an audio chat, open Windows Messenger, right-click the contact you'd like to speak with; then choose Call ➪ Computer. Alternatively, you could simply open a normal text chat window and then expand the entry labeled *Start talking* (at the right of the Conversation window). What you see should resemble Figure 14-20. You should have a normal Conversation window open, with the Speakers and Microphone options available.

You can use the Speakers slider to modify the volume of the speakers, adjust the Microphone option with its slider (or use the Mute button to toggle the microphone on or off). To stop a voice chat, simply click Stop talking.

An audio chat is an *invitation;* before you can begin speaking, the person you invite has to agree to join the conversation. On the receiving end, such an agreement consists of a standard Windows Messenger alert window, plus a new Conversation window (in which you see the invitation), as shown in Figure 14-21. When the second user accepts the invitation, the voice conversation begins.

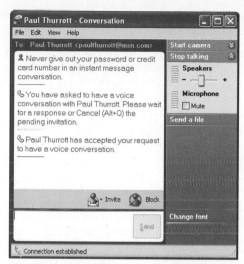

Figure 14-20: The Conversation window as an online conversation begins.

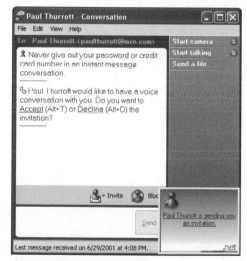

Figure 14-21: An invitation to join a conversation

Tip   You can still have a one-way voice chat if only one person has a microphone: The second user would simply have to type responses normally, using their keyboard.

Face-to-Face with Video Chat

Audio chat is certainly a step up from text chats; with Windows Messenger, you can also use *video chat* to enable that "video phone" feature long promised by the telephone industry. Video chat requires a camera of some sort — typically a Web camera, though DV camcorders and other devices often work fine too — and a separate microphone if you want to use voice as well. Typically, all the voice hardware you need is a headset for the audio portion (as you would for straight audio chat). You can mix and match capabilities as needed — for example, one user might have audio only while the second is using audio and video.

To use video chat, you have to install and configure a compatible video device of some sort; I use a fairly cheap, USB-based Logitech Web cam for this purpose. To ensure that the camera is installed and configured correctly, open up My Computer. You should see the camera listed under Scanners and Cameras, as shown in the bottom of Figure 14-22.

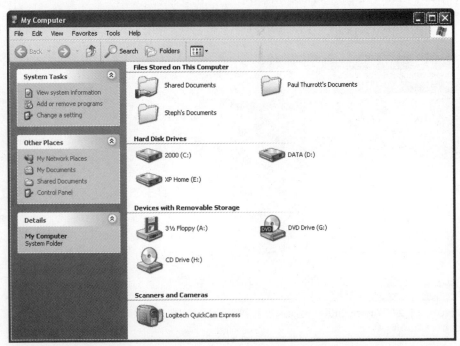

Figure 14-22: Installed scanners and cameras are listed at the bottom of your My Computer window.

When you double-click the camera icon, the window changes to show the output from the camera, as seen in Figure 14-23. You can use this window as a guide to adjust the focus on the camera, though other configuration options (such as brightness and tint) probably require software from the camera maker.

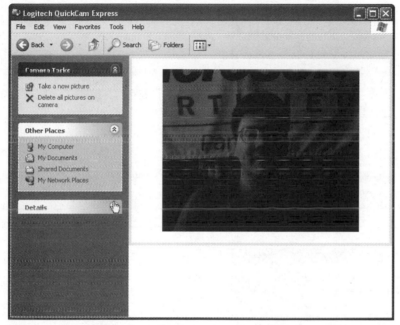

Figure 14-23: Output from the camera as it appears on-screen

Curiously, there is no way to initiate a video chat directly from Windows Messenger. Instead, you have to open a normal text chat and then click the Start camera button. The other person in the chat gets an invitation to accept or decline the video chat request. If accepted, the video window on the receiving computer displays the output from the sender's camera, as shown in Figure 14-24.

If both users have cameras, picture-in-picture (PIP) technology is used so the current user's image is shown in a small window in the lower right corner of the video window, as shown in Figure 14-25.

You can turn off the PIP effect by choosing Options and then unchecking Show My Video as Picture-In-Picture. You can also turn off video output by choosing Options ⇨ Stop Sending Video.

As with audio chatting, video chat is limited to two users.

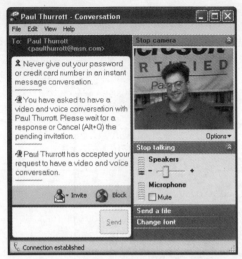

Figure 14-24: Video input from the sender appears on-screen. Not everyone will get the dashing results shown here.

Figure 14-25: User to user, face to face, thanks to picture-in-picture (PIP)

Other Uses for Windows Messenger

In addition to Windows Messenger's cool audio and video capabilities, this handy little utility can be used for a variety of other purposes; it's amazing to see how this once limited tool has evolved to be a central conduit for such a wide array of features. This section examines some other ways to use Windows Messenger. But Microsoft is enhancing Windows Messenger all the time. Check the Windows Update Web site (www.windowsupdate.com) and the Web site for this book (www.xpdigitalmedia.com) for more information about any updates: The product will literally be updated the day that Windows XP is publicly released.

MSN Alerts and other .NET Web services

With the release of Windows XP, Microsoft expects to offer a slew of .NET Web services through its MSN Alerts program. The idea is to provide customized alerts so you can be notified (for example) when your favorite baseball team plays a game, when the weather takes a turn for the worse, or what airlines offer the best deals on vacation flights (with price quotes from Expedia). For more information about MSN Alerts, visit the MSN Alerts Web site (alerts.msn.com).

Remote Assistance

Windows XP supports Remote Assistance, a new help-desk feature that allows you to cede control of your PC temporarily to another user so that person can fix a problem for you. Though Remote Assistance is likely to see most of its use in corporate settings, it's also a nice feature for the geek whose family needs help with their home computer.

Remote Assistance can be accessed in a variety of ways: Microsoft has added a Remote Assistance icon to the root of the More Programs menu in the Start Menu, but you can access it directly from Windows Messenger as well: Simply choose Tools and then Ask for Remote Assistance from the main Windows Messenger window to fire off the appropriate invitation. For more information about this feature and its myriad of options, please visit the Web site for this book (www.xpdigitalmedia.com).

Application sharing

Windows Messenger also offers the capability to share applications over a network (though this feature is fairly slow and grainy over the Internet). Application sharing is vaguely like Remote Assistance, except the remote user can only access an individual application, not the entire system.

Whiteboard

For collaboration on both text and graphics, Windows Messenger supports a *whiteboarding* feature as well: Two users can exchange information on a virtual whiteboard (which somewhat resembles Windows Paint), make changes on-screen, and see each other's changes taking effect.

I'll have more information about Windows Messenger's non-media features on the Web site for this book (www.xpdigitalmedia.com).

✦   ✦   ✦

Index

Continued

Continued

Continued

Continued

Continued